A Concise Introduction to Syntactic Theory

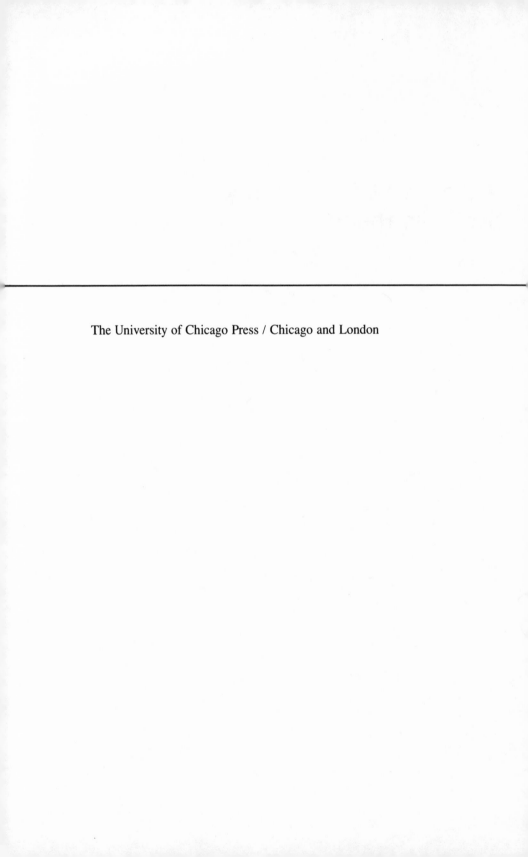

The University of Chicago Press / Chicago and London

A CONCISE INTRODUCTION TO SYNTACTIC THEORY

The Government-Binding Approach

Elizabeth A. Cowper

The University of Chicago Press, Chicago 60637
The University of Chicago Press, Ltd., London
© 1992 by The University of Chicago
All rights reserved. Published 1992
Printed in the United States of America

00 99 98 97 96 95 94   5 4 3
ISBN (cloth): 0-226-11644-1
ISBN (paper): 0-226-11646-8

Library of Congress Cataloging-in-Publication Data

Cowper, Elizabeth A.
    A concise introduction to syntactic theory: The government-
binding approach / Elizabeth A. Cowper.
        p.   cm.
    Includes bibliographical references and index.
    1. Government-binding theory (Linguistics)   2. Generative grammar.
3. Grammar, Comparative and general—Syntax.   I. Title.
P158.2.C6   1992
415—dc20   91–19943
                                                         CIP

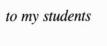
to my students

Contents

Preface

The theory of Government and Binding (GB) can reasonably be described as the major school of research in syntax in North America and most of Europe. While many other syntactic theories exist, a number of these define themselves, at least to some extent, in terms of how they differ from GB. Whether or not one adopts the GB approach, it is necessary to have some degree of familiarity with it in order to function effectively as a syntactician in North America today. In addition, many principles of GB have found their way into current phonological theories, so that a deep understanding of much current work in phonology requires at least a passing acquaintance with GB syntax.

This textbook is meant to be a short, clear, and coherent introduction to the theory—one that will provide an overall framework of knowledge, enable users to actually work syntactic questions out for themselves, and, most importantly, make it possible to read the primary literature without unnecessary confusion and discouragement. It is intended, on the one hand, as a course textbook to be used by upper-level undergraduates and beginning graduate students and, on the other hand, as a resource for linguists whose training has been in other theories and who want to learn the essentials of GB theory in a relatively painless way.

In order to achieve the goals of clarity and conciseness, it has proved necessary for the textbook to be somewhat streamlined, or even skeletal, in structure. Many very interesting questions have simply been ignored, so as to preserve the clarity and general coherence of what remains. It must therefore be emphasized that this textbook is *not* to be taken as a substitute for reading the primary literature in the area, nor is it to be taken as an exhaustive presentation of the theory. It should be used in preparation for attacking the literature. The instructor should feel free to supplement it with other readings, although I would caution against doing this too early. The book has worked well as the only textbook for a semester-long course, and students have gone on to do original research in the following semester. It is my hope that this textbook will make syntax seem exciting and do-able at the earliest stages and will serve as a handy security blanket during the initial forays into the glorious complexities of what my students have come to call "the real stuff."

I am grateful to many people for various kinds of help during the preparation of this book. First and foremost, I owe thanks to the dozens of students at the University of Toronto who served as guinea pigs over several years of classroom testing. I am especially grateful to those who were subjected to the very first draft and provided a great deal of useful feedback. A number of linguists, in particular Carol Georgopoulos, Diane Massam, and Leslie Saxon, used various versions of the manuscript in their classes and gave me valuable comments. An anonymous reviewer provided thorough and painstaking comments which improved the book significantly. Jack Chambers, of the University of Toronto, and Geoffrey Huck, of the University of Chicago Press, have my heartfelt thanks for their encouragement, good advice, and confidence in the book. Finally, I would like to thank my daughter, Judith Szamosi, for her help with the proofreading.

1 The Theory in Context

The theory of Government and Binding has developed out of a tradition going back to the 1950s, known variously as transformational grammar (TG), generative grammar, or generative-transformational grammar. While it is not the purpose of this textbook to give a detailed, or even thorough, history of the theory, I will give a short outline of how the theory has changed and developed over the years, so as to provide a context for what follows.

In section 1.1, some of the most fundamental goals and assumptions of the theory of generative grammar will be identified. These are the things which have remained constant throughout the history of the theory, even though just about every aspect of how the theory is structured and implemented has changed. In section 1.2, a number of major stages of the theory will be identified, and the major properties of each stage will be described. For a more comprehensive discussion of the development of the theory, see Newmeyer (1980).

1.1 Goals and Assumptions

The fundamental problem of linguistic theory, according to Chomsky, is that of "determining how it is possible for a child to acquire knowledge of a language" (Chomsky 1973:12). This question has remained at the core of work in generative grammar since its inception. In order to answer this question, we must first examine it and make sure we understand it precisely enough that it can guide our investigations in a meaningful way.

First, what is meant by "knowledge of a language"? I am not speaking here of the kind of explicit, conscious knowledge taught in elementary-school grammar classes. Rather, I mean the largely unconscious knowledge that makes us speakers of a language—the knowledge we use when we judge that (1) is a grammatical sentence of English while (2) is not.

(1)   Mary is dancing on the stage.
(2)   *Mary are danced the stage on.

Before we can begin to answer the question of how knowledge of a language can be acquired, we must have some notion of exactly what it is that is being acquired.

Knowledge, however, is not something we can observe directly. This is especially true in the case of language. Every normal human being is a native speaker of (at least) one language and thus by definition has acquired knowledge of that language. Most people, however, never study their native language in any conscious way. Just as people know how to walk without consciously knowing which muscles, nerves, and parts of the brain are involved, people know their native language without consciously knowing its structure. In contrast, people who know predicate logic, or chess, for example, normally do have an awareness of the structure of the system of rules governing what can be done in logic or in a game of chess.

Since we cannot observe knowledge of language directly, how then can we study it? What we can do is observe people as they use this knowledge in various ways—as they speak and understand their native language. In other words, we can observe the linguistic behavior of native speakers. Another thing we can do is ask people, including ourselves, to use their knowledge in judging whether particular sentences are acceptable sentences of their native language. From these types of linguistic behavior, we can then try to deduce the knowledge that enables them to perform the behavior. S. Jay Keyser, in class lectures in the late 1960s, put it very well: We are trying to figure out what it is that people **act as if** they know. Our job is therefore not merely to describe what people say, but, rather, to figure out what might be the knowledge which permits them to perform their linguistic behavior. We shall henceforth refer to this knowledge as the speaker's linguistic **competence** and to the behavior which we can observe as the speaker's linguistic **performance.**

The problem, of course, is that linguistic competence is not the only factor which influences linguistic performance. For this reason, not everything a native speaker of English says is an equally reliable indicator of that speaker's linguistic competence. A rather blatant example is given in (3).

(3)   Please don't shut the window on my [loud scream].

External events, such as a window shutting on someone's hand, can interrupt a speaker and force the abandonment of a sentence in midstream. No one would seriously propose that the sentence in (3) as it stands constitutes a grammatical sentence of English. Rather it is a sentence fragment, or an incomplete sentence, which happened to be uttered by someone on a particular occasion.

While it is fairly clear that (3) can be discarded as contaminated data, many cases are far less obvious. Consider, for example the sentences in (4) and (5).

(4)   a.   They talked to Sue and I about the accident.
        b.   Me and Sue saw the accident.
(5)   a.   They talked to I about the accident.
        b.   Me saw the accident.

Sentences like those in (4) are produced by speakers of English fairly frequently, while sentences like those in (5) are almost never observed. Nonetheless, most speakers of English would say that all four of the sentences are ungrammatical. The problem with all of these sentences has to do with the form of the pronoun *I/me*. Normally, when this pronoun occurs as the object of a verb or of a preposition, it takes the so-called objective form, *me*. When it occurs as the subject of a clause, it normally takes the so-called nominative form, *I*. Confusion tends to arise when this pronoun occurs in a coordinate structure containing the conjunction *and*. The question is, in constructing a grammar of English which is supposed to reflect the competence of native speakers of English, do we consider the sentences in (4) grammatical or ungrammatical? If we consider them grammatical, then the rule governing the choice of pronoun form will have to have in it a special subclause saying that in coordinate structures, the choice of form is freer. If we consider them ungrammatical, then we must explain why speakers often produce sentences like (4) and almost never produce sentences like (5).

The point here is that in order to develop a theory of competence, or a model of a native speaker's linguistic knowledge, we will, at every step of the way, be making judgments about the relevance of the data. These judgments are possible only in the context of the theory itself. The theory of linguistic competence will ultimately interact with other theories of memory, production, and comprehension, as well as with an understanding of external events (see (3) above) to account for particular instances of linguistic behavior. For the moment, we will simply say that generative grammar has been and continues to be primarily concerned with linguistic **competence.**

The next question that arises in our examination of Chomsky's question has to do with the model of knowledge, or grammar, we are constructing. What should the grammar do? According to Chomsky, the grammar must explicitly account for all of the grammatical sentences of the language under consideration. In other words, every grammatical sentence of the language must conform to all the requirements of the grammar, and every ungrammatical sentence must violate some requirement of the grammar. In this, generative grammars differ from the traditional and structuralist grammars that preceded them. Those grammars, again according to Chomsky,

> do not attempt to determine explicitly the sentences of a language
> or the structural descriptions of these sentences. Rather, such
> grammars describe elements and categories of various types, and
> provide examples and hints to enable the intelligent reader to de
> termine the form and structure of sentences not actually presented
> in the grammar. Such grammars are written for the intelligent
> reader. To determine what they say about sentences one must
> have an intuitive grasp of certain principles of linguistic struc
> ture. These principles, which remain implicit and unexpressed,

are presupposed in the construction and interpretation of such grammars. While perhaps perfectly adequate for their particular purposes, such grammars do not attempt to account for the ability of the intelligent reader to understand the grammar. The theory of generative grammar, in contrast, is concerned precisely to make explicit the contribution of the intelligent reader. (Chomsky 1973:8)

When a particular sentence conforms to all the requirements, or rules, of a generative grammar, we say that the grammar **generates** that sentence. If a sentence violates one or more requirements or rules of the grammar, then we say that the grammar fails to generate that sentence. If a grammar generates all the grammatical sentences of a language, and fails to generate any ungrammatical sentences, then we say that the grammar is **observationally adequate**—it successfully distinguishes between grammatical and ungrammatical sentences.

It is entirely possible that several very different observationally adequate grammars could be written for the same language. The goal of linguistic theory, however, goes beyond simply describing which sentences are grammatical and which are not. What we are trying to understand is not the language at all, but **knowledge of language** and how it can be acquired. Our grammar must therefore achieve more than observational adequacy. In addition to accounting for grammatical versus ungrammatical sentences, it must capture linguistically significant generalizations. In other words, it must provide the correct analysis for the sentences of the language—the analysis which corresponds to the native speaker's (unconscious) knowledge. For example, if two sentences are related to each other in a systematic way, as are the sentences in (6), then the grammar must explicitly account for that relation.

(6)   a.   Sue started the car.
      b.   The car started.

A grammar which accurately reflects the native speaker's knowledge is called a **descriptively adequate** grammar. It provides a model of the native speaker's linguistic competence. But recall that we are not simply trying to understand what knowledge of language is; we are trying to understand how knowledge of language can be acquired. The process of language acquisition can, for our purposes, be represented as in (7).

(7)

When a child acquires its native language, its knowledge, or competence, begins in an initial state (note that we have not yet said anything about what that initial state might be). As a result of the child's being exposed to language spoken in his/her environment, the competence gradually develops into an adult competence, which we call the final state.

A descriptively adequate grammar is a representation of the final state depicted in (7). A theory which also accounts for the initial state, and how it develops into the final state through exposure to linguistic data, is an **explanatorily adequate** theory—a theory which explains how it is possible to acquire knowledge of a language. The problem here is that, as far as we can tell, the linguistic data to which children are exposed are not by themselves sufficient to account for the development of the adult competence. Native speakers, in other words, know things which they could not possibly have learned from the language spoken around them. An example is given in (8).

(8) a. *Which book did Mary hire the person that ___ wrote ___?
     b. Who did Mary think that Anna saw ___?

The fact illustrated in (8) is stated informally in (9).

(9) In English, when a question word corresponds to a gap in a relative clause, the sentence is ungrammatical. If the gap is in a complement clause, the sentence is grammatical.

It is difficult to imagine how someone could learn this. Children do not make errors such as (8a), which means that there is no evidence of a stage of not knowing (9), preceding a stage of knowing (9). See Lightfoot (1982) for discussion of this issue.

There are many other aspects of linguistic competence which do not seem to be learnable from ordinary linguistic data in the child's environment. The conclusion to be drawn from this is that the child does not come empty-handed to the task of language acquisition. In other words, the initial state of linguistic competence has a role to play as well. In order to understand how language can be acquired, then, we must investigate the nature of the initial state of linguistic competence.

This initial state has been called the **biological endowment for language.** It must be common to all human beings, since all (normal) human beings are equally capable of acquiring any language. For this reason, it has also been called **universal grammar,** where by grammar we mean linguistic competence.

Recall that linguistic competence can only be investigated indirectly, by observing linguistic performance. Universal grammar is even more difficult to investigate. It is impractical to try first to develop a competence model for every language in the world and then look at what these grammars have in common. In addition, it is counterproductive. What we need to do is to develop models of specific languages at the same time as we are developing a model of universal grammar. The model of universal grammar will then inform us as we examine each language and can be revised where necessary. Conclusions based on the analysis of one language will narrow the possibilities for the analysis of other languages.

1.2 Stages in the Development of Generative Grammar

1.2.1 The Standard Theory

Chomsky's *Aspects of the Theory of Syntax,* published in 1965, defined the framework within which much syntactic research took place for the following decade. The structure of the model is shown in (10).

(10)

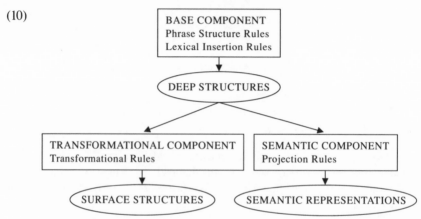

To illustrate how the grammar works, let us consider how the sentence in (11) would be derived.

(11)   The car was stolen by a young woman.

Phrase structure rules, such as those given in (12), apply to give the tree in (13).

(12)   S → NP AUX VP
         NP → (DET) (ADJ) N
         VP → V (NP)

(13)

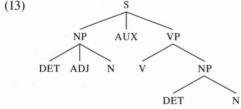

Rules of lexical insertion, which take account of the context in which a word occurs, apply to insert the lexical items into the tree in the appropriate places, giving (14) as the deep structure for the sentence.

(14)

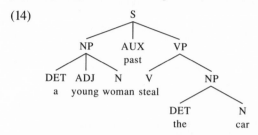

This deep structure serves as the input to the transformational component and to the semantic component. The transformational component contains transformational rules such as passive formation, affix-hopping and subject-verb agreement. Passive formation gives the intermediate representation shown in (15).

(15)

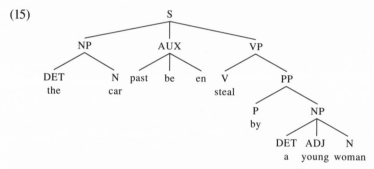

Affix-hopping and subject-verb agreement apply to give (16) as the surface structure.

(16)

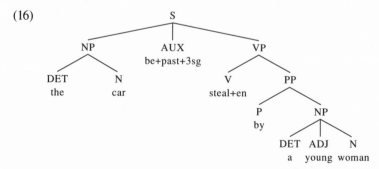

The structure in (16) serves as the input to the phonological component, which realizes the auxiliary verb as *was*, the main verb as *stolen*, and applies any phonological rules, giving the phonetic output.

Another example involves the transformations of reflexivization and equi-NP deletion, as well as affix-hopping and subject-verb agreement. The identical subscripts on the three instances of *Carol* indicate that all three noun phrases refer to the same person.

(17)   Deep Structure:

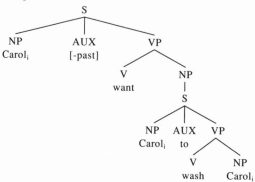

Reflexivization:

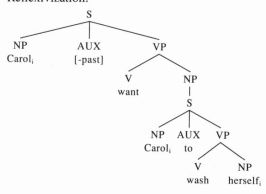

Equi-NP Deletion:

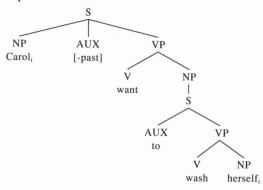

Affix-Hopping, Subject-Verb Agreement:

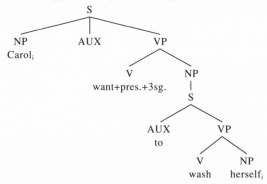

Meanwhile, the deep structure is interpreted by the projection rules of the semantic component. These rules combine the semantic representation of the various parts of the sentence to construct a semantic representation for the sentence as a whole. The important thing to note about this model is that the semantic representation is constructed entirely on the basis of the deep syntactic structure. It follows as an implicit claim, then, that the application of a transformation can have no effect on the meaning of a sentence. This implicit claim was articulated in Katz and Postal (1964) and came to be known as the Katz-Postal hypothesis.

What was universal about this model was not any specific phrase structure rules or transformations, but rather the structure of the model and the various categories (NP, V, etc.) that it made use of. The rules in each of the components were seen as language-particular and therefore to be learned by the native speaker in the course of language acquisition.

1.2.2 The Problem of Meaning

The Katz-Postal hypothesis ran into empirical problems almost immediately. Assuming for the purposes of this discussion that there is a transformation of passive formation which operates roughly as shown above, consider the sentences in (18).

(18)   a.   The editor didn't find many mistakes.
        b.   Many mistakes weren't found by the editor.

The only difference between (18a) and (18b) is that passive has applied in the derivation of (18b) and not in (18a). The presence of the verb *do* in (18a) is accounted for by another transformation which inserts *do* under certain circumstances. This means that the deep structures of (18a) and (18b) are the same and therefore that the semantic representations will also be the same. Unfortunately, the sentences are not synonymous. Sentence (18a) is true if there were, in fact, very few mistakes for the editor to find and the editor found all the mistakes there were. Sentence (18b) states that there were many mistakes that the editor failed to find. See Partee (1971) for a thorough discussion of this problem.

Clearly, it was not possible to maintain the model in (10) along with the assumption that (18a) and (18b) have identical deep structures. Some revision would have to be made. Either the model in (10) would have to be revised so as to allow the application of transformations to have some effect on semantic representations, or the analysis of (18a) and (18b) would have to be changed so that the two sentences had different deep structures. Both alternatives were pursued, the first by Chomsky and R. Jackendoff, among others, and the second by J. R. Ross, J. D. McCawley, and G. Lakoff, among others. It is impossible to do justice here to the many issues raised in the course of the debate between these two approaches. Relevant readings can be found in the references cited at the end of the chapter.

1.2.3 The Extended Standard Theory

In this section we will look at the model that developed out of the standard theory, revised so as to handle the empirical problems encountered by the standard theory and the Katz-Postal Hypothesis. Most of what is said here is taken from Jackendoff (1972), perhaps the clearest and most comprehensive treatment of the relation between semantics and syntax in this theory.

The overall structure of the model is given in (19).

(19)   SYNTACTIC COMPONENT   SEMANTIC COMPONENT

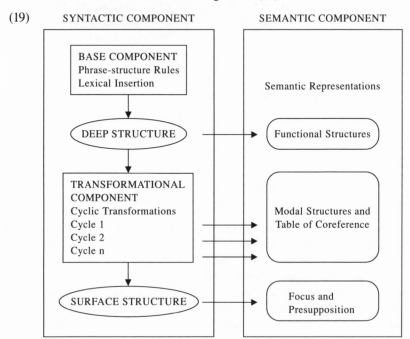

The structure of the syntactic part of the model is essentially the same as it was under the standard theory. Phrase structure rules and lexical insertion together produce deep structures. Deep structures are then subject to transformational rules, which apply (as they did in the standard theory) in a cyclic manner. The cycle governs the way rules apply to syntactic structures. The set of transformations applies first to the lowest (most subordinate) clause, then to the next lowest, and so on until they apply to the main clause. The output of the transformational component is the surface structure, which then undergoes phonological rules to produce the phonetic representation.

What makes the extended standard theory different from the standard theory is the relation of semantics to syntax. From the diagram in (19), it would appear that syntax and semantics have become intertwined in a more complicated way than they were in the standard theory. As we shall see, however, this model represents a significant move toward distinguishing the two components and making them autonomous from each other.

Let us first discuss the structure of the semantic component represented on the right-hand side of (19). The semantic representation of a sentence, claims Jackendoff, is not a single, uniform structure. It consists of several well-defined subparts, each of which contains a different type of information, and each of which is based on a different stage in the syntactic derivation. From deep structure we derive what Jackendoff calls functional structure. This structure contains, as the name implies, semantic functions and their arguments, and expresses the "who-did-what-to-whom" aspect of the meaning of the sentence. Notice that in (18a) and (18b) above, although the sentences are certainly not synonymous, in both cases the editor is the one doing the finding (or not finding), and mistakes are the things being found (or not being found). Thus it remains possible for this aspect of meaning to be derived from syntactic deep structures.

The second and third parts of the semantic representation are derived cumulatively, on the basis of what are called cycle-final structures. Cycle-final structures are pieces of syntactic structure, consisting of a particular clause and all the clauses it contains, at the point after all transformations have applied to that particular clause.

Modal structure has to do with the scope of negation and quantified elements (the elements causing problems for the Katz-Postal hypothesis in (18)), as well as with a number of other things. This structure is sensitive to whether or not transformations have applied, since it is based on cycle-final (that is, transformed) structures.

The table of coreference expresses which pairs of noun phrases in a sentence must refer to the same thing, which pairs must refer to different things, and which may or may not refer to the same thing. Like modal structure, the table of coreference is constructed on the basis of cycle-final structures. Consider as an example the sentences in (20).

(20)   a.   **Mary** saw **herself** in the mirror.
       b.   **Mary** saw **her** in the mirror.
       c.   **Mary** thinks that **she** is attractive.

In (20a), the reflexive pronoun *herself* must refer to the same individual as the noun phrase *Mary* in order for the sentence to be grammatical. In contrast, the non-reflexive pronoun *her* in (20b) must refer to someone other than *Mary* in order for the sentence to be grammatical. In (20c), the sentence is grammatical whether or not the pronoun *she* refers to *Mary*. Using the abbreviation *coref* to mean coreferential with, or referring to the same thing as, the table of coreference for (20a) will contain the specification [Mary +coref herself]. The table of coreference for (20b) will contain the specification [Mary −coref her]. The table of coreference for (20c) will not contain any specification for the pair [Mary, she], leaving these noun phrases free to be coreferential or non-coreferential. The sentences in (21), which have the same deep structure but different transformational histories, illustrate that the application of transformations can have an effect on the table of coreference.

(21)   a.   That Mary was fired doesn't bother her a bit. (*her* may or may not refer to Mary)
       b.   It doesn't bother her a bit that Mary was fired. (*her* cannot refer to Mary)

The last part of the semantic representation is derived on the basis of syntactic surface structures and has to do with focus and presupposition. The presupposition of a declarative sentence, very roughly, is that information which the speaker assumes that the hearer knows. The focus is the information which the speaker assumes that the hearer does not know. (Note that these very rough definitions hold only for declarative sentences.) Focus and presupposition depend on a number of factors, including stress pattern, and, as the transformationally related sentences in (22) and (23) show, are affected by the application of transformations such as passive formation and contrastive stress assignment.

(22)   a.   Mary drank the SHAVING LOTION. (not the peach brandy)
       b.   Mary DRANK the shaving lotion. (She didn't give it to her brother for his birthday.)
       c.   MARY drank the shaving lotion. (The pet alligator didn't.)
(23)   a.   The soldiers cleaned up the beach. (We knew that the soldiers were going to clean something up. I'm telling you that thing was the beach.)
       b.   The beach was cleaned up by the soldiers. (We know that the beach was going to be cleaned up. I'm telling you that the soldiers did it.)

The important thing here is not so much which aspects of meaning are based on which level of syntactic representation, but rather the idea that various syntactic levels may contain information relevant to the meaning.

1.2.3.1 THE AUTONOMY OF SYNTAX

Another major change introduced at this point was the idea that the syntactic component should be autonomous—that syntactic rules should be able to refer only to syntactic information. This is reminiscent of the idea of separation of levels in the American structuralist tradition. Specifically, Jackendoff pointed out that transformations such as reflexivization and equi-NP deletion, among others, which substituted pro-forms for full expressions, or deleted expressions under coreference with other expressions, made reference to information which is semantic rather than syntactic. For a full discussion of the problems associated with rules of this type, see Jackendoff (1972). Jackendoff proposed that transformations be constrained so as not to be able to mention reference or coreference, and that rules such as those listed in (24) should therefore be eliminated in favor of interpretative rules such as those creating the table of coreference.

(24) a. Reflexivization: converts a full noun phrase to a reflexive pronoun when there is an antecedent in an appropriate position. (John saw John $\Rightarrow$ John saw himself)
      b. Pronominalization: converts a full noun phrase to a pronoun when there is an antecedent in an appropriate position. (Mary wonders whether Mary will win $\Rightarrow$ Mary wonders whether she will win)
      c. Equi-NP deletion: deletes the subject of a subordinate clause when there is an antecedent in the next clause up. (John expects that John will win $\Rightarrow$ John expects to win)

What this means is that pronouns and gaps (like the empty subject of *to win* in (24c)) are present at deep structure. Jackendoff proposed that the subject of the embedded clause in *John expects to win* is an abstract element, Δ, which is interpreted by rules of coreference similar to those interpreting pronouns and reflexives. The introduction of abstract elements such as these marked a turning point in linguistic theory and paved the way for the development of the so-called Y-shaped model of grammar, sometimes known by the awkward name "Revised Extended Standard Theory."

1.2.4 The Y-shaped Model

Once abstract elements, or empty categories as they came to be known, were accepted as possible entities in syntactic representations, a major simplification of the model of grammar became possible. Instead of the model in (19), in which various syntactic levels served as input to the semantic component, the model in (25) was proposed.

(25)

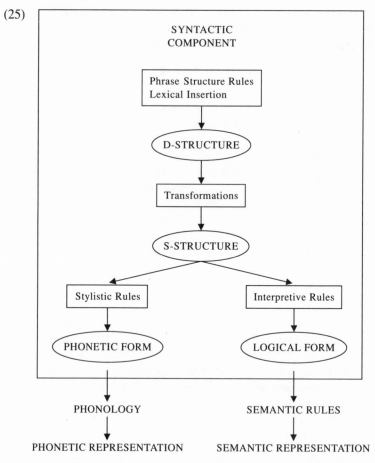

SYNTACTIC
COMPONENT

Phrase Structure Rules
Lexical Insertion

↓

D-STRUCTURE

↓

Transformations

↓

S-STRUCTURE

Stylistic Rules   Interpretive Rules

↓   ↓

PHONETIC FORM   LOGICAL FORM

↓   ↓

PHONOLOGY   SEMANTIC RULES

↓   ↓

PHONETIC REPRESENTATION   SEMANTIC REPRESENTATION

Notice that in this model, as in the standard theory, semantic representation is based on a single syntactic level. This time, however, the relevant level is not deep structure at all, but rather surface structure.

The picture in (25) actually overstates the similarities between this model and the standard theory. There are several reasons for this. First, the various rule components are very different in this model from what they were in the standard theory. In the standard theory, phrase structure rules were relatively unconstrained in terms of what a particular category could consist of. Here, phrase structure rules are constrained by X-bar theory (see chapter 2). In the standard theory, the transformational component consisted of a relatively large number of construction-specific rules, such as passive formation, question formation, relative clause formation, dative shift, subject-to-object raising, subject-verb inversion, and the like. Here, the transformational component contains only a very small number of very general transformations such as

Move NP and Move WH-Phrase (see chapters 5 and 7). Second, empty categories play a crucial role in the model depicted in (25). Not only are there empty elements such as the one in the subordinate subject position in *John expects to win,* but whenever an element is moved by a transformation, an empty element called a *trace* remains in the moved element's original position. For this reason, the output of the transformational component is no longer called surface structure. It is a more abstract level than the surface structure of the standard theory, and the name has been changed to reflect this. With empty categories such as the two just mentioned, the D-structure of a sentence is fully recoverable from the S-structure. This is what makes it possible for semantic interpretation to be done purely on the basis of S-structure. Finally, this model has a number of well-formedness conditions on representations, which did not exist in the standard theory. The standard theory had a number of conditions governing the applicability of rules, but no separate conditions on the representations themselves. The next section is devoted to a discussion of the significance of conditions on representations.

1.2.5 From Rules to Representations

As stated in the previous section, a major change in the theory was the shift in emphasis from rules to representations. In the standard theory, rules were very specific, as the example in (26) shows.

(26) Passive:
X NP V NP Y
1 2 3 4 5 ⇒ 1 4 be en 3 by+2 5

The rule in (26) is a version of the passive transformation for English. Note that the transformation explicitly mentions three English morphemes and is based on English word order. This means that any other language exhibiting a passive construction will have to have a different transformation to account for it. In a theory that relies on conditions on representations, it is possible to have a transformation such as the one given in (27) and discussed in some detail in chapter 5.

(27) Move NP.

The transformation in (27) makes no mention of word order. In fact, it is completely silent on the question of which NP should move, where it should move to, and under what circumstances. These questions are dealt with by the conditions on representations. The conditions hold at various levels, such as D-structure, S-structure, and Logical Form, but they hold regardless of whether any transformations have applied. An example of a condition on representations is the Case Filter, discussed in chapter 6. This filter states where lexically filled (that is, non-empty) noun phrases may occur at S-structure, and guarantees, for example, that *the car,* in (28) must undergo NP-movement from subordinate subject position to main clause subject position.

(28)   a.   *It seems the car to be rather dirty.
       b.   The car seems ___ to be rather dirty.

It turns out that the division of labor between very general transformations, such as NP-movement, and conditions on representations, such as the Case Filter, make it possible to achieve a greater level of consistency among the grammars of various languages. While specific matters of word order and grammatical morphemes forced standard theory transformations to be language-particular, it can be shown that all languages exhibit rules such as NP-movement and WH-movement. The conditions on representations, likewise, are essentially the same from language to language. Since our ultimate goal is to discover the nature of universal grammar, the increased generality achieved by the move from rules to representations is clearly a good result. This advance set the stage for a rather clearly articulated theory of universal grammar, which has come to be known as the "Principles and Parameters Approach."

1.2.6 Principles and Parameters

In this section, we will take a brief look at the view of universal grammar and language acquisition which underlies current research in generative grammar. In recent years, as researchers have come closer to attempting to achieve explanatory adequacy and to addressing the question of language acquisition, the nature and role of universal grammar has changed. In early years, it was often seen almost as a toolbox for the linguist, containing all the basic elements and operations found in grammars of the languages of the world. An individual grammar would make use of some, but not necessarily all, of the things found in universal grammar. This view is clearly incompatible with the idea that universal grammar constitutes the biological endowment for language, since the acquisition of a particular language would consist in large part of learning which elements not to use. Additionally, this view of universal grammar implies, rather implausibly, that the child acquiring a language has all the pieces needed to build a grammar of any language in the world, but no notion of how they are organized.

A more sophisticated view of universal grammar regarded it as a set of specifications or constraints which governed what a grammar of a language must look like. The problem with this approach was that it did not sufficiently reduce the amount of learning required of the child acquiring language. The Principles and Parameters Approach, while still in its early stages, seems to offer more hope that we will eventually achieve an understanding of the question of language acquisition. This approach sees universal grammar as having essentially the same structure as the grammar of a particular language. The difference is that at various points in the grammar, there are choices to be made, or parameters to be fixed, by the child acquiring a particular language. For example, one parameter has to do with the position of the head of a phrase with respect to its complements and modifiers. In English, the verb comes at the beginning of the verb phrase, while in other languages, such as Bengali and Japanese, the verb comes at the end of the verb phrase. This parameter has two values: phrases are either head-initial or head-final. It is still an open question whether this parameter is fixed once for each category, once for each class of categories (classes yet to be determined), or once for each language. With respect to phrase structure, then, universal grammar determines almost everything in the grammar of a particular language. The child must simply learn whether the head goes at the beginning or the end of the phrase. For each parameter in universal grammar, there will be a finite (and preferably very small) number of possible settings, and the information necessary to fix the parameter will be present in the linguistic data available to the child. Once the parameters have been fixed, the grammar of the language will be essentially complete.

Research on parameters is still in its infancy. The most well-developed set of parameters that I am aware of has been proposed for stress systems in the theory of metrical phonology (Dresher and Kaye 1990). In syntax, a number of parameters have been proposed, and some, notably the so-called null-subject parameter, have been the subject of research on language acquisition (Hyams 1986). What is mysterious about parameters in syntax is that there seem to be so few of them. It has been proposed (Chomsky 1989) that in fact all syntactic parameters are to be found in the lexicon, rather than in the grammar itself. If this were true, then the acquisition of the syntactic component of a particular language would consist essentially of learning the words of that language, where by learning a word we mean learning its meaning, its syntactic and morphological properties, and its phonological representation.

The theory of Government and Binding, then, is a theory of linguistic competence which fits into the principles and parameters approach to universal grammar. Questions of explanatory adequacy and language acquisition will not figure prominently throughout the rest of this book as we look at how the theory works. It should be borne in mind, however, that the ultimate goal of research in this theory is, and has been since the beginning, to understand how it is possible to acquire knowledge of language.

Readings

Chomsky, Noam. 1965. *Aspects of the Theory of Syntax*. Cambridge, Mass.: MIT Press.

———. 1973. *The Logical Structure of Linguistic Theory*. New York: Plenum.

———. 1986. *Knowledge of Language: Its Nature, Origin and Use*. New York: Praeger.

————. 1989. "Some Notes on Economy of Derivation and Representation." In I. Laka and A. Mahajan, *Functional Heads and Clause Structure: MIT Working Papers in Linguistics*, vol. 10. Cambridge, Mass.: Massachusetts Institute of Technology.

Dresher, B. Elan, and Jonathan D. Kaye. 1990. "A Computational Learning Model for Metrical Phonology." *Cognition* 34:137–95.

Hyams, Nina M. 1986. *Language Acquisition and the Theory of Parameters*. Dordrecht: Reidel.

Jackendoff, Ray. 1972. *Semantic Interpretation in Generative Grammar*. Cambridge, Mass.: MIT Press.

Katz, Jerrold J., and Paul M. Postal. 1964. *An Integrated Theory of Linguistic Descriptions*. Cambridge, Mass.: MIT Press.

Lakoff, George. 1971. "On Generative Semantics." In Danny D. Steinberg and Leon A. Jakobovits, *Semantics*, pp. 232–96. London: Cambridge University Press.

Lightfoot, David. 1982. *The Language Lottery*. Cambridge, Mass.: MIT Press.

McCawley, James D. 1968. "The Role of Semantics in Grammar." In Emmon Bach and Robert T. Harms, *Universals in Linguistic Theory*, pp. 125–69. New York: Holt, Rinehart and Winston.

Newmeyer, Frederick J. 1980. *Linguistic Theory in America*. New York: Academic Press.

————. 1983. *Grammatical Theory: Its Limits and Its Possibilities*. Chicago, Ill.: University of Chicago Press.

Partee, Barbara H. 1971. "On the Requirement that Transformations Preserve Meaning." In Charles J. Fillmore and D. Terence Langendoen, *Studies in Linguistic Semantics*, pp. 1–21. New York: Holt, Rinehart and Winston.

Ross, John Robert. 1970. "On Declarative Sentences." In Roderick A. Jacobs and Peter S. Rosenbaum, *Readings in English Transformational Grammar*, pp. 222–72. Waltham, Mass.: Ginn and Company.

————. 1972. "Auxiliare als Hauptverben." In Werner Abraham and Robert Binnick, *Generative Semantik*, pp. 95–115. Frankfurt am Main: Athenäum Verlag.

2 Categories and Phrase Structure

The earliest models of generative-transformational grammar (Chomsky 1965) contained a base component, whose output was the set of deep structures of a particular language. The base component consisted of two subcomponents, the categorial component and the lexical component. The categorial component contained phrase structure rules of the sort exemplified in (1).

(1) S → NP VP
     VP → V (NP) (PP)
     NP → NP S

The only constraint on phrase structure rules was that they be context-free. In other words they took the form in (2).

(2) A → X,
     where A is a single category, and X is a string of categories.

A theory such as this one clearly allows for many phrase structure rules that never occur. Some examples are given in (3).

(3) NP → S VP
     PP → NP VP DET

What is needed, then, is a theory which defines what phrase structure rules are possible in natural language. This definition should be as narrow as possible, so that anything it permits actually occurs in some language. In addition, we require a theory of syntactic categories which allows for just those categories which actually occur.

In this chapter, we will pursue these two goals, and ultimately develop a theory of phrase structure rules that corresponds essentially to the one proposed by Jackendoff (1977). It will be superior to the earlier model in two ways. First, it will be more empirically adequate, in that it will account for a wider range of data. Second, it will specify in more detail what types of phrase structures are possible in language. Recall that one of the tasks of universal grammar is to define as narrowly as possible the properties of a grammar of a human language. One aspect of a grammar that must be defined this way is the types of phrase structures involved.

2.1 The Notion "Head of a Phrase"

The phrase categories in (4) are fairly typical of those found in early generative grammars.

(4) a. NP → (DET) (ADJP) N
  b. VP → V (NP) ($\left\{\begin{matrix} ADVP \\ PP \end{matrix}\right\}$)*
  c. PP → P NP
  d. ADJP → (DEG) ADJ
  e. ADVP → (DEG) ADV

   Notice that the name of each of these phrase categories contains the name of a lexical category. This is no accident; a noun phrase must contain a noun, a verb phrase must contain a verb, and so on. In almost all cases, every other element of the phrase category is optional, while the element after which the phrase category is named is obligatory. Let us call the obligatory element in the phrase category the *head* of that category. In (5) below, the heads of all of the phrase categories are set in boldface type. Each element set in boldface type is the head of the phrase category immediately dominating it.

(5)

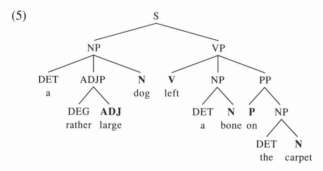

   In addition to being generally obligatory, the head of a category has other privileged characteristics. For example, it is the properties of the head that become properties of the phrase category as a whole. Consider the noun phrases in (6) and (7).

(6) a. the tall man
  b. the happy woman
  c. the brown dog
  d. the intelligent girl
(7) a. the brown dog
  b. the red car
  c. the white sugar
  d. the blue sky

In (6) all the nouns bear the feature [+animate]—in other words, they refer to living things. Any speaker of English would agree that the noun phrases in (6) are animate noun phrases. The adjectives in (7) are all adjectives of color, but it is much less acceptable to say that the noun phrases in (7) are color noun phrases. Another example is given in (8) and (9).

(8) a. under the porch
     b. in the garden
     c. on the stove
(9) a. beside the woman
     b. with the man
     c. for the child

The prepositions in (8) are all prepositions of location, and the prepositional phrases are clearly locative. The noun phrases in (9) are all animate, but there is no sense in which the prepositional phrases are animate.

We have now seen two examples in which semantic properties of the head of a phrase are also properties of the phrase as a whole. In recent years much work has been done on the basis of the double-barreled assumption that properties of the head are properties of the phrase, and properties of the phrase are properties of the head. This work has led to some rather interesting and sometimes surprising results involving new syntactic categories, which will be taken up in chapter 4. For now, however, we will stick with the phrase categories inherited from early transformational grammar.

In the case of NP, VP, ADJP and ADVP, it is possible for a phrase category to consist only of its head. This is illustrated in (10).

(10) a.   b.

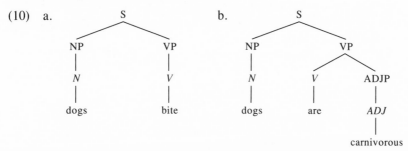

Thus, for the categories NP, VP, ADJP and ADVP, the only obligatory element is the head of the phrase. All other material is optional.

We could, at this point, elevate this observation to the status of a rule of universal grammar. There are two reasons for doing this. First, it places an immediate restriction on the types of phrase structures that languages can have and therefore takes an initial step toward defining what may be built-in, or innate, to children acquiring language. Second, by making such a strong claim, we are forcing ourselves to take a much closer look at data that seem to contradict it. Either we will discover that the data can, and should, be analyzed in such a way as to conform to the proposed universal grammar rule, or we will have to revise the rule of universal grammar. In either case, we will learn something, either about the particular language, or about universal grammar. Without a strong claim, we would have no particular reason to question, or examine more closely, an analysis which might be either wrong or very important to the determination of universal grammar.

The rule of universal grammar will look something like (11).

(11) $XP \rightarrow \ldots X \ldots$, where all material in '. . .' is optional and X is a variable ranging over lexical categories.

The rule in (11) is to be interpreted with both occurrences of X referring to the same lexical category.

Let us now examine the rules in (4) to see whether they all conform to the statement in (11). In fact, there is an immediate problem. The phrase structure rule for PP has an obligatory NP following the preposition.

(12) $PP \rightarrow P \; NP$

Thus PP seems to violate the generalization that everything but the head of a phrase is optional. This is the type of situation referred to above, which should lead to a re-examination of the analysis. Either we must make the rule for PP fit the generalization in (11) or we must somehow revise the generalization. It is preferable to retain the generalization, if possible, since any revision that allows for the phrase structure rule in (12) would widen the range of possible phrase structure rules. Thus, the language learner would have a wider range of possibilities to choose from in acquiring the language. Therefore, let us first look again at prepositions and PP's to see whether the generalization in (11) might actually hold for this category.

It is true that many prepositions require a following NP, as shown in (13).

(13)   a.   *She ran into.
        b.   *He cut the bread with.

However, consider the following sentences.

(14)   a.   He turned the lamp on.
        b.   She put the book down.
        c.   Sue sent the report over.
(15)   a.   He turned the lamp on its side.
        b.   She put the book down the garbage disposal.
        c.   Sue sent the report over the back fence.

There is a class of words which have traditionally been called particles. Some of these are shown in (14). In most cases, these words also belong to the class of prepositions, as shown in (15). Suppose that prepositions, like verbs, could be either transitive (take an object) or intransitive (take no object). As with verbs, some prepositions are always transitive, some are always intransitive, and some are both transitive and intransitive. Examples are given in (16)–(18).

(16) Intransitive only:
    a.   He threw the book away.
    b.   *He threw the book away the window.
(17) Transitive only:
    a.   *She ran into.
    b.   She ran into the house.
(18) Both transitive and intransitive:
    a.   Sue put her hat on.
    b.   Sue put her hat on the shelf.

If we assume that particles are, in fact, simply intransitive prepositions, then the structures of (a) and (b) are as shown in (19).

(19)   a.

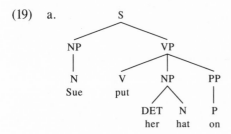

   b.

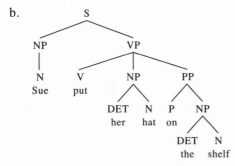

This analysis is attractive, in that it allows us to maintain the generalization in (11) and permits us to reduce the number of lexical categories needed in the grammar. It does, however, raise some questions about intransitive prepositions. First, intransitive prepositions frequently seem to alter the meaning of the verb. For example, when we turn a lamp on, we do not actually turn the lamp. Second, intransitive PP's, in contrast to transitive PP's, by and large participate in an alternation shown in (20) and (21).

(20) a. Marge put her hat on.
      b. Marge put on her hat.
(21) a. Marge put her hat on the shelf.
      b. *Marge put on the shelf her hat.

The meaning shift can be handled fairly easily. There are many expressions whose meaning is different from the combination of the meanings of the words in the expression; these are called idioms. Verb-preposition combinations such as *turn NP on, put NP down* (meaning denigrate), etc., can simply be listed in the lexicon with their meanings.

The word-order alternation in (20) can also be accounted for, but the account requires more theoretical apparatus than we have developed at this point. Essentially, the verb and the preposition undergo a restructuring process which allows them to jointly take an object NP. This process only works if the preposition does not have an object of its own.

We will adopt the hypothesis that particles are really intransitive prepositions, while acknowledging that many details remain to be worked out.

The phrase structure rule for PP can now be stated as in (22), the generalization in (11) can be maintained, and the category *particle* can be eliminated from the grammar.

(22) PP → P (NP)

Given this analysis, we can now say that in all of the cases examined so far, the only obligatory element in a phrase category is the head of that category. Thus it is possible to state a rule schema which describes the expansion of all phrase categories, as in (23):

(23) XP → (C$_1$) (C$_2$) . . . (C$_j$) X (C$_{j+1}$) . . . (C$_k$),
      where X = N, V, ADJ, ADV or P,
      and C$_i$ represents a non-head constituent.

2.2 Intermediate Structure within the Phrase Category

The phrase categories we have seen so far have only had two levels of structure: the level of the entire phrase and the level on which the head occurs, as illustrated in (24) below.

(24)

Since this structure has no hierarchical organization among the elements of the phrase category, it will be referred to as a flat structure. As we shall see, this type of structure is empirically inadequate, making a hierarchical structure, such as the one in (25), necessary.

(25)

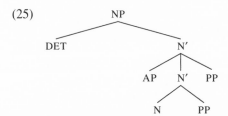

Let us look first at the internal structure of the noun phrase. Based on what we conclude from noun phrases, we will go on to examine the structure of the other phrase categories in the grammar. Consider the sentences in (26) below.

(26)   a.   I met the member of Parliament with gray hair.
       b.   *I met the member with gray hair of Parliament.

Under the analysis given in (24), the object noun phrases in (26) would both be given the structure shown in (27).

(27)

There is no way to predict that the noun phrase in (26a) is well-formed, while that in (26b) is ungrammatical. The flat structure treats both prepositional phrases as sisters of N. Since they belong to the same syntactic category, their order should be free, as it is with the two prepositional phrases in (28).

(28)   a.   A man [from Paris] [with blue eyes]
       b.   A man [with blue eyes] [from Paris]

It seems that, in (26), *of Parliament* is more closely tied to the head noun than is *with gray hair.*

There are many pairs of noun phrases which behave similarly to the ones just discussed. Some examples are shown in (29)–(31).

(29)   a.   We sold the box *of crackers* with the green label.
       b.   *We sold the box with the green label *of crackers.*
(30)   a.   The chairman *of the committee* in the blue suit.
       b.   *The chairman in the blue suit *of the committee.*
(31)   a.   A piece *of cake* on a plastic plate.
       b.   *A piece on a plastic plate *of cake.*

There is something that all of the italicized prepositional phrases in these examples have in common which distinguishes them from the other PP's in the data. According to Jackendoff (1977), these PP's are arguments of the nouns they follow. In other words, part of the meaning of these nouns is the fact that they take some kind of complement. A member must be a member of something; a chairman must be the chairman of something, and so on. In this way, these nouns are somewhat similar to transitive verbs, and the underlined PP's play a role similar to that played by the object of a verb. The other PP's, on the other hand, simply provide more information about the head noun. For this reason they are called modifiers. Since they restrict the set of things in the real world that the noun phrase can refer to, they are called restrictive modifiers.

Jackendoff has proposed that arguments are sisters of N, while restrictive modifiers are sisters of N'. His proposal, with some modifications not relevant to the point at hand, is illustrated in (32).

(32)

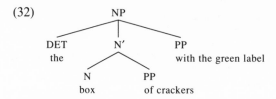

A structure like (32), together with the assumption that a PP is an argument if and only if it is a sister of N, accounts for the strict ordering of the PP's observed in (29)–(31) above.

This proposal, however, requires further motivation. It could also be proposed that PP's fall into two classes, PParg and PPmod, and that the phrase structure rule for NP looks like (33).

(33)   NP → (DET) (AP) N (PParg) (PPmod)* . . .

The rule in (33) also accounts for the strict ordering of PP's and retains the flat structure. I shall refer to it as the annotated flat structure.

Further motivation for the hierarchical structure can be found in the behavior of the pronoun *one*. This pronoun can represent part of a noun phrase, as (34) shows.

(34)   a.   Sue has a large dog, but Fred has a small one. (one = dog)
       b.   I live in an old white house and she lives in a new one. (one = white house)

One can also replace an N PP sequence, as shown in (35).

(35)   She likes the car with the white roof in the garage, not the one in the driveway. (one = car with the white roof)

However, there are some parts of noun phrases that cannot be replaced by *one*, as shown in (36).

(36)   a.   *I like the King of Sweden, but I can't stand the one of Denmark.
       b.   *I climbed to the top of the hill, but not to the one of the mountain.

Consider how the behavior of *one* could be described in terms of the two structures we have outlined. The hierarchical structure provides the following analyses of the noun phrases in (34)–(36).

(37)

(38)

(39)

(40)

(41)

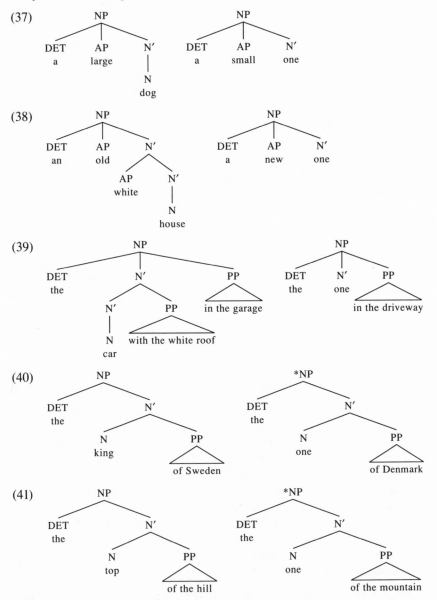

In all of the grammatical cases above, *one* has replaced all of the material dominated by an N′ node. In the two ungrammatical cases, *one* has replaced material dominated only by N. Thus if we adopt the hierarchical structure, we can simply say that *one* is a pronoun substituting for N'.

The annotated flat structure gives the following analyses.

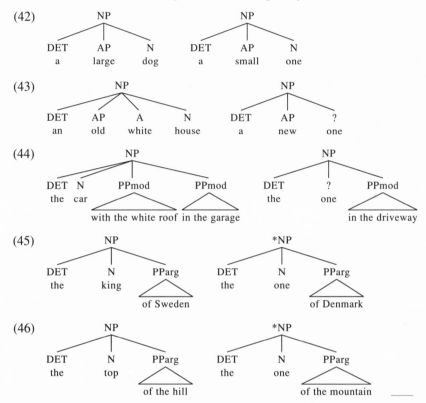

(42)

NP				NP		
DET	AP	N		DET	AP	N
a	large	dog		a	small	one

(43)

NP					NP		
DET	AP	A	N		DET	AP	?
an	old	white	house		a	new	one

(44)

NP					NP		
DET	N	PPmod	PPmod		DET	?	PPmod
the	car				the	one	
		with the white roof	in the garage				in the driveway

(45)

NP				*NP		
DET	N	PParg		DET	N	PParg
the	king			the	one	
		of Sweden				of Denmark

(46)

NP				*NP		
DET	N	PParg		DET	N	PParg
the	top			the	one	
		of the hill				of the mountain

With this type of structure, there is no obvious structural generalization describing the range of material that *one* can replace. It replaces N in (42), and the result is grammatical. However, when it replaces N in (45) and (46), the results are ungrammatical. In (43) and (44), *one* is replacing strings of material that do not even form constituents. (AP + N, N + PP). The only statement that holds true is that when there is a PParg in the noun phrase, *one* cannot replace the material preceding the PParg.

Let us therefore adopt the hierarchical approach to the structure of NP and assume that *one* can replace any N'. We can now use the distribution of *one* to learn more about the details of NP structure.

Consider the sentences in (47).

(47)   I want this big fuzzy pink rabbit, not
    a.   that one. (one = big fuzzy pink rabbit)
    b.   that little one. (one = fuzzy pink rabbit)

   c.   that little shiny one. (one = pink rabbit)
   d.   that little shiny blue one. (one = rabbit)

If we assume that *one* can only replace material which forms an N' constituent, then the structure of the noun phrase in (47) must be:

(48)

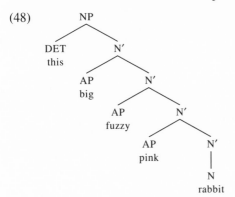

Now consider the sentences in (49).

(49)   I know that man with the bald head in the living room on the sofa, not
    a.   the other one. (one = man with the bald head in the living room on the sofa)
    b.   the one on the chair. (one = man with the bald head in the living room)
    c.   the one in the dining room on the chair. (one = man with the bald head)
    d.   the one with blond hair in the dining room on the chair. (one = man)

Again assuming that *one* can only replace N', the noun phrase in (49) has the structure shown in (50).

(50)

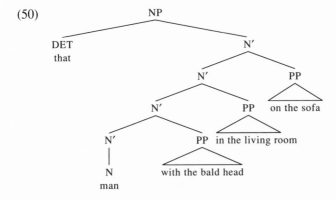

To make matters slightly more complicated, let us consider an example in which there is both a prenominal adjective phrase and a postnominal prepositional phrase.

(51) I want that big rabbit on the shelf, not
   a.   this one. (one = big rabbit on the shelf)
   b.   this little one. (one = rabbit on the shelf)
   c.   this one on the table. (one = big rabbit)
   d.   this little one on the table. (one = rabbit)

Upon careful examination of the various phrases that must be N′, we find ourselves in an apparently impossible situation. There is no way that *big rabbit* can form an N′ excluding *on the shelf*, while at the same time *rabbit on the shelf* forms an N′ excluding *big*. We must have at least two possible structures for the noun phrase in (51) to account for all of the facts in (51a–d).

(52) a.

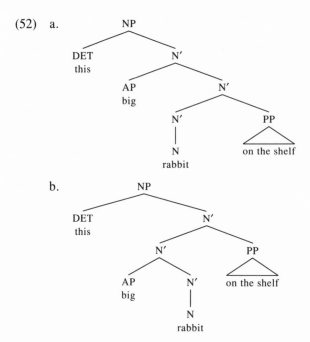

b.

Structure (52a) accounts for (51b) but not for (51c). Structure (52b) accounts for (51c) but not for (51b). Both structures can account for (51a) and (51d). What this means is that the first clause in (51) is ambiguous. In other words, it can have a number of different well-formed structures.

Before going on, let us write a phrase structure rule, or a set of rules, to describe the structures we have developed for the English noun phrase.

(53)   a.   NP → DET N′
       b.   N′ → N (PP)   (for argument PP's)
       c.   N′ → N′ (PP)
       d.   N′ → (AP) N′

Rules (53b) and (53c) can be collapsed into one using the brace notation, as shown in (54).

(54)   N′ → $\begin{Bmatrix} N \\ N' \end{Bmatrix}$ PP

We have determined that the English noun phrase has a hierarchical structure and that the intermediate node, N′, can occur more than once in the structure of a particular noun phrase. We have also determined, from the behavior of the English pronoun *one*, that N′ and N must be distinct levels. *One* substitutes for N′, but not for N. Let us now consider whether it is necessary for N′ and NP to have distinct labels. If it is not, then NP could be used as the label for the intermediate node.

First of all, are there any pronouns that substitute for NP but not N′? It turns out that there are. Consider the sentences in (55).

(55)   a.   I lost my jacket, but I found it later.
       b.   *I lost my new jacket, but at least I still have the old it.
       c.   I lost my new jacket, but at least I still have the old one.

The definite pronouns in English (*he, she, him, them, her, they,* etc.) substitute for NP, as shown in (55a), and crucially not for N′, as (55b) shows. Thus it seems that NP and N′ are indeed different and should be labeled differently.

We have seen that if there is an intermediate phrase category (N′) within the noun phrase, certain otherwise baffling facts about the order of PP's within NP, and the distribution of the pronoun *one*, can be explained. Turning to the verb phrase, we will see that it requires a similar type of intermediate category. Consider the following sentences.

(56)   a.   Sue asked Fred to cook dinner, and he did so.
       b.   Sue stirred the soup with a spoon, but Fred did so with a fork.
       c.   *Sue cooked lunch, and Fred did so dinner.

The phrase *do so* can substitute for an entire verb phrase, as in (56a), or for part of a verb phrase, as in (56b). However, it cannot substitute for a verb alone without its direct object, as illustrated in (56c). This phenomenon is similar to the situation found in noun phrases with the pronoun *one*, and it can be accounted for in a similar way. Suppose that the verb phrase, instead of having the flat structure illustrated in (57), is analyzed as in (58).

(57)

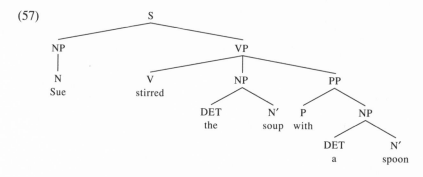

(58)

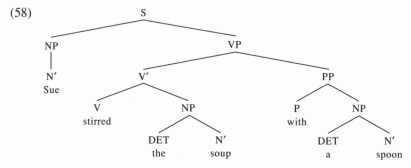

Given the structure in (58), the data in (56) can be accounted for if *did so* substitutes either for V′ or for VP, but not for V. Further evidence of this type of structure can be found in the possible orderings of elements within the verb phrase. The sentences in (59) show that although the order of elements within the verb phrase is relatively free, nothing can come between the verb and the direct object.

(59)   a.   Emily ate her soup quietly on Thursday.
       b.   Emily ate her soup on Thursday quietly.
       c.   *Emily ate quietly her soup on Thursday.
       d.   *Emily ate on Thursday her soup quietly.

If the direct object is dominated by V′, as in (58), then we can say that the order of elements dominated by VP is relatively free, while still forcing the direct object to remain next to the verb. The flat structure in (57) does not provide any way to single out the direct object from the rest of the postverbal elements in VP.

The notation we have used to describe the hierarchical structure of the verb phrase and the noun phrase is known as the "bar" notation. The lexical head of a category has no bars (N, V) and each level within the category has one more than, or the same number of bars as, the level immediately below it. A fully expanded noun phrase has the structure shown in (60).

(60)

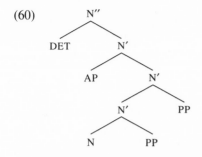

The term noun phrase, or NP, is used to refer to the entire category, or the category with the maximum number of bars. Another term often used is N^{max}. Thus, if the structure in (60) is correct, NP, N^{max} and N'' all mean exactly the same thing.

It will prove useful at this point to revise slightly our definition of the notion "head." There are actually three different ways in which a node can be a head. The term head, as we have been using it, refers only to the lexical head of a category, that is to the node which has no bars and is of the same category (N, V, etc.) as the phrase category itself. Thus, in (60) the head of N'' is N. Henceforth, this notion will be expressed by the terms "lexical head" or "X^0 head." Another sense expressed by the term "head of X^n" is the node *immediately* dominated by X^n which itself dominates the X^0 head of X^n. To refer unambiguously to this sense of head, we will use the term "immediate head." The term head on its own will mean *any* node dominated by X^n which dominates the X^0 head of X^n, including the X^0 head itself.

2.3 A Phrase Structure Grammar

The following is a phrase structure grammar which incorporates the various proposals made in this chapter and which makes use of the bar notation.

(61) $S \rightarrow N''\ V''$

$V'' \rightarrow V'\ (\left\{ \begin{matrix} P' \\ ADV' \end{matrix} \right\})^*$

$V' \rightarrow V\ (N'')$

$P' \rightarrow P\ (N'')$

$N'' \rightarrow (DET)\ N'$

$N' \rightarrow (ADJ')\ N'$

$N' \rightarrow \left\{ \begin{matrix} N' \\ N \end{matrix} \right\} PP$

$ADJ' \rightarrow (DEG)\ ADJ$

$ADV' \rightarrow (DEG)\ ADV$

2.4 Cross-category Generalizations

We have seen that both NP's and VP's must have a certain amount of internal structure, and we have expressed this structure by means of bar notation. In this section, we will examine other properties that the various categories have in common and will extend the notation to account for these properties.

2.4.1 Conjunction

Consider the sentences in (62)–(65) below:

(62) a.   John [bought a car on Monday] and [sold his bicycle on Tuesday].
      b.   Sue [buys] and [sells] antiques.
      c.   Fred [buys junk] and [sells antiques] in Vancouver.
(63) a.   The [large houses] and [small stores] were torn down.
      b.   The large [boxes of crackers] and [bottles of milk] were stolen.
      c.   [The tall man] and [a short woman] were dancing.
      d.   The [king] and [queen] of Sweden arrived.
(64) a.   The furniture was very [old] and [worn].
      b.   The house was [rather large] but [very crowded].
(65) a.   The little boy fell [off the chair] and [onto the floor].
      b.   The dog ran [up] and [down] the hill.

All of these sentences contain conjoined structures. In (62), verb phrases or parts of verb phrases are conjoined. Given the structure defined in the previous section, it is fairly easy to see how the various sentences in (62) are constructed.

(66) a.

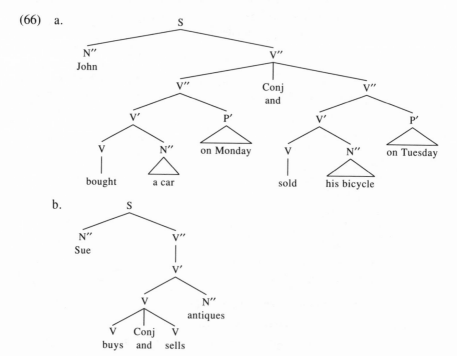

c.

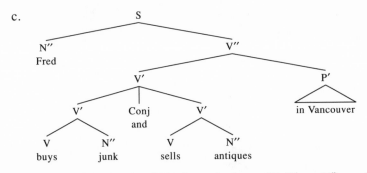

Notice that any of the levels within the verb phrase (V, V', or V") can be conjoined. The same is true for noun phrases, as shown in (63) and in (67) below.

(67) a.

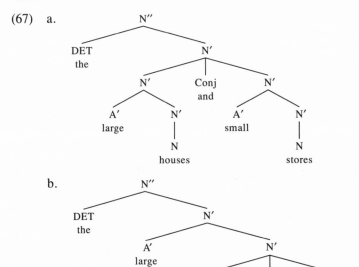

b.

c.

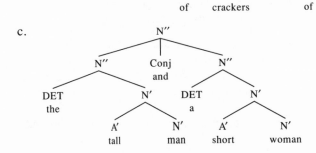

d.

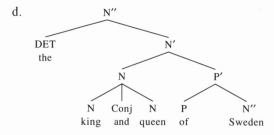

The sentences in (64) and (65) illustrate the same behavior for adjective phrases and prepositional phrases.

There are two ways to account for all of these conjoined structures. The first is to write a separate phrase structure rule for each possibility. This alternative would require a large number of phrase structure rules, such as those in (68).

(68)   a.   N″ → N″ Conj N″
       b.   N′ → N′ Conj N′
       c.   N → N Conj N
       d.   V″ → V″ Conj V″
       e.   V′ → V′ Conj V′
       f.   V → V Conj V
       g.   ADJ′ → ADJ′ Conj ADJ′
       h.   ADJ → ADJ Conj ADJ
       etc.

This approach has three flaws. First, a large number of phrase structure rules is required to express what is essentially a single property of language, namely that structures may be conjoined. Second, this analysis does not make any explicit generalizations about conjoined structures: which categories may be conjoined, and what do conjoined structures in general look like? By listing each category separately, the analysis predicts that no other categories will occur in conjoined structures. This prediction would be correct if there were certain categories in the grammar which, for no apparent reason, simply failed to occur in conjoined structures. However, the sentences in (69) suggest that perhaps all categories do occur in such structures.

(69)   a.   You should read [[this] or [that]] book by tomorrow. (determiner)
       b.   John [[can] and [will]] do the dishes. (modal verb)
       c.   Sue wants [[six] or [seven]] crayons. (numeral)

It would be more interesting to claim that, in principle, all categories may be conjoined, and then try to find an explanation for any particular category which cannot be conjoined. An analysis which simply lists those categories which do conjoin does not raise the question of why some do and some do not.

Also, by failing to treat the phenomenon of conjunction in a unified way, this analysis offers no principled account of the fact that the two conjoined categories are always the same and are always the same as the category dominating them. In other words, it fails to explain why conjoined structures such as those in (70) do not occur.

(70) a.   b.

Under the analysis given in (68), it is a complete coincidence that all conjoined structures consist of conjuncts of a single category, dominated by a node of the same category. Again, a better approach would be to claim that these categories are necessarily identical. If any counterexamples are found, these should be examined carefully and an explanation found for their unusual behavior. Thus, a superior analysis would do three things: eliminate unnecessary phrase structure rules, make interesting predictions about further data, and account for the fact that conjoined structures are of the same category as their conjuncts. The following approach has these three characteristics.

Let X be a variable ranging over all syntactic categories. Thus X can stand for N, V, ADJ, ADV, and P, and any other syntactic categories the grammar may contain. In addition, let i in X^i stand for any number of bars, including none at all. So N^i can stand for N, N′, or N″ (NP). The only constraint is that if i occurs more than once in a given expression, it stands for the same number of bars each time, and if X occurs more than once in a given expression, it stands for the same category each time. This constraint is simply the standard interpretation of a variable in any notational system that uses variables. Using X^i, we can now write one phrase structure rule for conjunction:

(71) $X^i \rightarrow X^i$ Conj X^i

This rule replaces all of the phrase structure rules in (68) and also makes predictions about other conjoined structures in the language. It predicts that any category at all may occur in a conjoined structure. In addition, it follows from the notation that all conjoined structures will consist of two occurrences of a given category, dominated by a node of the same category. This was made possible by introducing two variables, one ranging over categories (X), and the other ranging over numbers of bars (i). In the rest of this section, we will see further uses for these two variables.

2.4.2 Generalized Subject and Object Relations

The notions of subject and object have traditionally been used to describe the relations which noun phrases bear to verbs. So, for example, in (72), *Audrey* is the subject of *refused,* and *the offer* is the object of *refused.*

(72)   Audrey refused the offer.

Now consider the noun phrase in (73).

(73)   Audrey's refusal of the offer.

Intuitively, *Audrey* and *the offer* bear exactly the same relations to *refusal* in (73) as they do to *refused* in (72). Compare the structures in (74) and (75).

(74)

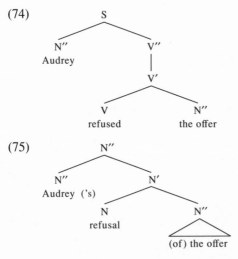

(75)

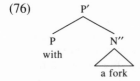

Notice that in both cases, the object is the noun phrase which is a sister of X^0 (V or N), and the subject is the noun phrase which is external to (not dominated by) X'.

The definition of object given here can easily be extended to include objects of prepositions, as shown in (76).

(76)

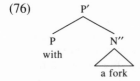

The noun phrase *a fork,* the object of the preposition, is a sister of P.

Now let us return to the elements which mark the subjects and objects of nouns. Obviously, nouns do not take "bare" subjects and objects as verbs do; the noun phrase in (77) is ungrammatical.

(77)   *Audrey refusal the offer.

Notice, however, that the missing elements are entirely predictable. The subjects of nouns are always marked with the possessive suffix *'s,* and the objects of nouns are always marked with the preposition *of.* The structure of the noun phrase should, strictly speaking, be as in (78).

(78)

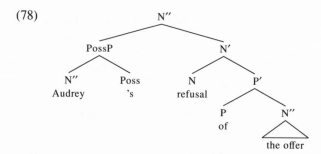

Since the possessive suffix and the preposition *of* function solely as markers for the subject and object, the structure in (78) can loosely be said to conform to the definitions of subject and object given.

Adjectives also take objects, as the sentences in (79) show.

(79)   a.   Eleanor fears nuclear war.
       b.   Eleanor is afraid of nuclear war.

In (79b), *nuclear war* bears the same relation to *afraid* as it does to *fears* in (79a).

(80)   a.   b.

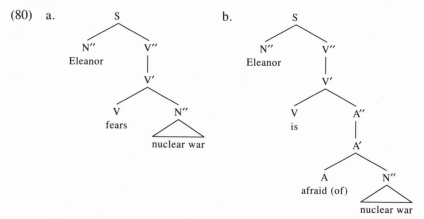

As with nouns, adjectives do not take "bare" objects. They are marked with the preposition *of* in the same way as with nouns, giving the structure in (81).

(81)

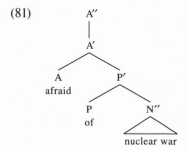

Thus, N, V, ADJ, and P all take objects. Objects of V and P occur as bare noun phrases, while those of N and ADJ occur as prepositional phrases.

We have seen that the major syntactic categories N, V, A, and P take objects and that V and N also take subjects. An obvious question to ask at this point is why P and A do not take subjects. Or can it perhaps be shown that they do, in fact, take subjects? Data such as (82) and (83) have been used to construct arguments that subjects occur with all major categories.

(82)   a.   I like [my steak rare].
         b.   I like [my steak to be rare].
(83)   a.   I prefer [George in a good mood].
         b.   I prefer that [George be in a good mood].

The bracketed expressions in (82a) and (83a) have been called small clauses. They differ from the full clauses in (82b) and (83b) in that they lack verbs. The nature of small clauses will be discussed in some detail later on; for the moment we will simply note that if the bracketed expressions in (82a) and (83a) are AP and PP respectively, the NP's *my steak* and *George* could conceivably be analyzed as the subjects of these categories. Thus, it may be possible to make the general claim that all major categories take subjects.

An object can be defined as the noun phrase which is a sister of X^0, for all major categories, and a subject as the noun phrase which is external to X'. Another question that deserves mention has to do with the position of the subject with respect to X''. In the case of N, the subject falls within X'', while with V, the subject lies outside X''. We are not yet in a position to do more than note this difference, but we will return to it in chapter 11.

In any case, the generalizations drawn about subjects and objects of various categories can be made only thanks to the category variable X.

Notice also that it now makes sense to talk about transitive and intransitive members of each category. Transitive and intransitive verbs are familiar, and transitive and intransitive prepositions have been introduced. Some examples of transitive and intransitive adjectives and nouns are given in (84).

(84)   a.   Adjectives
                i.   Transitive: afraid, fond, full
               ii.   Intransitive: happy, beautiful
         b.   Nouns
                i.   Transitive: refusal, destruction, theft
               ii.   Intransitive: departure, explosion, birth

2.5 Rule Schemata

The two variables introduced in the previous section make it possible to state in general terms exactly what types of phrase structure rules are possible. The rule schema in (85) is a refined version of that given in section 2.1.

2.5.1 The Major Rule Schema

(85) $X^n \rightarrow (C_1) \ldots (C_j) \, X^{n/n-1} \, (C_{j+1}) \ldots (C_k)$,
       where C_i is a maximal phrase category.

This schema allows only one type of non-head material, namely maximal phrase categories. Notice also that this rule schema allows the head, in a particular expansion, to have the same number of bars as the node dominating it. This is necessary to account for data like (86), which were discussed earlier in this chapter.

(86)   a.   *I met the king of France and Joe met the one of Spain.
       b.   I met the man with red hair and Trish met the one with the wig.
       c.   We arrested the man with red hair in apartment 3G, not the one in the penthouse.

In (86b), the prepositional phrases *with red hair* and *with the wig* are sisters of N', since *one* occurs with them. But (86c) shows that *with red hair* must be dominated by N', since *one* is interpreted as *the man with red hair*. The structure of *the man with red hair in apartment 3G* must be as given in (87).

(87)

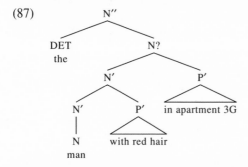

We thus know that N' can take N' as its head. But the rule schema in (85) allows any category to take an identical category as its head. If this prediction is correct, then we would expect to find structures like (88).

(88)

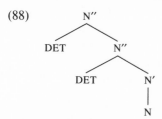

The structure in (88) would give rise to noun phrases such as those found in (89).

(89) a.   *This the house
      b.   *That you
      c.   *A her

Since such noun phrases do not seem to exist, we must conclude that N″ cannot serve as the head of another N″ node. In addition, (85) predicts that structures like (90) should occur, giving rise to noun phrases like those in (91).

(90)

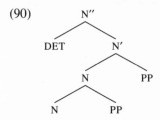

(91)   *A box of crackers of cookies

The important aspect of (91) is that both PP's, being sisters of N, are functional arguments in the sense of Jackendoff (1977). The ungrammaticality of (91) suggests that this is impossible. Thus it seems that the rule schema given in (85) is too general and that, at least in the case of noun phrases, the only category which can have an identical category as its head is N′. We thus provisionally revise (85) as (92).

(92) a. $X^n \rightarrow (C_1) \ldots (C_j) X^{n-1} (C_{j+1}) \ldots (C_k)$
      b. $X' \rightarrow (C_1) \ldots (C_j) X' (C_{j+1}) \ldots (C_k)$

2.5.2 The Conjunction Rule Schema.

(93) $X^i \rightarrow X^i \text{ Conj } X^i$

This schema also needs refinement. Notice that the structures generated by the conjunction rule as it stands must all involve exactly two conjuncts. There are, however, conjoined structures in English with three or more conjuncts. Examples are given in (94).

(94) a.   Trish, Kelly, and Emily watched the movie.
      b.   We should walk quietly, slowly, and carefully.
      c.   The children chopped, mashed, and pounded the bananas.
      d.   The toys are blue, green, yellow, orange, and red.

These sentences can, except for the fact that *and* does not always occur between pairs of elements, be generated by the conjunction rule we have, but consider the structures the rule assigns, for example, to the subject noun phrase in (95a).

(95)   a.

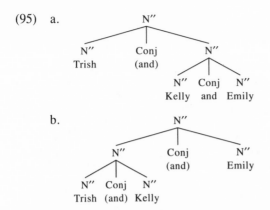

The conjunction rule predicts that the subject noun phrase in (95a) is ambiguous and that in each case two of the conjoined NP's are more closely associated to each other than either of them is to the third. These predictions fail to account for the fact that under one interpretation of (95a), indeed, the most natural interpretation, the subject noun phrase is simply a list of three elements. The following rule allows more than two conjuncts at a single structural level.

(96) $X^i \rightarrow X^{i*}$ CONJ X^i

This rule, by using the * notation, allows any number of conjuncts to appear in a conjoined structure. A conjunction appears before the last conjunct. Note that the binary branching structures in (95) can still be generated by the rule in (96). This is desirable, since there are conjoined structures in which some conjuncts seem to be more closely associated than others. One such example is given in (97).

(97)   Trish and Kelly, and Madelyn and George, were in charge of the entertainment.

A minor problem with (96) is that it allows for only one occurrence of a conjunction in any single conjoined structure, but this can be ignored, since it does not bear on any issues to come.

2.5.3 Affixes

A third rule schema that has been proposed (Jackendoff 1977) is given in (98).

(98) $X^i \rightarrow$ Affix V^i

This is called a deverbalizing rule schema, and it allows for structures like those in (99).

(99) a.   b.

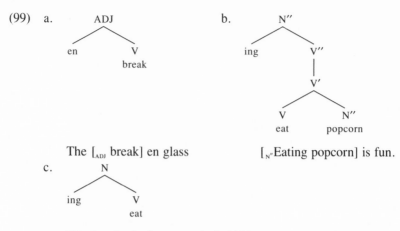

            The [$_{ADJ}$ break] en glass   [$_{N''}$Eating popcorn] is fun.

c.

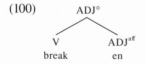

           The [$_N$eating] of popcorn is forbidden

There are two ways in which this rule schema differs from the other two we have seen. First, notice that the head is always some projection of V, while the dominating node is of a different category. In all of the other structures discussed, the head is, in fact must be, of the same category as the phrase node of which it is the head. Second, this rule schema violates the generalization that all non-head material must be Y^{max}, for some category Y. Jackendoff, in proposing this schema, was assuming that non-head material could be of two types: either Y^{max}, as above, or "a specified grammatical formative." The affixes shown in (99) are, in his approach, specified grammatical formatives. It has also been proposed that data like these should be accounted for by word formation rules which apply in the lexicon and that the syntactic component should not be concerned with processes, such as these, that change the syntactic category of a word or phrase. The various arguments will not be discussed here, as they are not crucial to our progress. We will assume the position taken in much recent work in morphology, such as that of Selkirk (1984), namely that affixes are added to stems by word formation rules operating in the lexical component of the grammar. The syntactic category of the word that results is determined by the affix, rather than the stem, and, as such, the head of a morphologically complex word such as *broken* is *-en*, not *break*. Thus the rule schema in (98) has no place in the syntactic component of the grammar. Morphologically, the structure of a word like broken in (99a) is shown in (100).

(100)   ADJ°

           V   ADJ^{aff}

      break   en

There are many interesting questions concerning the relationship between morphology and syntax, but they lie outside the scope of this chapter.

2.6 The Status of S

There is one phrase structure rule which does not fit, in an obvious way, any of the three schemata so far discussed. This is the expansion rule for S, given in (101).

(101) $S \rightarrow N'' V''$

In early work in this framework, two proposals were made. One, Jackendoff (1977), holds that V is the head of S and, thus, that S is really V'''. The other, Emonds (1976), claims that S is a special category with no unique head. In either case, there are problems. Let us consider Jackendoff's proposal first. If S is a projection of V, then N'' (the subject), being non-head material, ought to be optional. Thus sentences like (102) should be grammatical.

(102)   *Left this morning.

Clearly, S is an exception to the generalization that non-head material is optional. Another problem with Jackendoff's approach arises when one considers small clauses such as those given earlier.

(103)   a.   I like [my steak rare].
        b.   I prefer [George in a suit].
        c.   I consider [Eleanor a good doctor].

One analysis of small clauses holds that they are constituents of type S which have AP, PP, or NP in place of VP. If this analysis is to be maintained, then S cannot possibly be a projection of V. V'' is only one of several possibilities as the second constituent of S.

Emonds's proposal, on the other hand, has problems of its own. In treating S as a category that exceptionally lacks a unique head, he provides no explanation for its exceptional behavior. If one headless (or two-headed) category is allowed, why are there no others? Recently, proposals have been made which, at least partially, solve some of these problems, and we shall consider them in section 4.7. For the moment, we will adopt Emonds's proposal and assume the expansion given in (101). We thus have the following rule schemata:

(104)   a. $X^n \rightarrow (C_1) \ldots (C_j) X^{n-1} (C_{j+1}) \ldots (C_k)$
        b. $X' \rightarrow (C_1) \ldots (C_j) X' (C_{j+1}) \ldots (C_k)$
        c. $X^i \rightarrow X^{i*} \text{ CONJ } X^i$
        d. $S \rightarrow N'' V''$ (exceptional, to be discussed in chapter 4)

2.7 Narrowing the Possibilities

The rule schemata in (104) limit the set of possible phrase structure rules significantly, in comparison with the relatively unconstrained context-free system they replaced. It is desirable, however, to set even tighter limits. In particular, what are the possible values for n and i, and what are the possible instantiations of X?

We have seen, in the case of noun phrases, that there must be three distinct levels: N, N', and the maximal phrase category N" or NP. The most restrictive theory would allow exactly the same number of levels for all categories in all languages. We will therefore adopt such a theory, in the expectation that if it is wrong, data will soon emerge to falsify it. Thus the variable n in (104a) ranges over 1 and 2, while the variable i in (104c) ranges over 0, 1, and 2.

Let us now turn to the category variable X. Again, we would like to have as limited a set of syntactic categories as possible, while allowing for the variation which occurs among the languages of the world. In addition, we would like to be able to account for the fact that categories seem to group themselves into classes with respect to certain properties. For example, verbs and prepositions, but not nouns and adjectives, take N" direct objects.

(105) a. He ate the apple.
       b. She sat on the table.
       c. *He is afraid the dog.
       d. *The refusal the offer.

Verbs and adjectives also share certain properties. In some languages, it is impossible to find lexical items which are verbs but not adjectives, or vice versa. If a word takes verbal morphology, it behaves as a verb, but the same word can also be used as an adjective, with adjectival morphology. In Mende, a West African language, the traditional grammars do not even distinguish these two categories, using the term "neutral" to refer to words which behave like verbs and adjectives. In English, the similarities are not as obvious. One example is the passive participle, which has some verbal properties and some adjectival properties. In French, participial forms exhibit exactly the same number and gender agreement as adjectives do, while they seem to occur as the head of a verb phrase. A set of distinctive features has been proposed (Chomsky 1970), which allows us to refer to these classes. These are shown in (106).

(106)

	Noun	Verb	Adj	Prep
N	$+$	$-$	$+$	$-$
V	$-$	$+$	$+$	$-$

The feature $[-N]$ refers to the class of verbs and prepositions (those categories taking direct objects), while the class of verbs and adjectives is described by the feature $[+V]$. The participles referred to above might simply bear the feature $[+V]$, with no specification for $[\pm N]$. While other sets of category features have been proposed (Jackendoff 1977 and Reuland 1985), the features originally proposed by Chomsky are the simplest and still the most widely used. Note, however, that two binary distinctive features allow for only four distinct categories. The system of features clearly needs work, but it can be used as a starting point.

Readings

Chomsky, Noam. 1965. *Aspects of the Theory of Syntax*. Cambridge, Mass.: MIT Press.
————. 1970. "Remarks on Nominalization." In Roderick Jacobs and Peter Rosenbaum, *Readings in English Transformational Grammar*, pp. 184–221. Waltham, Mass.: Ginn & Company.
Emonds, Joseph. 1976. *A Transformational Approach to English Syntax*. New York: Academic Press.
Jackendoff, Ray. 1977. *X-bar Syntax: A Study of Phrase Structure*. Cambridge, Mass.: MIT Press.
Reuland, Eric. 1985. "A Feature System for the Set of Categorical Heads." In Pieter Muysken and Henk van Riemsdijk, *Features and Projections*, 1984. Dordrecht: Foris Publications.
Selkirk, Elisabeth. 1984. *Phonology and Syntax: The Relation Between Sound and Structure*. Cambridge, Mass.: MIT Press.

3 Thematic Relations and θ-Roles

3.1 General Introduction

Thus far, we have been concerned exclusively with phrase structure, that is with the hierarchical relations between elements of phrases and sentences. There is another type of relation that plays an important role in the grammar, which has more to do with meaning. Consider the sentences in (1).

(1) a. Jennifer ate the apple.
     b. The apple was eaten by Jennifer.

Notice that in (1a), the subject is *Jennifer,* while in (1b) it is *the apple.* In (1a), *the apple* is the object, while there does not seem to be an object in (1b). However, by merely describing the structural relationships in these two sentences, we are missing an important point. That is, both sentences describe the same event. In both sentences, *Jennifer* plays the role of *agent,* or doer of the action, and *the apple* plays the role of *patient,* or undergoer of the action. The roles of agent and patient, among others, are *thematic relations* that noun phrases can have. It should be fairly clear that any description that fails to take account of thematic relations is missing a large part of how sentences are put together.

Thematic relations were first described in the generative framework by Jeffrey Gruber in his 1965 doctoral dissertation. Jackendoff (1972) is an expansion and development from Gruber's work, and for years it remained the standard approach to the phenomenon. More recently, research in this area has been extremely productive, and many new insights have been gained.

We will begin with a brief synopsis of the central aspects of Jackendoff's (1972) theory of thematic relations, with some minor modifications, and then go on to look at the results of more recent work.

3.2 Individual Thematic Relations

The following is a list of thematic relations. Some were proposed by Jackendoff (1972), and some have come into general use since then.

Agent—initiator, doer of action
    —must be capable of volition (desire) or deliberate action

(2)   a.   Judith hit Emily.
      b.   A falling rock hit Emily.

Judith is the agent in (2a), but *a falling rock,* lacking the capacity for volition, is not an agent in (2b). In fact, (2b) has no agent at all. It is important to
note that in any particular sentence, an agent does not necessarily have to in-
tend to perform the action. In the examples in (3), the italicized noun phrases
are agents.

(3)   a.   *George* accidentally broke the glass.
      b.   Without meaning to, *Fred* insulted his sister.

An agent thus requires the *capacity* for volition, not volition itself in a particular sentence.

Goal—entity toward which motion takes place
         —motion may be concrete, as in (4a), or abstract, as in (4b)

(4)   a.   i.   Betsy went from Montreal to *Toronto.*
           ii.   Betsy gave the book to *Mary.*
      b.   i.   Betsy went from angry to *furious.*
           ii.   Betsy gave the highest mark to *Mary.*

Source—entity from which motion takes place
           —motion may be concrete or abstract

(5)   a.   i.   John went from *Montreal* to Toronto.
           ii.   *John* gave the book to Daniel.
      b.   i.   John went from *angry* to furious.
           ii.   *John* gave the highest mark to Daniel.

Notice that in (5aii) and (5bii), *John* is the agent as well as the source. This
shows that a given noun phrase may have more than one thematic relation.

Location—the place (concrete or abstract) where something is

(6)   a.   i.   Annie stayed in *Toronto.*
           ii.   *Annie* kept the book.
      b.   i.   Annie stayed *angry.*
           ii.   *Annie* kept all the glory for herself.

Experiencer—the individual who feels or perceives the event

(7)   a.   *Alan* likes cookies.
      b.   It seems to *me* that the words are mixed up.
      c.   *Jeremy* saw the eclipse.

Recipient—This is a subtype of the *goal* thematic relation. It occurs with
verbs denoting change of possession such as *give, donate,* and *receive.*

(8)   a.   We gave *George* a present.
      b.   *Fred* received flowers from Martha.

Instrument—the object with which an action is performed

(9)   a.   We cut the meat with *a knife*.
      b.   *This key* will open that door.

Benefactive—the one for whose benefit the event took place

(10) a.   I bought these flowers for *Sue*.
      b.   I cooked *him* dinner.

Theme—This is the least consistently used of all of the thematic relations. Strictly speaking, a theme occurs only with a verb of motion or location. (Recall that the motion or location can be concrete or abstract.) With a verb of motion, the theme is what moves. With a verb of location, the theme is the entity whose location is being described. Examples are given in (11).

(11) a.   The children gave *a book* to Sue.
      b.   Sue kept *the book*.
      c.   *Peter* stayed angry.
      d.   The man stole *a car*.

Over the years, *theme* has come to be used as a type of default thematic role—the label to give when no other label seems to fit. As Jackendoff (1987) points out, however, this is an inappropriate use of the term theme. He suggests that the terms *patient* and *percept* are more accurate labels for many instances of what have been called themes.

Patient—an entity which undergoes an action

(12) a.   The dog bit *the child*.
      b.   The arrow hit *the apple*.
      c.   The president fired *the treasurer*.

Percept—an entity which is experienced or perceived

(13) a.   Suzie saw *the monster*.
      b.   It seemed to Oliver *that there would not be any more food*.
      c.   *The stories* frightened the children.

A quick look through the example sentences for each of the thematic relations shows that each thematic relation can occur in many positions in a sentence. Therefore, it cannot be predicted which thematic relation a given noun phrase will have, given only its structural position. In fact, in order to establish the thematic relation of each noun phrase, we need to know what the verb means. Some verbs (murder, claim, explain) take an agent. Others (go, sell, buy, give) take sources and goals, and so on. This means that the *lexical entry* for each verb will have to specify how many NP's it takes and which NP gets which thematic relation. We will now look at how this information might be stored in the lexicon.

3.3 Lexical Entries for Verbs

It is intuitively obvious that if we know what a verb means, we know what thematic relations are borne by the noun phrases occurring with it.

3.3.1 A Simple Case

Consider, as an example, the verb *eat*. *Eat* takes an agent and a patient, as shown in (14).

(14)   [Sue] ate [the apple]
       agent   patient

A sentence like (14) might lead us to propose that the lexical entry for *eat* contain, among other things, the material in (15).

(15)   [NP_1 eat NP_2]
       NP_1 = agent
       NP_2 = patient

This could be restated somewhat more economically, as in (16).

(16)   eat   <*agent*, patient>

The agent in (16) is italicized to indicate that it corresponds to the external argument, or subject, of the verb.

3.3.2 Multiple Thematic Roles

As Jackendoff (1972) points out, the relation between noun phrases in a sentence and thematic roles is not one-to-one. In many cases, a single noun phrase bears more than one of the thematic roles listed above. Some examples are given in (17).

(17)   a.   Sue stole a book from Ellen.
            agent   theme   source
            goal
       b.   Katie jumped into the water.
            theme   goal
            agent
       c.   Sue sold a car to Mike for two thousand dollars.
            agent

source	theme	goal	—
goal	—	source	theme

While (17a) and (17b) are clear enough, (17c) deserves some comment. Notice that this sentence has two goals, two sources, and two themes. As Jackendoff (1972) points out, verbs such as *buy, sell,* and *trade* each describe two related events: the transfer of property from the agent to another individual, and the transfer of some other property from the other individual to the agent. The primary event is the one involving the transfer of the property named by the direct object. The horizontal line in (17c) is there simply to avoid confusion between the thematic roles relating to the primary event and those relating to the secondary event.

In addition to allowing multiple thematic relations on a single noun phrase, some verbs allow variation in the thematic relations assigned to a given noun phrase. Consider the sentences in (18).

(18)   a.   Susie rolled down the hill.
       b.   The rock rolled down the hill.

In (18a), *Susie* can be the agent, as well as the theme, of the verb *roll,* while in (18b), *the rock* is only the theme. It seems that the intransitive verb *roll* allows its subject to be either a theme or a theme/agent. While the choice is largely governed by the nature of the subject noun phrase, it is fair to say that the intransitive verb *roll* optionally assigns the thematic relation of agent to its subject.

Any adequate theory of thematic relations will have to answer the following questions:

1. Which thematic roles can be combined with which others? Why are some but not all combinations possible?

2. Which thematic roles can be assigned optionally (as with agent in (18) above)? What determines whether or not they get assigned?

3. Exactly what is the relation between the meaning of a lexical item and the list of thematic roles it assigns? Can one of these be predicted on the basis of the other?

3.4 Deriving Thematic Roles

This section is primarily devoted to answering, at least in a preliminary way, the third question in the previous section. We saw earlier that knowing which thematic roles a verb assigns is part of knowing what a verb means. We will now consider whether or not there is more to the meaning of a verb than the list of thematic roles associated with it.

Consider the sentences in (19).

(19)   a.   Alan gave the book to Sue.
       b.   Alan loaned the book to Sue.

In both of these sentences, *Alan* is the agent and the source, *the book* is the theme, and *Sue* is the goal. However, the sentences are not synonymous. In (19a), *Sue* becomes the owner of *the book,* while in (19b), *Sue* explicitly does not become the owner of *the book.*

One might attempt to capture the difference between *give* and *loan* by refining the thematic roles so as to distinguish between *goal/owner* and *goal/custodian*. This approach quickly leads to an unreasonable proliferation of thematic roles. The verb *send*, for example, is neutral as to whether the goal becomes the owner of the theme, and even allows for the possibility that the goal never received the theme at all. This is illustrated by the sentences in (20).

(20) a. Kathleen sent the book to Michael, but he never got it.
     b. *Kathleen gave/loaned the book to Michael, but he never got it.

We would thus need to distinguish actual or achieved goals from intended goals.

Another distinction that would have to be made within the thematic role of goal is shown in (21).

(21) a. Katherine went to Toronto
     b. The temperature fell to 0° C.

The goals in these sentences are neither owners nor custodians, but destinations. If the owner/custodian distinction is to be made, then the recipient/destination distinction will also have to be made.

Goal is not the only thematic role that would need refinement. Consider the sentences in (22).

(22) a. The soldier killed the captain.
     b. The soldier murdered the captain.
     c. The soldier assassinated the captain.

These verbs all assign the role of agent to their subject and patient to their object. As is well known, however, the agent of *kill* may or may not have intended to perform the action, while the agent of *murder* or *assassinate* must have intended to perform the action. *Murder* and *assassinate* are also different in that *assassinate* ascribes political motivation to its subject and some degree of importance to its object. While *intentional* agent seems not unreasonable as a subtype of *agent, politically motivated agent* and *important patient* seem rather far-fetched. There seems to be something fundamentally wrong with trying to pack the entire meaning of a verb into the thematic roles it assigns.

Because of considerations such as these, it is now fairly generally accepted that the labels given to thematic roles are simply abbreviations and that the content of a thematic role must be derived from an appropriate analysis of the meaning of the lexical item assigning that role. Jackendoff (1983; 1987) has developed a theory called Conceptual Semantics, from which one can derive the information carried by a list of thematic roles. In what follows, we will take a very brief look at some of the proposals made in this theory.

Jackendoff proposes two tiers in the conceptual structure, a thematic tier, which contains information about themes, sources, goals, and locations, and an action tier, which contains information about who (or what) is acting upon what (or whom). The thematic tier contains predicates such as GO and BE, path functions such as FROM, TO, TOWARD, VIA, UP, and DOWN, place functions such as IN, ON, and AT, and the predicate CAUSE. The action tier contains the predicate ACT, which may or may not be further specified by the feature VOL, meaning volitionally, or on purpose. The representation for "Sue hit Fred with a stick" is shown in (23).[1]

(23) [CAUSE (SUE, [GO (STICK, [TO (FRED)])])]
      [ACT (SUE, FRED)]

This approach allows for a rather elegant treatment of verbs like *roll*. Consider the sentences in (24).

(24) a. The ball rolled down the hill.
      b. Alfred rolled down the hill.
      c. Alfred rolled the ball down the hill.
      d. The wind rolled the ball down the hill.

The problem with this verb is that although it takes a theme, and potentially an agent, it does not always assign these roles to the same positions. In (24a), the theme is the subject and there is no agent. In (24b) the subject is both agent and theme. In (24c) there is both an agent and a theme role, but the roles are assigned to different noun phrases. While (24d) is very similar to (24c), *the wind* in (24d) seems somehow less of an agent than *Alfred* in (24c). Jackendoff's representations of (24a)–(24d) are shown in (25).

(25) a. [GO (BALL, [DOWN (HILL)])]
      b. [GO (ALFRED, [DOWN (HILL)])]
          [ACT/VOL (ALFRED)]
      c. [CAUSE (ALFRED, [GO (BALL, [DOWN (HILL)])])]
          [ACT/VOL (ALFRED, BALL)]
      d. [CAUSE (WIND, [GO (BALL, [DOWN (HILL)])])]
          [ACT (WIND, BALL)]

The core meaning of the verb *roll* is the representation in (25a), consisting simply of a thematic tier, with the predicate GO taking a thing and a path as its arguments. If the action tier is spelled out, as in (25b), then we get the agent+theme subject meaning of (24b). If the verb is transitive, as in (24c) and (22d), then there is a predicate CAUSE on the thematic tier. When CAUSE is present, the action tier may or may not contain the feature VOL, which corresponds to the difference between (24c) and (24d).

---

1. This is a simplified representation. Jackendoff has another tier in the representation, which corresponds to time, and allows the separation of subparts of an action.

The role of *agent*, then, corresponds to three things: the *causer* of an event, the *actor* in an event, and the one exercising *volition* with respect to an event. Degrees of agentivity will arise depending upon how many of these properties a particular noun phrase has.

While this area of research is extremely promising, it is in its very early stages. Different researchers are making different assumptions about the way to represent lexical semantics, and many inconsistencies and details remain to be worked out. In addition, those working in the theory of Government and Binding are continuing, for the moment, to assume representations with the more traditional list of thematic roles. For the remainder of this text, we will also use the traditional representations, keeping in mind that the thematic roles are merely abbreviations for material in the conceptual semantic representation. The interested student is referred to the readings listed at the end of the chapter.

3.5 θ-Roles

We have seen that an element may assign one or more thematic relations to a given noun phrase. While the investigation of exactly which combinations are possible, and exactly what semantic distinctions need to be made, is extremely interesting, this is a semantic, rather than a syntactic, issue. Syntacticians have adopted an idealization of thematic relations, which uses the notion *θ-role*. In much of the literature, the terms thematic relation and θ-role are used interchangeably, but this is a potentially dangerous error. Thematic relations are defined in semantic terms, and more than one may hold between a particular verb and a particular noun phrase. θ-roles, however, are defined in syntactic terms. A θ-role is the set of thematic relations assigned by a particular element to a particular position. A θ-role may thus be composed of one or more thematic relations, but crucially all of the thematic relations making up a single θ-role must be assigned by a *single* element to a *single* position. This idealization allows syntacticians to make reference to whether or not an element has been assigned any thematic relations without first having to work out a full theory of lexical semantics.

It will also turn out that what is important for syntactic theory is not how many thematic relations an element has, but rather how many θ-roles it has. This will be taken up again in chapter 5.

For the most part, then, we will be making reference to θ-roles rather than to specific thematic relations.

Readings

Gruber, Jeffrey. 1965. "Studies in Lexical Relations." Ph.D. diss., MIT, Cambridge; Indiana University Linguistics Club, Bloomington, Ind. Reprinted as part of Gruber (1976).

————. 1976. *Lexical Structures in Syntax and Semantics.* Amsterdam: North-Holland.

Hale, Kenneth, and Samuel Jay Keyser. 1987. "A View from the Middle." *Lexicon Project Working Papers 10.* Cambridge, Mass.: MIT Center for Cognitive Science.

Jackendoff, Ray. 1972. *Semantic Interpretation in Generative Grammar.* Cambridge, Mass.: MIT Press.

————. 1983. *Semantics and Cognition.* Cambridge, Mass.: MIT Press.

————. 1987. "The Status of Thematic Relations in Linguistic Theory." *Linguistic Inquiry* 18:369–412.

4 Predicting Phrase Structure

In the preceding two chapters, we have developed a set of rule schemata which constrain the types of phrase structure rules a language may have and briefly discussed the network of θ-roles which are assigned by verbs to their arguments. In this chapter, we will further examine the role of the lexicon in the grammar and show that much of the information carried by phrase structure rules can be predicted on the basis of information required in the lexicon. Ultimately, we will conclude that if the grammar contains both X-bar theory and a lexicon, individual phrase structure rules ought not to be necessary.

4.1 The Lexicon

Part of knowing one's language is possessing a vocabulary or list of words. This list of words is called a lexicon and consists of a set of *lexical entries,* one for each word. What information must a typical lexical entry contain? First, the speaker must know how the word is pronounced. Thus, the lexical entry must contain *phonological* information. Second, the speaker must know if the word is irregular in any way. For example, the lexical entry for *give* must note that the past tense is not **gived* (compare with the verb *live*), but *gave*. The lexical entry therefore contains *morphological* information. Third, the speaker needs to know what the word means—*semantic* information. Finally, the speaker needs to know what syntactic category the word belongs to and what restrictions, if any, the word places on the contexts in which it occurs in sentences of the language. This last type of information is *syntactic* information, which we will look at in some detail.

Traditionally (Chomsky 1965), the syntactic information in a lexical entry was expressed as follows.

(1)   give: +V
          [+____ NP PP]
          <+ animate subject>
          <+animate indirect object>

The first line, +V, states that the word in question is a verb. The material in square brackets is called a strict subcategorization statement. The dash represents the position of *give* with respect to the other elements. This rule states that *give* must be followed by a noun phrase, which is, in turn, followed by a prepositional phrase. Notice that the strict subcategorization statement refers only to the syntactic categories in the lexical item's context. The statements in angle brackets are selectional restrictions. These specify any semantic properties required of elements in the context.

Selectional restrictions, as such, have largely been eliminated from the syntactic component of the grammar in recent years. For example, the requirement that *give* take an animate subject can be made to follow from the fact that the subject of *give* is assigned the thematic role of agent. Agents must be capable of intention or volition, which is normally only characteristic of animate beings. Other selectional restrictions, such as the requirement that the object of *drink*, but not the object of *pour*, must be a liquid, have been incorporated into the meaning of the verb. Jackendoff (1987) gives the following representation for *drink*. Irrelevant details have been omitted for the sake of clarity.

(2)   drink

    ____ NP_j

    $[_{EVENT}$ CAUSE $(THING_i, [_{EVENT}$ GO $(LIQUID_j,$ [TO ([IN ([MOUTH OF $THING_i])])])])]$

Since in the semantic representation, the element corresponding to the object is specified as a liquid, only noun phrases referring to liquids can occupy the object position without causing a clash. The representation associated with the verb *pour*, by contrast, would not contain any reference to liquid.

We will adopt, as an initial approximation, the type of representation shown in (3).

(3)   give: $[-N, +V]$ category

        $[+$____ NP PP$]$ strict subcategorization

        (agent/source, theme, goal/recipient) θ-grid

        [SEMANTIC REPRESENTATION]

As discussed in the previous chapter, it is likely that the information contained in the θ-grid can be derived from the semantic representation. However, since Government-Binding theory assumes the existence of a θ-grid, we will make use of it, bearing in mind that this is an area where changes are in progress.

The θ-grid in (3) states that *give* is associated with three θ-roles, one an agent and source, the second a theme, and the third a goal and recipient.

Note that the category membership of the lexical item is stated in terms of the syntactic distinctive features mentioned in chapter 2. Thus, *give* is specified as $[+V, -N]$. To sum up, then, the syntactic portion of the lexical entry has, so far, three parts: first, a category specification in terms of syntactic distinctive features; second, a strict subcategorization statement or statements; and finally, a θ-grid.

4.2 Phrase Structure Rules and Strict Subcategorization

Both phrase structure rules and strict subcategorization statements contain information about the types of phrase categories a language has. For example, the phrase structure rule given in (4) admits a V′ containing a verb, a noun phrase, and a prepositional phrase.

(4)   V′ → V (NP) (PP)

The strict subcategorization statement in the lexical entry for *give* states that *give* occurs in a constituent consisting of a verb, a noun phrase, and a prepositional phrase. The general rule schema provided by X-bar theory predicts that such a constituent must bear the label V′. Only X^{max} can occur as non-head material, therefore V must be the head of the constituent in question. The only category which can have V as its immediate head is V′. Thus if *give* is ever to occur in an English sentence, English must allow structures of the sort given in (5).

(5)

$$
\begin{array}{ccc}
 & V' & \\
 & \diagup \mid \diagdown & \\
V & NP & PP
\end{array}
$$

In this sense, there is a redundancy between the phrase structure rule in (4) and strict subcategorization statements such as those shown in (6).

(6)   give: [+____ NP PP]
      sleep: [+____]
      hit: [+____ NP]
      go: [+____ PP]

The four structures in (6) are exactly the possibilities allowed by (4). This degree of redundancy strongly suggests that either the phrase structure rules, or the strict subcategorization statements, should be eliminated from the grammar. The question of which of the two should be done away with depends on which one can be predicted on the basis of the other. The phrase structure rule can be seen, essentially, as a summary of the subcategorization statements in the lexical entries of all of the verbs in the language. Thus the phrase structure rule contains no information that is not present in the strict subcategorization statements. In contrast, the strict subcategorization statements contain information not contained in the phrase structure rule. What they alone state is which verb occurs in which context. Thus, if one of these two things is to be eliminated from the grammar, the phrase structure rule is clearly the one that can be dispensed with.

An identical argument can be made for eliminating the phrase structure rule in (7).

(7)   P′ → P (NP)

Lexical entries such as those in (8) contain all the information necessary to predict what (7) says.

(8) a. into: $[-N, -V]$
            $[+\underline{\hspace{1.5em}} NP]$
     b. away: $[-N, -V]$
            $[+\underline{\hspace{1.5em}}]$

Similarly, the rules for A′ and N′ can be done away with.

We have seen that, at least in the case of X′, phrase structure rules contain only redundant information and should be eliminated from the grammar. The logical question to ask at this point is whether *all* phrase structure rules can be dispensed with in this way. There are two other types of expansions in the grammar. One is the expansion of X′ where the head is not X, but rather X′. The other is the expansion of X″.

All the examples of X′ having X′ as its head that we have seen involve modifiers. Stowell (1981) shows that almost any maximal projection can appear as a postnominal modifier. This is illustrated in (9).

(9) a. A man [$_{AP}$ more handsome than Adonis]
     b. A tree [$_{PP}$ with green leaves]
     c. A car [$_{VP}$ sitting in the driveway]
     d. A house [$_S$ that Sue wanted to buy]

X-bar theory tells us that any non-head material must be a maximal projection. Thus, a phrase structure rule such as the one in (10) adds no information to that provided by X-bar theory.

(10)
$$N' \longrightarrow N' \left\{ \begin{array}{l} AP \\ PP \\ VP \\ S \end{array} \right\}$$

The only maximal projection that seems not to be able to occur as a postnominal modifier is NP. In chapter 6 we will see that an independent property of NP's, their need for Case, will prevent them from occurring in this position.

Let us now turn to prenominal modification. Prenominal modification is much more restricted than postnominal modification. Only adjective phrases are possible and only a limited range of adjective phrases at that. Consider the noun phrases in (11).

(11) a. A tall tree
      b. A [very tall] tree
      c. *A [taller than Sue] tree
      d. *A [happy about the weather] child

The generalization seems to be that a prenominal adjective phrase must have its adjective head as its rightmost element. Two questions arise at this point. First, what is the appropriate structural analysis of permissible pre-nominal AP's? Are they AP's at all, or are they some nonmaximal category? If they are nonmaximal, how do they conform to X-bar theory? Second, how are these modifiers introduced? We are not yet in a position to answer either of these questions in a revealing way. The best we can do at this point is propose an ad hoc subtype of adjective phrase and write a phrase structure rule that introduces it as a prenominal modifier.

As for modification in the verb phrase, the picture is very similar. Post-verbal modification is allowed with almost any maximal projection, as shown in (12).

(12) a. Marie wrote the book [$_{ADVP}$ as quickly as she could].
      b. Marie wrote [$_{PP}$ with a new pencil].
      c. Marie wrote [$_S$ as if she had nothing else on her mind].
      d. Marie wrote [$_{VP}$ sitting on the floor].

Preverbal modification is much more restricted, as shown in (13).

(13) a. Cian has quietly gone to sleep.
      b. *Cian has [more quietly than Alan] gone to sleep.
      c. *Cian [with a pencil] wrote his paper.

Finally, let us consider the expansion of X''. In noun phrases, the non-head material in X'' includes possessors, determiners, and quantifiers. Although strict subcategorization does not appear to be involved here, it seems to be the case that all of these elements serve a common function. In all cases, they specify the definiteness and serve to identify the referent, if any, of the noun phrase. Thus it might be possible to give a semantically based account of those elements which occur as non-head daughters of N''.

Although many details remain to be worked out, it is clearly worthwhile to pursue the goal of eliminating phrase structure rules from the grammar in favor of strict subcategorization statements and/or other independent principles. We will thus assume that this can ultimately be done.

4.3 Strict Subcategorization and θ-Roles

Having shown that, given strict subcategorization statements in the lexicon, phrase structure rules are largely redundant, let us now examine the status of the strict subcategorization statements themselves. We have assumed that the lexical entries for verbs such as *hit, swim,* and *put* contain the following information.

(14) a. hit: [+V, −N]
                [+___ NP]
                (agent, patient)

b. swim: [+V, −N]
    [+____]
    (agent/theme)
c. put: [+V, −N]
    [+____ NP PP]
    (agent, theme, location)

The first thing to notice is that the θ-grid in each case has one more element than the strict subcategorization statement. This is because each of these verbs assigns a θ-role to its subject, in addition to assigning θ-roles within V′. Some verbs, such as *seem,* do not assign a θ-role to the subject position, and in such a case, there are exactly as many elements in the θ-grid as there are in the strict subcategorization statement.

(15) seem: [+V, −N]
      [+____ (PP) S]
      ((experiencer), percept)
      It seems (to me) [s that George is ill].

Thus, if we could somehow mark, in the θ-grid, which if any of the θ-roles are assigned outside V′, then we could predict from the θ-grid the number of elements in the strict subcategorization statement. Let us indicate the V′-external θ-role by italicizing it in the θ-grid.

(16) a. hit: [+V, −N]
          [+____ NP]
          (*agent,* patient)
      b. swim: [+V, −N]
          [+____]
          (*agent/theme*)
      c. put: [+V, −N]
          [+____ NP PP]
          (*agent,* theme, location)

There does indeed seem to be some redundancy between the strict subcategorization statement and the θ-grid. Let us now consider what other information is provided by the strict subcategorization statement and see how much of it can be predicted on the basis of other considerations.

One type of information that the strict subcategorization statement provides is *categorial* information—whether the contextual material required is NP, PP, AP, etc. Is such a specification necessary, or even desirable? Consider the prepositional phrase argument in the lexical entry for *put.* The prepositional phrase must describe a location, as specified by the θ-grid. But is it necessary for the location to be expressed by a PP? Consider the sentences in (17).

(17)   a.   He put the book [$_{ADVP}$ there].
       b.   I put the car [$_S$ where the truck had been].
       c.   You'll have to put it [$_{ADJP}$ lower], or I won't be able to reach it.

In fact, any category which can express a location can occur with *put*. Thus the strict subcategorization statement, by explicitly requiring a PP, is overly specific. All that is necessary is an argument expressing location. The same is true of other θ-roles. Any constituent which can refer to an animate, potentially volitional entity can satisfy the requirement for an agent, and any constituent which can refer to an object undergoing motion or having location can satisfy the requirement for a theme. In fact, only noun phrases seem to be able to satisfy these requirements.

Thus it seems that the categorial information in the strict subcategorization statement is in some cases predictable, as in the case of themes, patients and agents, and in some cases overly specific, as in the case of locations.

A second type of information carried by the strict subcategorization statement is the order in which the elements occur both with respect to the verb and with respect to each other. A couple of general statements will suffice to provide this information for the language as a whole, eliminating the need to state it for each lexical item. First of all, the verb is always the leftmost element in V'. This means that any V'-internal arguments will always follow the verb. Second, NP's must always be next to the verb. This means that in any case where more than one element occurs in V' after V, the NP element must come first. The second of these statements will later be shown to follow from the theory of Case; the first can be shown to be true not only of V', but of all X'-level categories in English. Consider the data in (18).

(18)   a.   [$_{N''}$ the [$_{N'}$ [$_N$ picture] of Fred]]
       b.   [$_{P'}$ [$_P$ on] [the roof]]
       c.   [$_{A'}$ [$_A$ full] [of peanuts]]

It can be stated, very generally, that in English the lexical head of a category is the leftmost element in the immediately dominating X'.

It appears, then, that the categorial and ordering information in strict subcategorization statements is unnecessary. Thus it seems that the strict subcategorization statements could, in fact, be eliminated in favor of the θ-grid.

Before adopting this position, however, we should address the question of whether the redundancy between strict subcategorization statements and the θ-grid could be eliminated by doing away with the θ-grid in favor of strict subcategorization statements. Such a move would entail predicting the θ-role of a particular argument on the basis of either its category or its position with respect to other arguments. There are several problems with this approach. First, the θ-grid frequently contains a specification for an X'-external argument. Since the strict subcategorization statement is limited to X'-internal elements, there would be no way to specify whether or not there was an external θ-position and what θ-role that position received. Second, although it is true that themes and patients are always NP's, it is not true that V'-internal NP's always have a consistent θ-role. Recall the example in (15) where the V'-internal NP was an experiencer. Third, a PP argument can be a source, goal, location, or agent. There is no way of choosing among these θ-roles on the basis of either category information or linear order. Finally, as we saw in (17), some verbs allow a variety of categories to satisfy a particular θ-role requirement. To state the facts for *put* in categorial terms would require a disjunctive statement like (19) and would completely miss the generalization that *put* simply requires an argument specifying location.

(19) $[+\underline{\quad}NP \left\{ \begin{array}{c} S \\ ADVP \\ ADJP \\ PP \end{array} \right\}]$

Since it does not seem possible to eliminate the θ-grid in favor of strict subcategorization statements, and since the converse is apparently quite feasible, we will assume that strict subcategorization statements are to be eliminated from the grammar and the θ-grid retained. Recall, however, that we saw in section 4.2 that strict subcategorization statements did not make phrase structure rules completely unnecessary, and that much work in this area remains to be done.

4.4 Consequences

4.4.1 The Role of X-bar Theory

The abandonment of individual phrase structure rules changes the role played by the X-bar theory developed in chapter 2. Instead of serving as a set of well-formedness conditions on phrase structure rules, it must now be seen as directly constraining tree structures—in other words, as a condition on representations. This is actually an improvement, for the following reason. As long as X-bar theory functions only to constrain phrase structure rules, it has no role to play in the grammar itself. It operates during the acquisition of a grammar to guide the learning of phrase structure rules and then effectively retires.

If, however, there are no phrase structure rules, then X-bar theory remains an integral part of the adult grammar. In addition, the acquisition task is significantly simplified. The language learner need only fix the parameters given in (20d) and (20e) below and then learn the lexical items of the language. No phrase structure rules need to be learned.

Another advantage of viewing X-bar theory as a set of constraints on structures rather than on rules will become apparent in the next chapter, when the transformation of NP movement is introduced. It will turn out that the output of NP movement always respects the constraints of X-bar theory. This is to be expected if X-bar theory holds of structures, but is not at all necessary if it only holds of phrase structure rules.

We will now assume that, instead of being derived by the application of phrase structure rules, syntactic structures are *projected* from the lexicon in accordance with the principles of X-bar theory. Thus, instead of being stated in terms of rule schemata, X-bar theory can be stated in something like the following terms.

(20) a. Every X must be the head of an X^{max}.
    b. Every X^{max} must have a head of category X.
    c. Every nonmaximal X^n must be dominated by X^{n+1} (except X', which may be dominated by X').
    d. X is left (right) peripheral in X'.
    e. X' is left (right) peripheral in X''.

4.4.2 The Nature of θ-Role Assignment

We saw that *put* required a location argument, whose syntactic category was immaterial as long as the argument in question was capable of expressing location. Marantz (1984) has argued that there are two types of elements in the θ-grid. First, there are those which are directly assigned their θ-roles by the element bearing the θ-grid. Second, there are those which are required, but which must in some sense inherently have the relevant θ-role. Compare, for example, the theme and the source in (21).

(21) Fred bought [$_{NP}$ the book] [$_{PP}$ from Sue].

There is nothing about *the book*, in and of itself, that indicates that it is a theme in (21). In contrast, the prepositional phrase *from Sue* is clearly a source, even when it is seen out of context. Thus, Marantz claims, the verb *bought* directly *assigns* the θ-role of theme to *book*, while it merely requires (or in this case allows) the presence of a source. It is the preposition *from* that assigns the θ-role of source to *Sue*.

Given this distinction between θ-roles which are directly assigned by the verb, and those which are merely required or allowed, the θ-grid can carry the following information.

(22) a. How many θ-roles are arguments of X and what these θ-roles are.
    b. Which, if any, of the θ-roles is external to X' (indicated by *italics*).
    c. Which, if any, of the θ-roles is assigned directly by the verb (indicated in **boldface**).
    d. Which, if any, of the θ-roles is optional (indicated by parentheses).

Some examples of θ-grids are shown in (23).

(23) a. put: (*agent,* **theme,** location)
      b. steal: (*agent/goal,* **theme,** (source))
      c. go: (*agent/theme,* (source), (goal))
      d. surprise: (*percept,* **experiencer**)
      e. seem: (**percept,** *experiencer*)

4.5 The Structure of S: A Projection of INFL

Recall from chapter 2 that the expansion rule for S, given in (24), was an exception to the main phrase structure rule schema, repeated here in (25).

(24) $S \rightarrow NP\ VP$

(25) $X^n \rightarrow (C_1) \ldots (C_j)\ X^{n-1}\ (C_{j+1}) \ldots (C_k)$

We are now in a position to resolve the question of S. It has been proposed that the head of S is neither NP nor VP, but an element called INFL. INFL is the element that determines the finiteness (tensed or infinitival) of the clause containing it. This proposal seems odd at first, but it has several attractive consequences. The argument in its favor has to do with constraints on where selectional restrictions may hold. Recall from the beginning of the chapter that selectional restrictions are not considered to be part of the syntactic component of the grammar. However, there are syntactic constraints on what they can refer to.

4.5.1 The Importance of the Notion "Head"

Notice that subcategorization statements, as well as selectional restrictions, are rather limited in what they may say. For example, there do not seem to be any verbs which require that their direct object be modified by an adjective. Nor are there any verbs which require, for example, that their direct object be modified by a prepositional phrase referring to size or by a definite determiner. In fact, subcategorization statements and selectional restrictions refer only to the *heads* of categories in the immediate context. The immediate context seems to be the sisters of the element bearing the restriction. Consider the structure in (26).

(26)

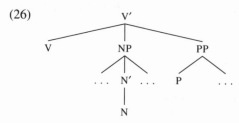

A selectional restriction borne by a verb occurring in this structure may specify semantic properties of the heads of the categories immediately dominated by V'. In other words, a verb may place semantic restrictions on the noun in its direct object or on the preposition in any PP within V'.

With these limitations in mind, let us now consider verbs that take clausal complements.

4.5.2 Why INFL Is the Head of S

Consider the data in (27)–(29).

(27) a. *Sue wanted [that John would leave early].
   b. Sue wanted [John to leave early].
(28) a. Alan insisted [that Joe had washed the dishes].
   b. *Alan insisted [Joe to have washed the dishes].
(29) a. George expected [that Sue would buy the car].
   b. George expected [Sue to buy the car].

These sentences all contain verbs that take sentential complements. The difference in grammaticality between the (a) sentences and the (b) sentences in (27) and (28) shows that some verbs require that their complements be finite, while others require nonfinite, or infinitival, complements. The difference between a finite and an infinitival clause derives from the nature of INFL. If we are to maintain the generalization that selectional restrictions can refer only to the heads of categories that are sisters to the element bearing the restriction, we are forced to adopt the hypothesis that INFL is the head of S.

A problem remains, however. If neither NP nor VP is the head of S, why are these elements obligatory? According to the theory of phrase structure, non-head material should be optional. What we need to do is to show that the presence of NP and VP in S, if it is indeed obligatory, follows from something else. If some other factor requires the presence of NP and VP, then as far as phrase structure theory is concerned, these elements are indeed optional, and S conforms to the restrictions of the theory.

The answer to this can be found partly in semantic well-formedness and partly in morphology. It is fair to say that S corresponds to the semantic category of proposition. A well-formed proposition consists of a predicate and any arguments it may take. Any S which did not contain a predicate would thus be semantically ill-formed. Now, why must the predicate be a VP? Predicates can also be expressed by other categories, such as AP and even NP, as shown in (30).

(30) a. Mary is **happy.**
   b. Dumbo is **an elephant.**

The need for a VP can be made to follow from the morphology of INFL. INFL carries features of finiteness ([$\pm$ tense]) and tense ([$\pm$ past]). To the extent that INFL is phonetically realized, it occurs as an affix on the first verb in the clause. It is a well-established principle of morphology that affixes cannot occur independently; they must be attached to a stem to form a word. Thus, if INFL were to occur without VP, the result would be morphologically ill-formed. There would be an affix with no word to attach itself to. Therefore, a verb phrase is required by an independent principle of morphology. Now, consider what information INFL carries in addition to features for finiteness and tense. INFL also carries features for person and number, which depend on the person and number features of the subject NP. So, if there were no subject NP, there would be no source for the person and number features which INFL must bear. It seems, then, that the presence of NP and VP in S can, in fact, be made to follow from other principles and that it is therefore unnecessary for a specific phrase structure rule to state explicitly that they are obligatory.

4.5.3 Refinements in the Structure of S

If we assume that INFL (I) is the head of S, then S should be written as I^{max}, or IP. Given X-bar theory, the next question that arises has to do with the number of bars in I^{max}. There are three possibilities, which are illustrated in (31).

(31)

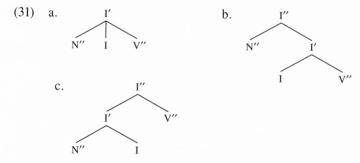

Since we have already seen that other categories in English require X^{max} to have two bars, we will tentatively exclude (31a). Unless there is direct evidence to the contrary, we will assume that the behavior of INFL parallels that of the other categories.

In order to decide between (31b) and (31c), we can proceed in two ways: first, by examining the structure of other categories in the language and, second, by looking for direct empirical evidence in the behavior of INFL.

4.5.3.1 Cross-categorial Comparison—X′

All of the other categories in English that we know of (N, V, A, P), have a head-initial X′. These are illustrated in (32).

(32)   a.   the [$_{N'}$ [$_N$ king] of France]
       b.   [$_{V'}$ [$_V$ eat] the eggs]
       c.   [$_{A'}$ [$_A$ afraid] of dogs]
       d.   [$_{P'}$ [$_P$ on] the bus]

If we adopt (31b), then INFL also has a head-initial I'. The structure in (31c) has a head-final I'.

4.5.3.2 Cross-categorial Comparison—X″

With the possible exception of V″, all categories in English exhibit a head-final X″, as shown in (33).

(33)   a.   [$_{N''}$ the [$_{N'}$ king of France]]
       b.   [$_{A''}$ rather [$_{A'}$ tired of dancing]]
       c.   [$_{P''}$ right [$_{P'}$ on the table]]

Again, (31b) but not (31c) allows INFL to follow the same pattern. In general, English syntactic categories have the structure shown in (34).

(34)

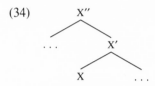

4.5.3.3 Internal Evidence

Since INFL is not a lexical category—the members of this category are not lexical items—it is not entirely straightforward to examine its behavior. First of all, recall that INFL is realized as an inflectional affix on the first verb in the clause. Thus it seems to be very closely tied to the verb phrase, suggesting that perhaps (31b) is the correct structure. On the other hand, INFL also contains person and number features which must match those of the subject noun phrase. One way to approach this question is to look at languages where INFL does not intervene between the subject noun phrase and the verb phrase, in other words, languages where INFL is either sentence-initial or sentence-final. One such language is Japanese. In Japanese, the X-bar schema is entirely head-final, giving a structure such as (35).

(35)

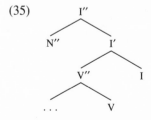

In Japanese, the only possible structure has INFL more closely associated to the verb phrase than to the subject noun phrase, corresponding to (31b). We will therefore adopt (31b) as the structure for I″ in English.

4.6 Summary

We have seen that phrase structure rules at the X' level are clearly redundant. We have claimed that, as far as possible, all individual phrase structure rules at all levels ought to be eliminated. Further, we have shown that strict subcategorization statements are also redundant and should be eliminated from the lexicon. In order to pare down the rules of grammar and lexical specifications in this way, we had to make the following new assumptions.

(36) a. X-bar theory, in general, is part of universal grammar. It constrains tree structures directly, rather than acting as a constraint on the form of phrase structure rules. Individual languages may specify whether the head is the leftmost or rightmost element in its immediately dominating projection.

b. The θ-grid for a given lexical item X can specify which, if any, arguments are external to X'.

c. A general principle (Case theory, see chapter 6) accounts for the fact that NP arguments of X occur only adjacent to X in X'.

Finally, we have determined that the abstract element INFL is the head of the formerly exceptional category S (now I''). I'' conforms to the generalizations about phrase structure stated in (20) above.

Readings

Chomsky, Noam. 1965. *Aspects of the Theory of Syntax.* Cambridge, Mass.: MIT Press.

Jackendoff, Ray. 1987. "The Status of Thematic Relations in Linguistic Theory." *Linguistic Inquiry* 18:369–412.

Marantz, Alec. 1984. *On the Nature of Grammatical Relations.* Cambridge, Mass.: MIT Press.

Stowell, Timothy A. 1981. "Origins of Phrase Structure." Ph.D. diss. MIT, Cambridge, Mass.

5 NP-Movement

We have seen that the lexical entry of each verb specifies the θ-roles that the verb assigns to its arguments. Thus, a verb such as *eat* assigns the role of *agent* to its subject and the role of *theme* to its object,[1] as shown in (1):

(1) Fred ate the apple.
     agent   theme

However, *eat* also occurs in sentences like those in (2), where the thematic relations are somewhat different.

(2) a. [The cake] was eaten by [a stray bear].
         theme   agent
         (agent and theme both present, but arranged differently)
     b. [The cake] had already been eaten.
         theme
         (no agent present)

The sentences in (2), together with (1), illustrate that even for one verb, the arrangement of thematic relations can vary from sentence to sentence. The statement in (3) accounts for sentences (1) and (2).

(3) eat: <*agent,* **theme**>
     be eaten: <*theme,* agent>

The following examples will begin to show a general pattern in the way the arrangement of thematic relations varies.

(4) a. Laura   kept the money.
         location   theme
         agent
     b. The money was kept by Laura.
         theme   location
                                 agent
     c. The money was kept.
         theme

---

1. Here and henceforth, we shall be using names such as agent and theme for θ-roles. It should be borne in mind that these are merely convenient abbreviations and have no theoretical status.

(5) a.   John received the stolen goods.
           goal   theme
           agent
     b.   The stolen goods were received by John.
           theme   goal
                                           agent
     c.   The stolen goods were received.
           theme
(6) a.   The committee sent flowers.
           source   theme
           agent
     b.   Flowers were sent by the committee.
           theme   source
                            agent
     c.   Flowers were sent.
           theme

There is a general pattern exhibited by sentences (4)–(6) above. In the (a) sentences, the subject bears one or more thematic relations, one of which is *agent*. Exactly the same thematic relations are borne by the noun phrase following the preposition *by* in the (b) sentences. In the (c) sentences, where there is no by-phrase, no NP in the sentence bears these thematic relations. Similarly, the object in the (a) sentences bears the thematic relation of *theme*. This relation is borne by the subject in the (b) and (c) sentences.

Given the patterns in (4)–(6) above, it seems that many verbs would have to have lexical entries in two parts such as the one for *eat* in (3). One part would set forth the thematic relations for the active verb (*eat*) and the other part would set forth the thematic relations for the passive verb (*be eaten*). The relationship between the active and passive parts would be the same in each case, as illustrated in (7).

(7) VERB: $(\theta_1, \boldsymbol{\theta_2})$
      be VERBed: (θ_3, θ_4)

θ_1 is always identical to θ_4 and θ_2 is always identical to θ_3. We will return shortly to a way of capturing the generalization expressed in (7). First, however, let us examine some other cases where verbs seem to assign thematic relations differently in different sentences.

(8) a.   It seems that Jessie has eaten the cake.
     b.   Jessie seems to have eaten the cake.
(9) a.   It is likely that Jessie will steal the cake.
     b.   Jessie is likely to steal the cake.

In these sentences, there are two verbs which assign thematic relations. In (8a), *eat* assigns the role of *agent* to *Jessie* and the role of *theme* to *the cake*.

In (9a) *steal* assigns the roles of *goal* and *agent* to Jessie, and the role of *theme* to *the cake*. The verb *seems* in (8a), and the adjective *likely* in (9a), assign the role of *percept* to the entire subordinate clause. We can represent these thematic relation assignments as in (10) below.

(10)   a.   It seems [that Jessie has eaten the cake].
                     [agent   theme   ]
                     ‾‾‾‾‾‾‾‾‾‾‾‾‾‾‾‾‾‾‾‾‾‾‾‾‾‾‾‾‾‾‾‾‾
                     percept
       b.   It is likely [that Jessie will steal the cake].
                     [goal   theme   ]
                            agent
                     ‾‾‾‾‾‾‾‾‾‾‾‾‾‾‾‾‾‾‾‾‾‾‾‾‾‾‾‾‾‾‾‾‾
                     percept

Now turn to sentences (8b) and (9b). In these sentences, *Jessie* is the subject of the main verb, *seem* in (8b) and *be likely* in (9b). Nonetheless, *Jessie* is the agent of *eat* in (8b), and the agent of *steal* in (9b). What about the thematic relation or relations assigned by *seem* and *be likely* in (8b) and (9b)? Recall that in the (a) sentences these verbs took the entire subordinate clause as percept. More precisely, these verbs take the *event* described by the subordinate clause as percept. It seems reasonable to say that, in the (b) sentences as well, the main verb takes the *event* (Jessie's eating the cake, or Jessie's stealing the cake) as its percept. In this way, we capture the fact that the (a) and (b) sentences describe exactly the same events or states of affairs. It is unclear, however, exactly how the thematic relations are going to be assigned in the case of the (b) sentences. Consider the diagram in (11).

(11)   percept   rest of percept
                      ‾‾‾‾‾‾‾‾‾‾‾‾‾‾‾‾‾‾‾‾
       [Jessie] seems [to have eaten the cake].
       agent   theme

In order for *eat* to assign the thematic relation of *agent* to *Jessie* in this case, the lexical entry for *eat* would have to contain something like the material in (12).

(12)   NP$_1$ VERB to eat NP$_2$
       NP$_1$ = agent
       etc.

Notice, however, that almost any verb can occur in the place of *eat* in a sentence like (8). The sentences in (13) provide a few examples.

(13)   a.   John seems to have built himself a better mousetrap.
       b.   Lisa seems to have hired an idiot.
       c.   Tom seems to have passed out.

The relevant generalization is the following: in a sentence like (11), the subject of *seem* (or *be likely*) receives the thematic relation it would receive if it were the subject of the verb in the lower clause.

We have now seen two cases where a single verb assigns thematic relations differently in different sentences. In both cases, a general pattern emerged that was true for many verbs. We will now look at a way of accounting for these general patterns, without adding cumbersome and redundant material to the lexical entries of a large number of verbs.

5.1 Accounting for θ-Roles

Assume that each verb has exactly one θ-grid in its lexical entry. This assumption immediately simplifies the lexical entries of all verbs. It also makes it impossible to have lexical entries such as the one illustrated in (2). Clearly, then, this assumption will force some revisions in the grammar, so that the grammar as a whole still accounts for the data we have been concerned with. Let us explore what these revisions might be. We will again use the verb *eat* as an example. Assuming that the active form of *eat* is more basic than the passive form, the θ-grid associated with the active verb will be the one that appears in the lexical entry of the verb. *Eat* will therefore assign the role of agent to an NP in subject position and the role of theme to an NP in object position. Any other arrangement of θ-roles that appears with *eat* in English sentences will have to be produced by rearranging this lexical pattern. The process of rearranging material is called a *transformation*.

Consider the sentence "the cake was eaten." Since *the cake* bears the θ-role of *theme*, it will have to originate in object position. Since it occurs in subject position it will have to move from object position to subject position. It is derived as shown in (14).

(14)   _____ was eaten the cake
                            theme   (θ-role assignment)
        the cake was eaten _____   (transformation moving NP to subject
        theme   position)

Sentences containing verbs like *seem* are handled as shown in (15). *John* receives the θ-role of *agent* from the verb *steal* and then moves to subject position in the higher clause.

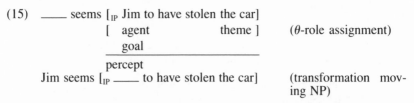

(15)   _____ seems [$_{IP}$ Jim to have stolen the car]
                [agent   theme]   (θ-role assignment)
                    goal
                    percept
        Jim seems [$_{IP}$ _____ to have stolen the car]   (transformation moving NP)

Thus, if θ-role assignment is restricted so that each verb has only one θ-grid, it is necessary to claim that noun phrases, in some cases, move from the position where they receive their θ-role to some other position in the sentence. The account of a sentence thus consists of two types of structure. The first of these, called D-structure, is the level which determines θ-role assignment. The second, S-structure, represents the actual word order of the sentence as it is spoken. The terms D-structure and S-structure derive historically from *deep structure* and *surface structure,* the two levels of syntactic representation in the standard theory (Chomsky 1965). However, the levels of D-structure and S-structure differ in several respects from their historical sources. Deep structure in the standard theory came to be viewed as the interface between syntax and semantics. It served as the input to transformations, which derived the surface structure, and to projection rules, which derived the semantic representation. The theory of Government and Binding relates syntax to meaning rather differently, as shown in the diagram in (16).

(16)

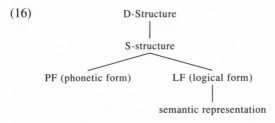

Here, S-structure is the level at which sound (beyond PF) and meaning (beyond LF) are linked.

A second difference between deep structure and D-structure has to do with the way they are formed. Deep structure arises by the application of phrase structure rules, followed by the process of lexical insertion. D-structure, on the other hand, is projected from the lexicon, according to the principles of X-bar theory.

S-structure and surface structure also differ from each other. Surface structure was the final output of the syntactic component; it contained no abstract elements and required only the application of the rules of the phonology to turn it into phonetic representation. S-structure is a more abstract entity. As will be shown in the next few chapters, it contains a variety of abstract elements that do not show up in the spoken sentence. It has even been proposed that certain stylistic rules may apply after S-structure, so that S-structure may have a structure or word order which differs from the final output. In addition, as we saw above, S-structure is the level that links sound to meaning.

Having made these terms explicit, let us return to the phenomenon under discussion: the transformation of NP-movement. Examples are given in (17) and (18).

(17)   D-Structure:
        ____ seems [____ to have been defeated the motion] NP-movement ⇒
                                                        theme
        ____ seems [the motion to have been defeated ____] NP-movement ⇒
        S-structure: the motion seems [____ to have been defeated ____]

(18)   D-structure:

_____ was believed [_____ to have been sold the house] NP-movement ⇒
                                                theme
_____ was believed [the house to have been sold _____] NP-movement ⇒
S-structure:
The house was believed [_____ to have been sold _____]

Notice that in (18), although *the house* is the subject of the main verb *be believed* at S-structure, it receives its θ-role from the verb *sell* in the subordinate clause at D-structure.

5.2 Observations on NP-Movement

Having shown that NP-movement is necessary if we wish to maintain the assumption that each verb can have only one θ-grid in its lexical entry, we will explore in more detail how this rule works and its consequences for the grammar as a whole. First, we will try to state explicitly some observations about the way NP-movement seems to behave and look closely at the derivation of various types of passive sentences. These statements will be merely observations, with no status as constraints or rules in the grammar. We will then develop some general constraints, to be incorporated into the theory, which account for the observed properties of NP-movement.

5.2.1 Movement is Structure-preserving

The first thing to notice is that when an NP moves, it always seems to move to a position where an NP could occur in a D-structure. In both of the cases we have seen, the NP moves to subject position. Thus, the structure resulting from NP-movement is always a structure which conforms to, or is compatible with, the D-structure configurations of the language. In this sense, NP-movement is a *structure-preserving* process.

5.2.2 Movement Is Upwards Only

Another fact to notice about NP-movement is that the movement is always "upwards" in the structure. The tree structures in (19) and (20) illustrate this.

(19)

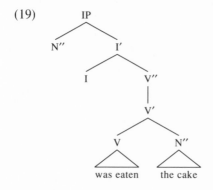

(20)

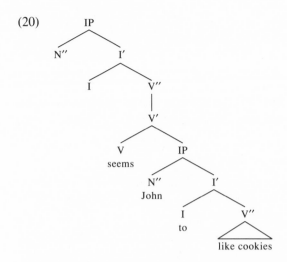

In (19), *the cake* moves up from inside to outside V". In (20), *John* moves from the subordinate to the main clause. We have not seen any examples where an NP moves from a main clause into a subordinate clause, or from outside some V" to inside that V". We will return to the question of why movement should only take place in an upwards direction; for now we will simply note that this seems to be the case.

5.2.3 Movement Is to a Non-θ-position

A slightly less obvious aspect of NP-movement is that it always moves an NP from a position where it receives a θ-role (a θ-position) to a position to which no θ-role is assigned, referred to as a non-θ-position. Consider first the cases involving *seem* and *be likely*.

5.2.3.1 CONSTRUCTIONS WITH *SEEM* AND *BE LIKELY*

(21)   a.   It is likely that Kelly will win.
       b.   Kelly is likely to win.

In both of these cases, *likely* assigns only one θ-role. In (21a), the subordinate clause [that Kelly will win] is the percept of *be likely*. In (21b), the subordinate clause [Kelly to win] is the percept. (Recall that NP-movement always comes after θ-role assignment.) Notice that the main clause subject position in (21a) is occupied by the pronoun *it*. This *it* is rather special. Unlike the *it* in subject position in (22a), the *it* in (21a) doesn't refer to anything. Thus (23a) makes sense while (23b) is nonsense.

(22)   a.   It is large and heavy.
       b.   It is likely that Kelly will win.
(23)   a.   What is large and heavy?
       b.   *What is likely that Kelly will win?

In (23) the *referent* (thing referred to) of *it* in the corresponding declarative sentence in (22) is being questioned. In (22a), *it* has a referent, so the question in (23a) is reasonable. Since *it* in (22b) has no referent, it makes no sense to question the referent, as (23b) attempts to do. The only function that *it* serves in (22b) is that of a placeholder. It is there because English sentences must have subjects. Thus, in a sentence like (24), there is nothing missing which carries any meaning; the sentence is ungrammatical because it lacks a subject noun phrase.

(24)   *Is likely that George will leave early.

Interestingly enough, in languages such as Italian and Spanish, where overt subject pronouns are not required, there is no placeholder pronoun. This is shown in (25), using Spanish.

(25)   a.   i.   Creo   que María está cansada.
                      believe-1sg. that M.   is   tired
              ii.   Yo creo que María está cansada.
              'I believe that Maria is tired.'
        b.   i.   Estan   cansados.
                      be-3pl. tired-pl.
              ii.   Ellos estan cansados.
              'They are tired.'
        c.   i.   Es   difícil   leer   este libro.
                      is-3sg. difficult to-read this book
              ii.   *El es difícil leer este libro.
              'It is difficult to read this book.'
        d.   i.   Parece   que María está cansada.
                      seem-3sg. that Maria is   tired
              ii.   *El parece que María está cansada.
              'It seems that Maria is tired.'

(25a) and (25b) show that overt subject pronouns are unnecessary even when there is a subject which has a referent. The (ii) sentences in (25a) and (25b) show that subject pronouns may be used, primarily for emphasis. Now consider (25c) and (25d). These differ from (25a) and (25b) in that the subject pronoun cannot occur. The most reasonable account of this is to say first that no θ-role is assigned to subject position in (25c) and (25d). Second, Spanish has no placeholder pronoun; all overt pronouns in Spanish are referential. Thus a non-θ-position in Spanish will be empty unless an NP moves into it through the application of NP-movement. By contrast, English subject pronouns are obligatory, and English has a placeholder pronoun. It thus makes sense to say that verbs like *seem* and *be likely* do not assign a θ-role to their subjects. We can refer to the subject position in this case as a non-θ-position. The notation used for this in recent literature is $\bar{\theta}$ (θ-bar)-position. Thus, a θ-position is a position to which a θ-role is assigned, and a $\bar{\theta}$-position is a position to which no θ-role is assigned. We can therefore say that in constructions with *seem* and *likely* where NP-movement takes place, the NP moves to a $\bar{\theta}$-position. After a discussion of passive sentences, we will see that NP-movement is always into a $\bar{\theta}$-position. We will see later why this must be true.

5.2.3.2 PASSIVE CONSTRUCTIONS

The passive cases are somewhat more complicated than the *seem* cases. We will look first at passive sentences with no agent—that is with no by-phrase following the verb.

(26)   The car was stolen

Since *the car* bears the θ-role of theme, which *steal* assigns to object position, the D-structure of (26) must be (27).

(27)   _____ was stolen the car

There is no agent in this sentence, so the only θ-role assigned is that of theme, as in (28).

(28)   _____ was stolen the car
                        theme

When NP-movement applies, the NP moves to subject position. Since no θ-role was assigned to this position, movement in this case is to a $\bar{\theta}$-position. So far, the situation is essentially parallel to the *seem* cases examined above. However, look at a passive sentence containing an agent phrase, such as (29).

(29)   The car was stolen by Adam.

The first question that arises has to do with the D-structure of sentences like (29). Specifically, where does the agent NP *Adam* originate? There are two reasonable possibilities.
A. The D-structure of (29) is (30):

(30)   Adam was stolen the car [$_{PP}$ by _____].

In this case, there are two instances of NP-movement involved in the derivation of (29). First, *Adam* moves into the by-phrase, leaving subject position empty. Then *the car* moves into subject position. θ-roles are assigned at D-structure exactly as they would be in the active sentence.
B. The D-structure of (29) is (31):

(31)   _____ was stolen the car by Adam

In this case, *Adam* gets its θ-role, not from the verb directly, but from the preposition *by*. *The car* is assigned its θ-rule in the normal way. Subject position is empty at D-structure, and the only movement that takes place is that of *the car* into subject position.

There are, as we will see, advantages and disadvantages to both alternatives. However, we will, after some discussion, adopt alternative B.

ADVANTAGE OF ALTERNATIVE A

θ-role assignment is exactly the same for active and passive verbs. This allows us to retain, in a completely straightforward way, the assumption that each verb is lexically associated with exactly one θ-grid.

DISADVANTAGES OF ALTERNATIVE A

1. NP-movement of *Adam* violates the generalization that movement is always structurally upwards. Thus the phenomenon of movement is less constrained than we had thought.

2. Movement of *the car* violates the generalization that movement is always into a $\bar{\theta}$-position. Under alternative A, subject position is a θ-position for passive verbs. If movement into a θ-position is permitted, then we will have to worry about why derivations like (32) produce ungrammatical sentences.

(32)   _____ seems [$_{IP}$ Adrian to like cookies]   NP-movement $\Rightarrow$
        Adrian seems [$_S$_____ to like cookies]   NP-movement $\Rightarrow$
        *Adrian seems [$_{IP}$ cookies to like _____]

Notice that the second movement, that of *cookies* to subject position in the subordinate clause, would be blocked if movement had to be to a $\bar{\theta}$-position. The subordinate clause subject position is a θ-position, since it receives a θ-role from *like*. This situation is essentially identical to the derivation required under Alternative A, in that an NP is moving to an empty NP position which was formerly occupied by another NP. That other NP received its θ-role in that position at D-structure. It is difficult to see how the theory could be made to allow the derivation illustrated in (30) while at the same time blocking something like (32).

3. If (30) is the D-structure of (29), then sentences like (33) will also be produced.

(33)   *John was stolen the car.

Since prepositional phrases are, in general, optional, there is no reason that the [$_{PP}$ by _____] phrase has to occur. If it does not occur, then there is nowhere for *John* to move to. Thus no movement can take place, and the S-structure remains the same as the D-structure, giving (33). We have no explanation for the ungrammaticality of (33).

ADVANTAGES OF ALTERNATIVE B

1. Since the only movement involved is from object to subject position, we can maintain the generalization that movement is always structurally upward.

2. Since the subject position of a passive verb is always a $\bar{\theta}$-position, we

can maintain the generalization that movement is always to a $\bar{\theta}$-position. Sentences like (32) will not arise.

3. Sentences like (33) above will also not be produced. Agents of passive verbs are always generated at D-structure in a post-verbal *by*-phrase. Subject position, being a $\bar{\theta}$-position, will always be empty at D-structure in a passive sentence. In other words, passive sentences will never contain an agent unless they also contain the preposition *by*.

DISADVANTAGES OF ALTERNATIVE B

1. θ-role assignment with passive verbs is somewhat different from θ-role assignment with active verbs. Specifically, the agent θ-role is assigned differently in the two cases. Unless some reasonable explanation can be found for this difference, we must weaken the claim that every verb has exactly one θ-grid in its lexical entry. Weakening this claim removes some of the motivation for having a rule of NP-movement in the first place.

2. Since the agent in a passive sentence seems to receive its θ-role, not from the verb itself, but rather from the preposition *by*, it is unclear exactly how the relation between the agent and the verb is to be established. In particular, it is hard to see how those thematic relations which depend crucially on the verb are to be assigned. For example, with *steal*, the agent is also the goal. With *send*, the agent is also the source. It is easy to have *by* assign the role of agent, but in order to assign these other roles, it is necessary to know which verb is involved.

As we have seen, both alternatives have advantages and disadvantages. The consequence of adopting alternative A is that the theory must allow a much wider range of movement types. If we adopt alternative B, however, there are some specific problems related to θ-role assignment in passive sentences which must be worked out.

5.2.3.3 θ-ROLE ASSIGNMENT IN PASSIVE SENTENCES

As stated in the previous section, the assumption that subject position in passive sentences is invariably a $\bar{\theta}$-position raised a problem with regard to the θ-grid for any verb appearing in both active and passive sentences. In this section, we will look at one possible solution to this problem.

What is required here is an understanding of the role of passive morphology, that is, the participial suffix on the verb. There are two reasons to examine passive morphology. The first is that it may help provide an answer to the question of what happens to the agent in a passive sentence. The second is that there must be some reason for the presence of the participial suffix. If it had no function, then we would expect sentences like (34) to be grammatical.

(34)   *Jennifer was see by Emily.

There are several views of passive morphology in recent literature (Jaeggli 1986; Baker 1988; Baker, Johnson, and Roberts 1989; Grimshaw 1989). While these approaches differ in interesting ways, they all have in common the idea that passive morphology makes the subject θ-role unavailable for assignment to an argument of the verb, where by argument here we mean subject or object position. The θ-role does not disappear entirely, as shown in (35).

(35)   The bicycle was stolen.

Although no agent is expressed in (35), the sentence clearly means that some person or persons stole the bicycle. The agent in (35) thus has the status of an implicit argument. In a passive sentence with an agent such as (29), the agent noun phrase, although not itself an argument of the verb, can be thought of as being identified with the implicit argument of the verb.

The foregoing is in no way a complete analysis of agents in passive constructions. Its purpose is merely to show that the problems facing Alternative B are not insurmountable. Since Alternative A would force us to widen significantly the possibilities for NP-movement, whereas Alternative B permits a more constrained view of this transformation, we will adopt Alternative B. The observation that began this section can thus be maintained: movement is always to a $\bar{\theta}$-position.

5.2.4 Movement is to an Empty NP Slot

Another fact about NP-movement is that it always moves the NP to an NP position that is unoccupied, or empty. In the passive sentence we looked at, subject position was empty before NP-movement took place. In the sentences with *seem* and *be likely*, the main clause subject position was also empty before movement took place. It is difficult to imagine what would happen if the theory were to allow an NP to move into a filled NP position. Consider the sentence in (36).

(36)   *Jeremy seems [Fred to like cookies]

If NP-movement were to apply in this sentence, moving *Fred* into subject position in the higher clause, what would the resulting structure be? There isn't room for both *Fred* and *Jeremy* in the main clause subject position. So either *Jeremy* would disappear, or perhaps *Fred* would disappear. In either case, the D-structure, and thus the network of θ-roles, would no longer be recoverable from the S-structure. We will not explore this any further here, but simply observe that NP-movement only takes place if the position to which the NP moves is empty.

5.3 NP-Movement and X-bar Theory

The observation that NP-movement is structure-preserving can be accounted for relatively easily. Recall from chapter 4 that once phrase structure rules are eliminated from the grammar, X-bar theory becomes a well-formedness condition on phrase structures themselves. If X-bar theory holds, not just of

D-structures, but also of structures derived by movement rules, then the output of NP-movement will have to conform to X-bar theory. NP-movement will thus automatically be structure-preserving.

5.4 The θ-Criterion

We have seen that each noun phrase in a sentence receives a θ-role and that some NP-positions do not receive a θ-role ($\bar{\theta}$-positions). These $\bar{\theta}$-positions were, in the cases we looked at, empty at D-structure. We are now ready to make these observations explicit, in the form of a condition on well-formed derivations. This condition will be known as the θ-criterion.

THE θ-CRITERION (FIRST APPROXIMATION)

1. At D-structure, every NP with a referent must receive a θ-role. If there is a lexical NP without a θ-role at D-structure, the sentence is ungrammatical.

2. An NP can only receive a θ-role once. If it receives a θ-role at some later stage in the derivation, then the sentence is ungrammatical.

Clause (1) of the θ-criterion blocks sentences like (37) and (38).

(37) *Daniel seems that Glenn is tired.

(38) *Daniel was eaten the cake.

In both of these sentences, *Daniel* is in a $\bar{\theta}$-position at D-structure. Thus it receives no θ-role and clause (1) of the θ-criterion is violated. Clause (2) blocks derivations like (39) and (40).

(39) _____ took the car.   NP-movement $\Rightarrow$
      *The car took _____.

(40) _____ believed [$_{IP}$ Rosemary to have taken the car]
                                                             NP-movement $\Rightarrow$
      *Rosemary believed [$_{IP}$ _____ to have taken the car]

In these cases, movement is from one θ-position to another. In (39), *the car* receives the role of theme at D-structure and then moves to subject position, where it receives the role of agent/goal. This violates clause (2) of the θ-criterion. In (40), *Rosemary* receives the role of agent at D-structure and then moves into subject position in the main clause, where it receives the role of experiencer. Again, clause (2) is violated.

A simpler statement of the θ-criterion is given in (41).

(41) Every referring NP must bear exactly one θ-role.

If we assume that once an NP receives a θ-role, it retains it, even when moved, then it is sufficient to say that the revised θ-criterion holds at all levels (that is, at D-structure and at S-structure). If the θ-criterion holds at D-structure, then every referring NP must originate in a θ-position. If it holds at S-structure, then no NP can move to a θ-position, since that would result in the NP having more than one θ-role. Thus the revised θ-criterion is empirically equivalent to the original version.

The θ-criterion is one of several general principles which determine exactly which NP movements are possible. We will explore other such principles as we go on.

5.5 Traces

5.5.1 NP-Movement Leaves a Trace

One of the general assumptions made in current syntactic work is that D-structures must be recoverable from S-structures. In order to ensure this, it has been proposed (Fiengo 1977) that when an NP moves, it leaves a trace, as follows.

(42) $[_{NP}$] was taken $[_{NP}$ the book]
$[_{NP}$ the book]$_i$ was taken $[_{NP}$]$_i$

When *the book* moves from object to subject position, the empty noun phrase left in object position is given an *index* (i), which is the same as the index borne by *the book*. In other words, the empty noun phrase is *coindexed* with *the book*. If two noun phrases, lexically filled or empty, are coindexed, this means they refer to the same thing, or are *coreferential*. Traces are usually written as t_i, but the meaning is exactly the same as $[_{NP}$]$_i$.

5.5.2 Coindexing

There are various types of noun phrase that must be coindexed with another noun phrase. In more traditional terms, these are elements that must have an *antecedent*. These elements cannot refer directly to something in the real world, but depend on their antecedents for reference. Some examples are shown in the following sentences.

(43) a.   Peter$_i$ hurt *himself*$_i$
      b.   *I$_j$ hurt *himself*$_i$
      c.   *Himself*$_i$ saw Peter$_i$
(44) a.   The girls$_i$ congratulated *each other*$_i$
      b.   *John$_j$ congratulated *each other*$_i$
      c.   *Each other*$_i$ congratulated the girls$_i$
(45) a.   Sue$_i$ wants [$[_{NP}$]$_i$ to leave]
      b.   *Sue$_i$ wants [$[_{NP}$]$_j$ to leave]
      c.   *$[_{NP}$]$_i$ wants [Sue$_i$ to leave]

The (a) sentences illustrate appropriate occurrences of reflexive pronouns (43), reciprocal pronouns (44), and null pronouns (45). Null pronouns are similar to traces in that they are phonologically empty NP-positions, but they differ from traces in that they have their own θ-role. They cannot, therefore, arise as traces do, by the operation of NP-movement. Null pronouns are discussed in more detail in chapter 10.

In the sentences above, the noun phrases in question have antecedents with which they are coindexed. The (b) sentences show that if these elements have no antecedent, the sentences are ungrammatical. Note that (45b) is to be understood as Sue wanting someone else (not Sue) to leave. The (c) sentences illustrate that it is not enough merely for an antecedent to occur in the same sentence as the element in question. We will investigate the required structural relationship in more detail later. For now, I will simply state the condition governing the structural relationship required between such elements and their antecedents so that we can use it in further discussion of movement processes.

5.5.3 Anaphors and C-command

First, however, a couple of terms must be defined, at least in a preliminary way.

ANAPHOR

An anaphor is a noun phrase which must be coindexed with an antecedent in order for the sentence containing it to be grammatical. Examples of anaphors are reflexive pronouns (43), reciprocal pronouns (44), and null pronouns (45). See chapter 10 for a full discussion of anaphors.

C-COMMAND

A node α c-commands a node β if every maximal projection dominating α also dominates β, and α does not itself dominate β. An example is shown in (46).[2]

(46)

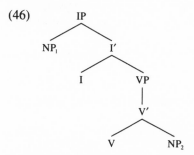

In this example, NP_1 c-commands I', I, VP, V', V, and NP_2. VP c-commands I and NP_1. V and NP_2 c-command each other. Crucially, NP_2 does not c-command NP_1. We are now in a position to state the structural relationship required between anaphors and their antecedents.

---

2. It should be noted that there is some confusion in the literature regarding this term. The original definition of c-command was as follows: A c-commands B if every **branching node** dominating A also dominates B, and A does not itself dominate B. However, c-command is widely used with the definition given in the text. Where it is important to distinguish these two structural relations from each other, c-command is reserved for **branching node** c-command, and m-command is used for **maximal projection** c-command. In this text, only the **maximal projection** version is required, and it will normally be called c-command.

C-COMMAND CONDITION ON ANAPHORA

An anaphor must be coindexed with an antecedent which c-commands it.
The (a) sentences in (43)–(45) satisfy this condition. In the (b) sentences,
the anaphors have no antecedents, and in the (c) sentences, the antecedents do
not c-command the anaphors.

5.5.4 Traces as Anaphors

Exactly what is a trace? We know that it is an element left behind when a noun
phrase moves. However, that statement cannot be the whole truth. One objection to the notion of traces has been that they are merely ad hoc elements
which serve to incorporate into a single tree structure the derivational history
of a sentence. If this were true, then trace theory would be merely a way of
hiding, in an apparently simple representation, an extremely powerful device.

In order to refute this objection, we must show that traces are, in fact,
"real" things which exhibit testable properties. The properties of traces will
be discussed in some detail in chapter 10, but I will make some preliminary
remarks here.

First of all, we have said that traces are empty NP-positions. Let us assume
that they are, in fact, NP's that happen to be phonologically null. They should
therefore share properties with other phonologically null NP's. Second, we
saw that a trace is coindexed with the element that moved. Assuming that coindexing is the relationship between coreferential elements, and that obligatory coindexing is what defines an anaphor, then traces should share properties
with anaphors. In fact, traces should *be* anaphors.

If a trace is an anaphor, then the c-command condition on anaphora should
apply. Thus the moved NP, which serves as the antecedent for the trace, must
c-command the trace. This would account nicely for one of the generalizations we observed earlier about movement—namely, that movement is always
structurally upward. If movement were structurally downward, as in (47) below, then the moved NP would not c-command the trace. The c-command
condition on anaphora would thus be violated.

(47)   John saw e

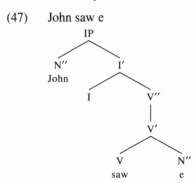

*t$_i$ saw John$_i$

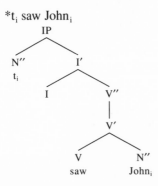

(Note: e is an abbreviation for an NP that is empty from D-structure on, as opposed to a trace (t), which arises through the application of a transformation.) If we assume (a) that movement leaves behind a coindexed trace, (b) that traces are anaphors, and (c) that anaphors are subject to the c-command condition, then we can predict that movement will always be structurally upward.

5.6 Traces, Chains, and the θ-Criterion

The assumption that NP-movement leaves a trace raises the possibility of looking at the θ-criterion in a slightly different way. We said that θ-roles are assigned to NP's at D-structure and are carried along if NP-movement applies. On the other hand, in the ungrammatical (39), repeated here as (48), we said that *the car* received a θ-role in object position, and then again in subject position, *after* NP-movement.

(48)   *The car$_i$ took t$_i$.

We can simplify the account somewhat by assuming that θ-roles are assigned, not to specific noun phrases, but rather to NP-positions. Thus, in (48), the theme θ-role is assigned to object position, while the agent θ-role is assigned to subject position. The trace thus bears the theme role and the moved NP, *the car,* bears the agent role.

Now let us define an NP and any traces coindexed with it as a *chain.* Thus, in (49), all of the italicized elements, taken together, form a chain.

(49)   *The horse$_i$* was believed [*t$_i$* to have been poisoned *t$_i$*]

The highest element in the chain (*the horse* in (49)) is called the *head* of the chain. The lowest element (the trace after *poisoned*) is called the *tail,* or *foot,* of the chain.

The statement of the θ-criterion can be revised as in (50).

(50)   Every chain must bear exactly one θ-role.

Notice that it is no longer necessary to assume that a noun phrase carries its θ-role along with it when it moves. θ-roles are assigned to positions, so that every chain must contain exactly *one* element which is in a θ-position. Since the θ-criterion holds at all levels, including D-structure, this guarantees that the θ-position must be the position occupied by the NP at D-structure, that is, the *tail* of the chain.

5.7 Summary

We have seen that it is necessary to assume a transformation of NP-movement which moves noun phrases from one position to another in the structure of a sentence. We also developed several conditions governing NP-movement and made some assumptions about the mechanism of NP-movement. These are summarized in (51).

(51) a. X-BAR THEORY: This is a set of well-formedness conditions on trees, which holds at D-structure and S-structure. It has the effect of requiring movement to be structure-preserving.

    b. TRACES: When an NP moves, the empty NP left behind is coindexed with the moved NP. This coindexed empty NP is a trace and behaves as an *anaphor.*

    c. THE C-COMMAND CONDITION ON ANAPHORA: An anaphor must be coindexed with an antecedent which c-commands it.

Principles (b) and (c) ensure that NP-movement is always structurally upwards.

    d. RECOVERABILITY: Although this principle was not developed in detail, but merely mentioned, its effect on NP-movement is clear. If D-structures must be unambiguously recoverable from S-structures, then NP-movement can never have the effect of obliterating any information in the tree. This means that movement must always be to an empty position.

    e. THE θ-CRITERION: Every chain must have exactly one θ-role. This holds at D-structure and at S-structure.

       Principle (e) ensures that NP's originate in θ-positions and move only to $\bar{\theta}$-positions.

Readings

Baker, Mark. 1988. *Incorporation: A Theory of Grammatical Function Changing.* Chicago, Ill.: University of Chicago Press.

Baker, Mark, Kyle Johnson, and Ian Roberts. 1989. "Passive Arguments Raised." *Linguistic Inquiry* 20:219–52.

Chomsky, Noam. 1965. *Aspects of the Theory of Syntax.* Cambridge, Mass.: MIT Press.

Fiengo, Robert. 1977. "On Trace Theory." *Linguistic Inquiry* 8:35–62.

Grimshaw, Jane. 1990. *Argument Structure.* Cambridge, Mass.: MIT Press.

Jaeggli, Osvaldo. 1986. "Passive." *Linguistic Inquiry* 17:587–622.

6 Government and Case

This chapter examines two subtheories that play an important role in constraining the results of NP-movement. They are also involved in other syntactic phenomena, but for the moment we will concentrate on their effect on structures involving NP-movement.

THE PROBLEM

We know that nonreferential *it* can be used to fill a $\overline{\theta}$-subject position, as in (1) below.

(1)   a.   It seems that Sue is tired.
      b.   It is believed that Sue is a genius.

We must therefore account for why, in sentences like (2) and (3), nonreferential *it* cannot be used. Why must NP-movement apply to produce (2b) and (3b)?

(2)   a.   *It seems Sue to be tired.
      b.   Sue$_i$ seems t$_i$ to be tired.
(3)   a.   *It was stolen a car.
      b.   A car$_i$ was stolen t$_i$.

Notice that all of these sentences satisfy the θ-criterion. In (2), *Sue* receives its θ-role from *be tired,* and in (3), *a car* is assigned its θ-role by *steal.* Nonetheless, these NP's cannot remain in their D-structure positions; they must undergo NP-movement. We will see that certain NP positions, although they are θ-positions and can be lexically filled at D-structure, have another property which forces them to be empty at S-structure.

6.1 Where Do Lexical NP's occur?

First let us examine the positions where lexical NP's *can* occur at S-structure. These fall into three main categories.

(4)   a.   Subject of a finite verb.
      b.   Direct object of an active verb.
      c.   Object of a preposition.

There is one other position which we will ignore. This is the so-called topic position, as in (5).

(5)   *John,* I've never been able to understand.

We shall look at each of the positions in (4) in turn and then formulate a general way of distinguishing them from other positions.

6.2 Subject of a Finite Verb

First of all, what is a finite verb? A finite verb is a verb that is marked, or *inflected,* for person, number, and usually tense. English has a relatively sparse inflectional system for most verbs, with a few exceptions such as the verb *be,* illustrated in (6).

(6)   I walk   I am
      you walk   you are
      she walks   he is
      we walk   they are
      I walked   I was
      you walked   you were
      she walked   he was
      we walked   they were

Infinitives (to walk, to be) are not inflected for person, number, tense, etc. Suppose that we represent the inflection markings by the element called INFL (inflection), which occurs between the subject and the verb phrase, as in (7).

(7)

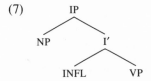

This approach allows us to say that the difference between an infinitival and a finite clause is simply the nature of INFL. There are basically two types of INFL, one which occurs in finite clauses, and the other occurring in nonfinite clauses. The difference between these two types has been described using the feature [±tense]. Finite clauses have a [+tense] INFL, while nonfinite clauses have a [−tense] INFL. The reason for using the feature [±tense] is that in finite clauses, a morpheme indicating tense appears on the first verbal element, as shown in (8).

(8)   a.   walk*s*/walk*ed*
      b.   ha*s*/ha*d* walked
      c.   *is*/*was* walking, etc.

In nonfinite clauses there is no such tense morpheme. The fact that INFL occurs directly before the verb phrase accounts automatically for the fact that the person/number/tense markings always show up on the first verbal element in the clause, as shown in (9).

(9) a. He *sings/sang* madrigals.
     b. He *has/had* sung madrigals.
     c. He *is/was* singing madrigals.
     d. He *has/had* been singing.
     e. He *can/could* have been singing.

Let us therefore assume that a finite clause is characterized by the presence of a [+tense] INFL between the subject and the verb phrase. We can now say that if a [+tense] INFL is present, then the subject may be lexically filled at S-structure, as in (10a). If no [+tense] INFL is present, then the subject must not be lexically filled at S-structure. NP-movement must apply, producing (10c).

(10) a. D-structure:
          [e [+tense] seem [that Cleo [+tense] like cookies]]
          Surface form:
          It seems that Cleo likes cookies.
      b. D-structure:
          [e [+tense] seem [Cleo [−tense] like cookies]]
          Surface form:
          *It seems Cleo to like cookies
      c. D-structure:
          [e [+tense] seem [Cleo [−tense] like cookies]]
          S-structure:
          [Cleo$_i$ [+tense] seem [t$_i$ [−tense] like cookies]]
          Surface form:
          Cleo seems to like cookies.

6.3 Direct Object of an Active Verb

Here we must figure out why *active* verbs allow lexically filled direct objects at S-structure while *passive* verbs do not. What difference is there between these two types of verb that might account for their differing behavior? The first thing to notice is that passive participles (beaten, eaten, lost, etc.) have certain properties in common with *adjectives*. Thus they sometimes occur in prenominal (before the noun) position, as in (11).

(11) a. The broken glasses
          (compare: The glasses were broken by the waiter.)

b.   A stolen car

(compare: The car was stolen by a junkie.)

Adjectives, as we shall see, can in some cases take a type of direct object. However, this direct object is different at S-structure from the direct object of an active verb. Consider the sentences in (12)–(14).

(12)   a.   Abby fears the police.
       b.   Abby is afraid *of* the police.
(13)   a.   John likes Mary.
       b.   John is fond *of* Mary.
(14)   a.   The bottle contains milk.
       b.   The bottle is full *of* milk.

It seems reasonable to say that the adjectives *afraid, fond,* and *full* assign θ-roles in essentially the same way as do the corresponding verbs *fear, like,* and *contain*. Thus *the police* bears the role of percept in both (12a) and (12b). In some loose sense, then, the adjectives in (12)–(14) take objects. However, unlike active verbs, adjectives do not take "bare" direct objects. The noun phrase bearing the object role must be in a prepositional phrase.

We have seen three characteristics shared by passive participles and adjectives. First, they both may occur in prenominal position. Second, they both can assign a θ-role to something in, loosely speaking, object position. Third, neither of them can have a "bare" direct object at S-structure. There are, however, systematic differences between passive participles and adjectives. These differences are somewhat obscured by the fact that some adjectives look just like passive participles. Wasow (1977) has proposed several tests which distinguish between so-called passive adjectives and passive participles.

First, adjectives, but not passive participles, can be negated with the prefix *un-* when the corresponding active verb has no form beginning with *un-*. This is illustrated in (15).

(15)   a.   The children hurt Roxy.
       b.   Roxy was hurt by the children. (passive participle)
       c.   *The children unhurt Roxy.
       d.   *Roxy was unhurt by the children. (passive participle)
       e.   Roxy was unhurt. (adjective)

Second, passive participles have the same θ-grids as the active verbs they are related to, except that the agent θ-role has been made unavailable for assignment to the subject.

Adjectives, including passive adjectives, have θ-grids that are not necessarily predictable from the θ-grid of the related verb. Consider the two passive adjectives *untaught* and *unsent*. The verbs *teach* and *send* both take an agent, a theme, and a goal, as shown in (16).

(16) a. Katie taught arithmetic to the children.
      b. Marcie sent the letter to Garfield.

Both verbs permit two passive constructions, as shown in (17) and (18).

(17) a. Arithmetic is taught to the children by Katie.
      b. The children are taught arithmetic by Katie.
(18) a. The letter was sent to Garfield by Marcie.
      b. Garfield was sent the letter by Marcie.

But the passive adjectives do not behave identically, as shown in (19) and (20).

(19) a. *Arithmetic is untaught.
      b.   The children are untaught.
(20) a.   The letter was unsent.
      b. *Garfield was unsent.

We can conclude from this that passive participles, while superficially similar to passive adjectives, are in fact different. Thus, passive participles are like verbs in that they inherit the θ-grids from the corresponding active verbs. They are like adjectives in that they can occur in prenominal position and cannot take a bare NP object. They are not, however, identical to either active verbs or adjectives. Recall from chapter 2 that verbs bear the features $[+V, -N]$, while adjectives are $[+V, +N]$. The feature that these two categories have in common, then, is $[+V]$. Let us assume, provisionally, that passive participles are simply $[+V]$, with no specification for the feature $[\pm N]$.

We can now state the fact that active, but not passive, verbs can take lexically filled direct objects at S-structure, as follows: A lexical NP can occur at S-structure in a position next to and c-commanded by $[+V, -N]$. Since passive participles lack the feature $[-N]$, they do not sanction a lexical NP in their object position. The structures in (21) illustrate the difference between active and passive sentences.

(21) a.

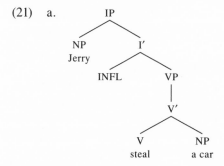

b.

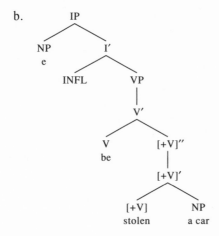

In (21a), the first maximal projection above *steal* is VP. VP dominates *a car,*
so *steal* c-commands *a car.* Thus *a car* can remain where it is. In (21b) the only
[+V, −N] element is the verb *be.* *A car* is not next to and c-commanded by
be. It is next to and c-commanded by *stolen,* which is merely [+V]. Thus *a
car* cannot remain where it is; that NP position cannot be lexically filled at
S-structure.

6.4 Object of a Preposition

Not much needs to be said here, other than that an NP can be lexically filled at
S-structure if it is next to and c-commanded by P. Notice that in (22), the first
maximal projection above the preposition is PP. Since PP dominates NP, the
preposition c-commands the noun phrase.

(22)

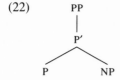

Recall that prepositions bear the features [−V, −N].

6.5 Government—A Definition

We can now unite the three NP positions which can be lexically filled at
S-structure with a general statement, as follows. A noun phrase can be lexi-
cally filled at S-structure if it is next to and c-commanded by INFL[+tense],
[+V, −N], or P. The next question to ask is what property INFL[+tense],
V, and P share which distinguishes them from other categories, such as N,
Adj, and passive participles, which cannot take bare lexical NP's. We have

seen that verbs and prepositions, but not passive participles, are [−N]. Adjectives and nouns are [+N]. The feature [−N] therefore seems promising as the defining criterion we are looking for. However, we have not as yet determined what features INFL[+tense] bears. Let us provisionally assume that INFL[+tense] also bears the feature [−N], leaving open the question of what other features it may also have.

Thus, lexical NP's can occur in positions next to and c-commanded by a [−N] element. We will now go on to refine our understanding of the structural relationship between the [−N] element and the lexical NP. Consider (23).

(23)   *It seems [s Sue to be crazy]

The question here is why *Sue* cannot occur in subject position in the lower clause. Although INFL in the lower clause is [−tense], *Sue* nonetheless is next to and c-commanded by *seems,* as (24) shows.

(24)

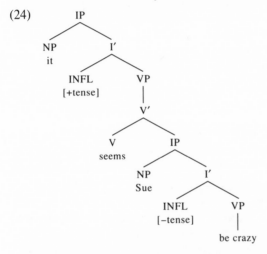

The apparently crucial difference between (24) and a structure like (25) below is that in (24), the verb and the noun phrase are in separate clauses, while in (25) the two elements are in the same clause.

(25)

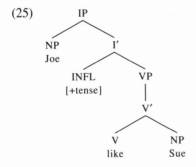

The notion of c-command is too broad to define precisely the structural relationship we need. What is required is a relationship which includes c-command, but which also incorporates some notion of *locality*.

Now consider (26).

(26)   *Joe put on the table the book.

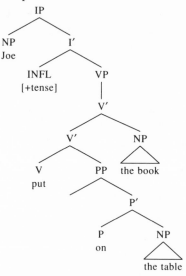

The book in (26) is not next to and c-commanded by V, but it is next to and c-commanded by PP. PP bears the feature $[-N]$, since it is the maximal projection of P. Thus our current statement predicts that (26) should be grammatical. Again, our definition is too permissive. We need to restrict the $[-N]$ element somehow, so that only $[-N]^0$ will sanction a lexical NP.

Let us call the structural relationship we are trying to define *government*. The statement sanctioning lexical NP's will thus have the following form.

(27)   a lexical NP may occur in a position next to and governed by a $[-N]$ element.

So far, we know the following about government.

(28)   GOVERNMENT: A FIRST APPROXIMATION
        α governs β iff
        a. α is X^0, for some X
        b. α c-commands β
        c. α and β are in the same clause.

Now consider (29).

(29)   *I resent Fred brother.

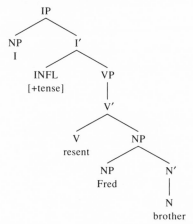

In this sentence, there are two noun phrases that are next to and c-commanded by the verb. These are *Fred* and the entire NP *Fred brother.* Given our definition of government, the sentence should be grammatical. In fact, *Fred* is what is causing the sentence to be ungrammatical. It must be marked with the possessive suffix *'s;* it cannot stand as a bare NP. Thus it seems that clause (c) of the definition of government given in (28), which stipulates that the two elements must be in the same clause, needs to be refined. One way to incorporate the locality required for government is to revise clause (c) as in (30) below.

(30)   GOVERNMENT
         α governs β iff
         a.   α is X⁰, for some X
         b.   α c-commands β
         c.   For all maximal projections γ, if γ dominates β then
               γ dominates α.

What clause (c) now states is that the lexical NP (β) cannot be separated from the governor (α) by any other maximal projections. In other words, maximal projections act as *barriers* to government. Since we are assuming that IP is a maximal projection, whose head is INFL, the definition in (30) prevents government from holding across clause boundaries. In (29), the higher NP *Fred brother* prevents the verb from governing the lower NP *Fred.*

Having defined, at least provisionally, the notion of government, let us now turn again to the distribution of lexical NP's. We can now say that lexical NP's may occur if they are governed by and adjacent to [−N].

6.6 Abstract Case

Having defined where lexical NP's may occur, let us now ask *why* they should occur in just these positions. In order to explain this, we will appeal to another property of NP's: the fact that they bear *Case*. In many languages, noun forms consist of two parts: a stem and a morpheme which indicates the syntactic role of the NP. In Latin, for example, the noun meaning 'woman' has the following forms:

(31)   femi**na**: nominative
        used when the noun is the subject of a finite verb, as in
        Femina virem amat
        woman man   loves
        'The woman loves the man'
(32)   femin**am**: accusative
        used when the noun is the direct object of a verb, as in
        Vir   feminam amat
        man woman   loves
        'The man loves the woman'
(33)   femin**ae**: dative
        used when the noun is the indirect object of a verb,
        or the object of certain prepositions
        Vir   feminae librum dedit
        man woman   book   gave
        'The man gave the book to the woman'
(34)   femin**ae**: genitive
        used for possession, as in
        Vir   librum feminae capit
        man book   woman   takes
        'The man takes the woman's book'
(35)   femin**aa**: ablative
        used when the noun is the object of certain prepositions, as in
        Vir   cum feminaa advenit
        man with woman arrives
        'The man arrives with the woman'

Thus the *Case* of a noun phrase depends on whether it is governed by INFL[+tense] (nominative), V (accusative), or P (dative, accusative, ablative). In languages like Latin, a noun must have Case. If there is no Case, the noun is simply not a well-formed word.

It has been proposed that the distribution of lexically filled NP's in all languages should be accounted for by appealing to the notion of Case marking. In some languages, such as Latin, Case marking is visible in the form of suffixes. In other languages, such as English, Case marking is invisible except for some marking in the pronoun system, as shown in (36).

(36)   I, you, he, she, we, they (nominative)
       me, you, him, her, us, them (objective)
       my, your, his, her, our, their (genitive)
       In English, genitive Case can also be seen on most nouns, as in *Mary's*.

Let us assume, then, that Case assignment is universal and works as follows:

(37)   INFL[+tense] assigns nominative Case to the noun phrase it governs.
       V and P assign objective Case to the noun phrases they govern.

In some languages, the particular cases assigned by V and P may vary depending on which verb or preposition is involved. In English, there is no reason to assume such variation.

Genitive Case is assigned in a rather different way, and we will not be concerned with it. We will simply assume that noun phrases in prenominal position receive genitive Case. Chomsky (1981) assumes a rule explicitly assigning genitive Case in just this context.

6.7 The Case Filter

If we assume that Case is assigned to an NP at S-structure when that NP is governed by and adjacent to $[-N]$, then it is possible to constrain the distribution of lexically filled NP's in a very simple way, as in (38).

(38)   The Case Filter:
       *NP, where NP has a phonological matrix but no Case.
       (Note: "lexically filled" and "having a phonological matrix"
       are essentially synonymous.)

This filter applies at S-structure and has the following effect. If a lexically filled NP is not governed by a $[-N]$ element, then it has no Case. Any sentence containing a lexically filled NP with no Case will be blocked by the Case Filter. Let us return to the examples that prompted the discussion, to show the Case Filter at work.

(39)   *It seems [Sue to be tired]

Sue in this case is not governed by a [+tense] INFL, since the lower clause is nonfinite. It is not governed by the higher verb since it is protected by IP. Thus it receives no Case. At S-structure, the Case Filter will mark the sentence as ungrammatical.

(40)   e INFL seems [Sue to be tired]
       Sue_i INFL seems [t_i to be tired]

In (40), at D-structure, *Sue* receives a θ-role, but no case. After NP-movement, *Sue* is in a position governed by INFL[+tense] in the main clause and thus receives nominative Case. The ungoverned subject position in the lower clause is now empty, so the Case Filter, applying at S-structure, will not block the sentence.

(41)   *It INFL[+tense] be stolen a car.

A car receives a θ-role from *steal*, but since *a car* is governed, not by V, but by a passive participle, it receives no Case. The Case Filter thus marks the sentence as ungrammatical.

(42)   e INFL[+tense] be stolen a car
        A car$_i$ INFL be stolen t$_i$

At D-structure, *a car* receives a θ-role, but no Case. NP-movement puts *a car* in subject position, where it is governed, and thus assigned nominative Case, by INFL. The caseless position is empty at S-structure, so that the Case Filter will not block the sentence.

6.8 Exceptional Case Marking

Consider the following sentences:

(43)   a.   David believes that the children are geniuses.
        b.   David believes the children to be geniuses.
(44)   a.   David thinks that the children are geniuses.
        b.   *David thinks the children to be geniuses.

In the (a) sentences above, *the children* is governed by INFL[+tense] in the lower clause and thus receives nominative Case. In the (b) sentences, *the children* is in subject position in an infinitival clause. There is no [+tense] INFL in the clause. If the definition of government in (28) is correct, then *the children* will receive no Case, since it is protected from the higher verb by IP. Although (44b) is ungrammatical as expected, (43b) is perfectly grammatical. We must conclude that *the children* in (43b) is getting case from somewhere. The sentences in (45) provide a clue as to where this case might be coming from.

(45)   a.   Sue believes that *we* are geniuses.
        b.   Sue believes *us* to be geniuses.
        c.   *Sue believes *we* to be geniuses.

Notice that in (45a), the subject of the lower clause bears nominative Case. This is to be expected, since it receives nominative Case from INFL. However, in (45b), the subject of the lower clause bears objective Case. The ill-formedness of (45c) shows that nominative Case would be ungrammatical here. We saw earlier that objective Case is assigned by V (and also P). An examination of sentences (45b) and (43b) reveals that the subject of the lower clause is, in fact, next to and c-commanded by V, as shown in (46).

(46)

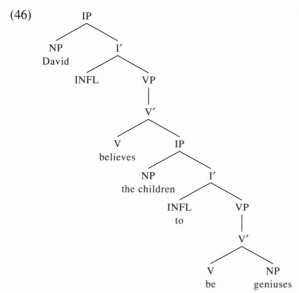

The only problem is that the verb in question does not govern the noun phrase to which it seems to be assigning Case. In general, Case cannot be assigned across a maximal projection, as shown in (44b). (Note that (43b) and (44b) have exactly the same structure.) However, it seems that certain verbs, contrary to normal principles, *can* govern, and assign case to, an NP across a maximal projection. Other such verbs are *expect, want,* and *show.* The lexical entry for each of these verbs will have to contain the information that the verb can, exceptionally, govern an NP in another clause. Notice, however, that the NP must still be adjacent to the verb. The sentences in (47) show that if anything comes between the verb and the lower clause subject, case marking fails and the sentence is ungrammatical.

(47) a. *We believe firmly Vanessa to be a genius.
      b. *We expect very soon him to arrive.

6.9 The Role of Government

We have developed the structural relation of government with specific reference to Case assignment and have restricted our definition to cover only government by an X^0 category. In fact, government plays a much larger role in the theory as a whole. For example, it has been claimed that θ-roles are assigned under government, in that the element assigning the θ-role must govern the position to which the θ-role is assigned. This idea raises serious questions, which we shall not discuss, about the assignment of θ-roles to subject position in a clause (note that the verb does not govern anything outside VP). Government is involved in constraining the movement of X^0 elements, which we will look at in chapter 8. The Empty Category Principle, taken up in chapter 9, is an extension of the notion of government. Government, or more precisely the absence of government, is crucially involved in the distribution of null pronouns, as we shall see in chapter 10. Thus, while we have worked out the basic properties of the government relation on the basis of Case assignment, it must be emphasized that government and Case are two separate aspects of the theory.

6.10 Summary of Principles

1. *Government:* α governs β iff
    a. α is X^0, for some X
    b. α c-commands β
    c.   For all maximal projections γ, if γ dominates β then γ dominates α.
2. *Case Assignment:* An NP receives Case at S-structure if it is governed by and adjacent to $[-N]$. $[-N]$ elements are INFL[+tense], V and P.
3. *The Case Filter:* *NP, where NP has a phonological matrix but no Case.

Readings

Chomsky, Noam. 1981. *Lectures on Government and Binding*. Dordrecht: Foris Publications.

Culicover, Peter, Thomas Wasow, and Adrian Admajian. 1977. *Formal Syntax*. New York: Academic Press.

Massam, Diane. 1985. "Case Theory and the Projection Principle." Ph.D. diss., MIT, Cambridge, Mass.

Travis, Lisa. 1984. "Parameters and Effects of Word Order Variation." Ph.D. diss., MIT, Cambridge, Mass.

Wascow, Thomas. 1977. "Transformations and the Lexicon." In Culicover, Wasow, and Akmajian (1977).

7 Transformation—WH-Movement

In this chapter, we will look at another movement process which differs in some superficial respects from the NP-movement dealt with in chapter 5. Although we will ultimately conclude that these two processes are instances of a single rule, we will begin by considering them separately.

7.1 Surface Facts—Motivation for Movement

Consider the sentences in (1).

(1) a. What did they see?
     b. Who are they dancing with?
     c. With whom are they dancing?
     d. When did they leave?
     e. What did they put on the table?

There are two aspects of these sentences that cannot be handled by the grammar we have. First, a verbal element precedes the subject. Second, a question word or phrase occurs at the beginning of the sentence. Ignoring the problem of the verbal element for the moment, consider the problem of the question words. Notice that in addition to the question word at the beginning of the sentence, there is a **gap** elsewhere in the sentence. The sentences in (1) are more properly represented as in (2) below.

(2) a. What did they see [$_{NP}$ e]?
     b. Who are they dancing with [$_{NP}$ e]?
     c. With whom are they dancing [$_{PP}$ e]?
     d. When did they leave [$_{ADVP}$ e]?
     e. What did they put [$_{NP}$ e] on the table?

The gaps shown in (2) are in positions to which θ-roles are assigned. The θ-roles assigned to these positions are, in fact, borne by the question words at the beginning of the sentences. Thus *what* in (2a) is the percept of *see*.

Since the θ-criterion holds at D-structure (at all levels, in fact), and since the question words bear the θ-roles assigned to the positions of the gaps, it follows that the question words must have originated in the gap positions and must have been moved to the beginning of the sentences by some transformation.

7.2 One Movement Rule or Two?

One question that arises immediately is whether this transformation is the same as the rule of NP-movement we have been dealing with.

7.2.1 Rationale

Initially, the answer seems to be no, since NP-movement moves only noun phrases, and question words and phrases can be not only noun phrases, but also prepositional phrases (2c), and adverb phrases (2d). Let us assume for the moment, then, that the rule involved is something specific to questions. This rule is commonly known as WH-movement, since question words in general begin with the letters "wh" in English. Having decided to assume that the two movement processes are different rules, we must now examine them to see which properties they share and in which ways they differ. As with NP-movement in chapter 5, we will only be making observations at this point. The observations in the next section have no status in the theory. They are merely facts and generalizations the theory will have to account for.

7.2.2 Differences and Similarities

NP-movement always moves an NP from a θ-position to a $\bar{\theta}$-position. WH-movement seems to be similar in this respect, since the gap at S-structure is in a θ-position, and the surface position of the WH-word is not a θ-position.

NP-movement leaves behind a coindexed trace, which must be c-commanded by the moved NP. If we assume, as before, that D-structures must be recoverable from S-structures, then WH-movement must also leave behind a coindexed trace, as in (3).

(3)

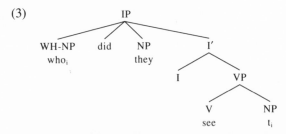

The first maximal projection dominating the WH-phrase is IP. Since IP dominates the trace, the c-command condition is satisfied.

NP-movement always moves an NP out of a non-case position, ultimately to a position that receives Case. WH-movement differs from NP-movement in two ways involving Case, as follows. First, the WH-word, if it is a noun phrase, can always receive Case in its pre-WH-movement position, as shown in (4).

(4) a.   They INFL do see what   (objective)
     b   They INFL be dancing with who   (objective)
     c.   They INFL be dancing with whom   (objective)
     d.   They INFL do leave when   (not NP, no case)
     e.   They INFL do put what on the table   (objective)

In fact, if the WH-word cannot receive Case before moving to the beginning of the sentence, the sentence will be ungrammatical. Consider the
derivations in (5).

(5) a.   It INFL do seem [who to want the book]
          nominative   objective
          WH-movement & verb morphology:
          *Who$_i$ does it seem t$_i$ to want the book?
     b.   e INFL seem [who to want the book]
          NP-movement:
          who$_i$ INFL seem [t$_i$ to want the book]
          nominative
          WH-movement & verb morphology:
          who$_i$ t$_i$ seems [t$_i$ to want the book]
          Who seems to want the book?

In (5a), the *who* is in a non-case position at D-structure. It moves directly to
a position at the beginning of the sentence. This new position cannot be subject position, since *it* occurs in subject position. *Who* thus does not receive
nominative Case from INFL in the main clause. There is no other governor
from which it can receive Case, so it violates the Case Filter and the sentence
is ungrammatical. In (5b), however, *who* first moves from a non-case position
to subject position in the main clause. This is an instance of NP-movement. In
main clause subject position, it is governed by and receives nominative Case
from INFL. It then undergoes WH-movement. At S-structure, since *who*
has received Case, it does not violate the Case Filter and the sentence is
grammatical.

Thus we can say that whereas NP-movement is always from a non-case
position and ultimately to a case position, WH-movement is always from a
case position to a non-case position.

Sentence (5b) also raises a point with regard to NP-movement, WH-
movement, and θ-positions. In (5b), a single noun phrase undergoes both
NP-movement and WH-movement. In a case like this, only the D-structure
position of the NP is a θ-position. Thus, only the first instance of movement
is from a θ-position to a $\bar{\theta}$-position. Any further movements are from a
$\bar{\theta}$-position to another $\bar{\theta}$-position. Crucially, however, all movements are *to*
a $\bar{\theta}$-position.

To summarize, then, here are the similarities and differences discovered so
far between NP-movement and WH-movement.

(6)   NP-movement   WH-movement
         a.   movement is to a $\bar{\theta}$-position (true of both types)
         b.   movement leaves a coindexed trace (true of both types)

c. restricted to NP's	NP's, PP's, ADVP's can move if they are WH-words or phrases
d. movement is out of a **non-case** position	movement is out of a **Case** position
e. movement is to a **Case** position (final movement)	movement is to a **non-case** position

7.3 Derived Structure for WH-Movement: IP and CP

We have simply been assuming that WH-movement moves the WH-word to sentence-initial position, directly dominated by IP. We will now see that in fact the structure resulting from WH-movement is not (7), but (8).

(7)

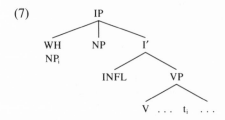

(8)

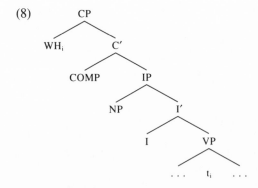

The argument will proceed as follows. First, we will show that there is a category called complementizer (COMP) which occurs outside IP. X-bar theory indicates that COMP head its own maximal projection (CP). We will then show that moved WH-phrases interact in interesting ways with the complementizer and argue that WH-phrases move to specifier position in CP.

7.3.1 COMP and IP

There is a set of words which introduce subordinate clauses. In traditional grammars, these words were called subordinate conjunctions, but we will call them complementizers. Examples are shown in (9).

(9) a. The committee claimed *that* the results were inconclusive.
     b. They wonder *whether* the children are hungry.
     c. Sue asked *if* the house was finished.

First, it can be shown that the sequence COMP NP INFL VP is a constituent, since it can occur in a coordinate structure, as shown in (10). Recall from chapter 2 that only constituents can be conjoined.

(10) Sue claimed [[that the work was done] and [that she had not been paid]].

Second, it can be shown that the sequence NP INFL VP, without COMP, must also be a constituent, since it too can occur in a conjoined structure.

(11) John said that [Mary had arrived] and [Sue had left].

Since all conjoined structures must fit the schema in (12), the sentences in (10) and (11) provide partial evidence for the structure in (8). In particular, they argue that COMP is external to IP, and that COMP and IP together form a constituent.

(12) $X^i \rightarrow X^{i*}$ CONJ X^i

Sentence (10) has the structure in (13), and sentence (11) has the structure in (14).

(13)

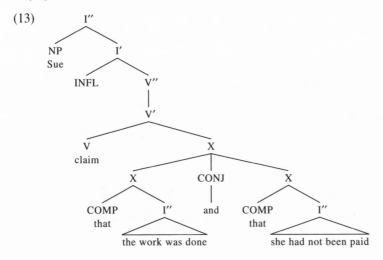

(14)

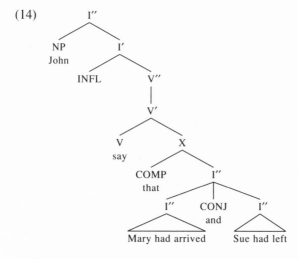

We have now seen that COMP must be a sister, rather than a daughter, of I″ and that a new category, which we have called X, dominates COMP and I″. The next step is to to determine the nature and internal structure of X.

7.3.2 The Structure of Subordinate Clauses

X-bar theory tells us that every X^0-level category heads a maximal projection and that every maximal projection (except in coordinate structures) has a unique head. It follows from X-bar theory that any non-head element must be a maximal projection. How does this bear on the structure of clauses introduced by complementizers? We determined in the previous section that these clauses have the structure shown in (15).

(15)

According to X-bar theory, X is a projection either of COMP or of IP. If it is a projection of IP, then COMP, being non-head material, must be a maximal projection. If X is a projection of COMP, then IP, being non-head material, must be a maximal projection. The two possible structures are shown in (16).

(16)   a.   b.

Recall the arguments given in chapter 6 for INFL being the head of S. In that chapter, we saw that clause types depended on the nature of INFL and that contextual restrictions related only to the heads of categories that were sisters of the element bearing the restriction. We will now use the same type of argumentation to show that COMP, rather than I″, is the head of X.

Consider the following sentences:

(17) a. George explained [that the children were misbehaving].
      b. George explained [why the children were misbehaving].
(18) a. *George wondered [that the children were happy]
      b. George wondered [whether the children were happy].
(19) a. George thought [that the boys were outside].
      b. *George thought [whether the boys were outside]

These sentences illustrate two things. First, they show that the difference between an embedded question and an embedded statement, or declarative, is expressed in the complementizer. We shall express this difference by means of a feature [±WH] which complementizers are specified for. A [+WH] complementizer introduces an embedded question, while a [−WH] complementizer introduces an embedded declarative. Second, they show that some verbs (such as *wonder*) require an embedded question as a complement sentence, other verbs (such as *think*) require an embedded declarative, while still others (like *explain*) may take either an embedded question or an embedded declarative. Given that these sorts of contextual restrictions can hold only between an X^0 category (the verb in the main clause) and the heads of its sisters, it follows that the complementizer must be the head of the subordinate clause. Using C as the abbreviation for complementizer, this forces us to adopt the structure in (20).

(20)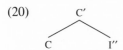

We can also show that the complementizer, in turn, places restrictions on the nature of INFL. Consider the data in (21).

(21) a. I believe *that* Sue has left.
      b. I would prefer *for* Sue to leave.
      c. *I believe *that* Sue to leave
      d. *I would prefer *for* Sue will leave

These data show that the complementizer *that* takes only a [+tense] IP, while the complementizer *for* takes only a [−tense] IP.

Given that complementizers have properties ([±WH]) which satisfy the lexical requirements of higher verbs and that complementizers also have lexical requirements which are satisfied by INFL, it makes sense to treat both COMP and INFL as heads.

The next question that arises has to do with the maximal projection of C. All other categories that we have seen in English have the following structure:

(22)

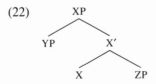

If COMP conforms to this generalization, then the structure for the COMP phrase must be as in (23).

(23)

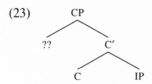

This structure has a position, indicated by ??, that does not occur in the embedded clause structures we have been using until now. According to X-bar theory, this position must be occupied by a maximal projection. It does not appear to be a θ-position, however, since complementizers do not assign θ-roles and since any θ-role assigned by a higher verb would be assigned to the CP as a whole. It also appears not to be a Case position, since we have no reason to assume that complementizers assign Case and a higher verb would not be able to assign Case through CP.

The position labelled ?? is thus a non-case, non-θ-position, at the beginning of a subordinate clause, which can accommodate a maximal projection. Looking back at the data in (1) and (2) and to the properties of WH-movement listed in (6), we see that these are exactly the properties of the moved WH-phrase.

Therefore, let us assume that when a WH-phrase moves to the beginning of a clause, it moves to the specifier position in CP. We now turn to one consequence of this assumption.

An earlier analysis of WH-movement (Chomsky 1977:85) had WH-phrases moving, not to specifier position, but to the complementizer position itself. In that analysis the interpretation of X-bar theory was somewhat less strict, and the complementizer was not assumed to be the head of the clause. While that analysis was less elegant from a structural point of view, it accounted for certain facts rather handily. Consider the data in (24).

(24) a.   Bonnie explained *that* we should do the work.
      b.   Bonnie explained *what* we should do.
      c.   *Bonnie explained *that what/what that* we should do

The data in (24) show that lexical complementizers and clause-initial WH-phrases are in complementary distribution. If they occupy the same structural position, as was the case in the earlier analysis, their complementary distribution is immediately accounted for. Since our theory places the complementizer and the moved WH-phrase in different structural positions, we will have to find another explanation. We will leave this question until chapter 9, and turn now to other instances of WH-movement.

7.4 Further Instances of WH-Movement

7.4.1 Indirect Questions

We have seen WH-movement at work in direct questions in the preceding section. The alert reader may have noticed that it also occurs in indirect questions, such as (25) below.

(25) a. Sue wonders [who$_i$ [t$_i$ ate the cookies]].
     b. It is unclear [what$_i$ [they want t$_i$]].
     c. Eddie wouldn't say [why$_i$ [he was so depressed t$_i$]].

7.4.2 Relative Clauses

Another case of WH-movement is to be found in relative clauses. Relative clauses are embedded sentences which modify noun phrases, as in (26). They have the structure shown in (27).

(26) I found the book [which$_i$ [you lost t$_i$]]

(27)

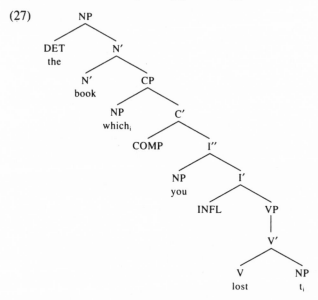

Although WH-movement is involved in both questions (direct and indirect) and relative clauses, there are several differences between the two constructions. We shall examine these and then look for ways of accounting for them.

7.5 Inventory of WH-Words

The WH-words involved in questions are not exactly the same as those involved in relative clauses.

(28)

	Questions	Relative Clauses
NP(animate)	who whom	who whom φ that (see below)
NP(inanimate)	what	which φ that (see below)
ADVP	when where why how	when (the time when . . .) where (the place where . . .) why (the reason why . . .) *how (*the way how) φ that
DET/ADJ	whose which	whose

The most straightforward way of accounting for these facts is to list each of the WH-words in the lexicon. The lexical entry for each word will simply state, among other things, whether the word is a relative pronoun, a question word, or both.

The feature [±WH], proposed to distinguish interrogative from declarative complementizers, is an obvious mechanism by which to distinguish question words from relative pronouns.

7.6 The Problem of *that* and φ

7.6.1 That *as a Complementizer*

That, as we have already seen, is a complementizer, as in sentence (29).

(29)   Sue said [$_{CP}$ that [$_{IP}$ the proposal was interesting]].

The question to deal with now is whether *that* in (30) should be analyzed as a relative pronoun, or as a complementizer.

(30) The house [$_{CP}$ that [$_{IP}$ she bought e]] is beautiful.

First of all, notice that although the other NP-relative pronouns can occur with prepositions, *that* cannot.

(31) a.   The man [to whom [I gave the book]] . . .
      b.   The book [from which [I took the question]] . . .
      c.   *The man [with that [I did the work]] . . .

This seems to indicate that *that* is not a noun phrase, since noun phrases in general can occur in prepositional phrases. Let us therefore assume that *that* in relative clauses is a complementizer, rather than a relative pronoun, and explore the consequences of this assumption. First, however, one more assumption needs to be made clear about relative clauses with real relative pronouns. Recall that when the WH-word moves into specifier position in CP, it leaves behind a coindexed trace, as shown in (32).

(32) I saw the man [$_{CP}$ who$_i$ [$_{IP}$ Sue hired t$_i$]].

In order for the sentence to receive the correct interpretation, the relative pronoun must also be related to *man,* since, in some sense, *man* and *who* are coreferential. We will assume that this relation is expressed by coindexing and that this coindexing simply happens at some point. We will not worry about the nature of this coindexing mechanism if there is one. Example (32) therefore has the representation shown in (33).

(33) I saw the man$_i$ [$_{CP}$ who$_i$ [$_{IP}$ Sue hired t$_i$]].

We now return to the consequences of having *that* as a complementizer in relative clauses.

7.6.2 *Where is the WH-word? A Nonlexical WH-word*

If *that* is a complementizer, then there is no visible WH-word in the relative clause. The question immediately arises as to whether WH-movement has taken place at all. For reasons that will become clear in section 7.7, it must be assumed that WH-movement has, in fact, taken place. Let us assume that there is an empty, or silent, REL-NP which can undergo WH-movement. The derivation of sentences like (30) will be as in (34).

(34) The house [$_{CP}$ that [$_{IP}$ she bought [$_{NP-REL}$ e]]] is beautiful.
      WH-movement
      The house$_i$ [$_{CP}$ [$_{NP-REL}$ e]$_i$ that [$_{IP}$ she bought t$_i$]] is beautiful.

WH-movement moves the empty NP into specifier position in CP, leaving a coindexed trace behind. The empty NP has an antecedent, since it is co-indexed with *the house*.

If we treat *that* as a complementizer, and propose an empty WH-word, another set of data follows automatically. As we shall see, if *that* is treated as a relative pronoun, the other set of data is unaccounted for.

7.6.3 Relative Clauses with Empty COMP

Consider sentences like (35).

(35)   He bought the house [$_{CP}$ [$_{IP}$ he wanted e]].

In (35), there is clearly a gap after *wanted*. If *that* is treated as a complementizer, sentences like (34) are accounted for in the following way. First, *that*-complementizers are normally optional. Thus, sentences like (36a) and (36b) are both possible.

(36)   a.   He said [that [he was leaving]].
         b.   He said [ϕ [he was leaving]].

If *that* complementizers are normally optional, and if the *that* that occurs in relative clauses is a complementizer, then we would expect that it should be optional as well. In addition, if there is an empty WH-word, we would expect derivations like (37) to occur.

(37)   He bought the house [$_{CP}$ [$_{IP}$ he wanted [$_{NP\text{-}REL}$ e]]].
         He bought the house [$_{CP}$ [$_{NP\text{-}REL}$ e]$_i$ [$_{IP}$ he wanted t$_i$]].

Such sentences do, in fact, exist, as (35) shows. If *that* were a relative pronoun, however, the existence of sentences like (35) would be unexpected. They would have to be derived in some other way—perhaps by introducing a rule deleting WH-words. In any case, more would have to be said about them. We will thus adopt the assumption that *that* in relative clauses is a complementizer.

7.7 Long Distance WH-Movement

The cases of NP-movement that we have seen were relatively local, in that the S-structure position of the moved NP was either in the same clause as its D-structure position, as in (38), or in the immediately higher clause, as in (39).

(38)   Mary$_i$ was invited t$_i$ to the party.
(39)   Anna$_i$ seems [$_{IP}$ t$_i$ to have found the treasure].

With WH-movement, however, there are sentences in which the S-structure position of the WH-phrase is several clauses higher than its D-structure position. Examples are given in (40).

(40)   a.   Who$_i$ did [$_{IP}$ Joe say that [$_{IP}$ Sue thought [$_{IP}$ she loved t$_i$]]]?
         b.   I met the man who$_i$ [$_{IP}$ Joe said [$_{IP}$ Sue thought [$_{IP}$ she loved t$_i$]]].

The structures of the sentences in (40) are shown in (41).

(41) a.

```
              CP
          ┌───┴───┐
         NP       C'
         who_i ┌──┴────┐
               C        IP
              did    ┌───┴───┐
                    NP        I'
                    Joe   ┌───┴───┐
                        INFL      VP
                               ┌───┴───┐
                               V        CP
                              say       C'
                                     ┌──┴───┐
                                     C       IP
                                    that  ┌───┴───┐
                                         NP        I'
                                         Sue   ┌───┴───┐
                                               I        VP
                                                    ┌───┴────┐
                                                    V         CP
                                                 thought      C'
                                                           ┌──┴───┐
                                                           C       IP
                                                               ┌───┴───┐
                                                              NP        I'
                                                              she   ┌───┴───┐
                                                                    I        VP
                                                                         ┌───┴───┐
                                                                         V        NP
                                                                       loved      t_i
```

b.

```
        IP
     ┌──┴──┐
    NP     I'
     I  ┌──┴──┐
        I      VP
           ┌───┴───┐
           V        NP
          met   ┌───┴───┐
               DET       N'
               the   ┌───┴───┐
                     N'        CP
                    man    ┌───┴───┐
                          NP        C'
                         who_i  ┌──┴───┐
                                C       IP
                                    ┌───┴───┐
                                   NP        I'
                                   Joe   ┌───┴───┐
                                         I        VP
                                              ┌───┴───┐
                                              V        CP
                                            said       C'
                                                    ┌──┴───┐
                                                    C       IP
                                                        ┌───┴───┐
                                                       NP        I'
                                                       Sue   ┌───┴───┐
                                                             I        VP
                                                                  ┌───┴───┐
                                                                  V        CP
                                                              thought      C'
                                                                        ┌──┴───┐
                                                                        C       IP
                                                                            ┌───┴───┐
                                                                           NP        I'
                                                                           she   ┌───┴───┐
                                                                                 I        VP
                                                                                      ┌───┴───┐
                                                                                      V        NP
                                                                                    loved      t_i
```

In both of these sentences, there are three clause boundaries (IP nodes) between the gap left by WH-movement and the surface position of the WH-word. Sentence (42) show that when NP-movement moves a noun phrase this far, the result is atrociously ungrammatical.

(42) a.   *Sue_i seems that [_{IP} John knows that [_{IP} Mary believes [_{IP} t_i to love Fred]]].

b.

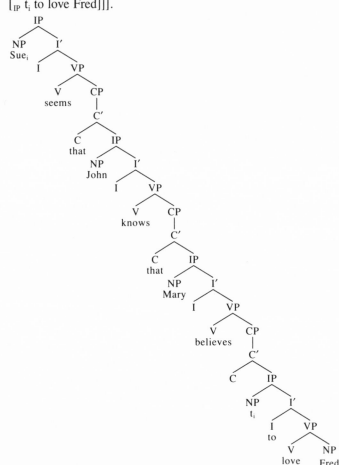

One might conclude from this that NP-movement is subject to some sort of locality condition which does not apply to WH-movement. However, WH-movement is not entirely unconstrained, as we see in the next section.

7.7.1 WH-Movement Blocked

Here we see that there are some cases where WH-movement must be blocked. Consider the sentences and structures in (43).

(43) a.   *Sue bought the suit which I know the tailor who made.

```
              IP
             /  \
          NP      I'
          Sue    /  \
                I    VP
                     |
                     V'
                    /  \
                   V    NP
                bought /  \
                     DET    N'
                     the   /  \
                         N'    CP
                        suit  /  \
                            NP      C'
                          which_i  /  \
                                  C    IP
                                      /  \
                                    NP     I'
                                    I     /  \
                                         I    VP
                                              |
                                              V'
                                             /  \
                                            V    NP
                                          know  /  \
                                              DET    N'
                                              the   /  \
                                                  N'    CP
                                                tailor /  \
                                                     NP     C'
                                                   who_j   /  \
                                                          C    IP
                                                              /\
                                                          t_j made t_i
```

b.   *I sold the book which
     you told me where Kate put.

```
           IP
          /  \
       NP      I'
       I      /  \
             I    VP
                  |
                  V'
                 /  \
                V    NP
              sold  /  \
                  DET    N'
                  the   /  \
                      N'    CP
                    book   /  \
                          NP      C'
                        which_i  /  \
                                C    IP
                                    /  \
                                  NP     I'
                                  you   /  \
                                       I    VP
                                           /    \
                                          V'      CP
                                         /|      / \
                                        V NP   AP    C'
                                     told me where_j / \
                                                    C   IP
                                                       /  \
                                                     NP     I'
                                                    Kate   /  \
                                                          I    VP
                                                              /  \
                                                             V'    AP
                                                            /  \   t_j
                                                           V    NP
                                                         put    t_i
```

In the sentences in (40), the WH-word moves across three clause boundaries, and the result is grammatical. In (43), the WH-word moves across two
clause boundaries, and the result is ungrammatical. Either something besides
locality is involved, or we are looking at WH-movement the wrong way, or
both. Let us examine sentences (40) and (43) more closely to find any difference on the basis of which we might predict the difference in grammaticality.

7.7.2 Successive Movements—The Subjacency Condition

Recall that WH-movement always moves a WH-phrase to the specifier of a
CP node. What if WH-movement moved the WH-phrase to the closest CP-
specifier, and then to the next CP-specifier, and so on, until it reached its surface position? One might then expect that a filled CP-specifier intervening between the underlying and surface positions of the WH-phrase would block
WH-movement and make such a sentence ungrammatical. With this in mind,
look at the intervening CP-specifiers in (41) and (43). In (41), the two CP-
specifiers between who_i and its trace are empty. In (43a), however, the CP-
specifier intervening between $which_i$ and its trace contains the WH-phrase
who. In (43b) the intervening CP-specifier contains the WH-phrase *where*.

It seems, then, that we can account for the apparently inconsistent behavior
of long-distance WH-movement by assuming that WH-movement is in fact
local, but that a WH-phrase may move through a succession of empty CP-
specifiers. WH-movement apparently cannot skip over a CP-specifier, nor is
there room in a single CP-specifier for two WH-phrases.

While these observations have often been stated as a condition on the application of movement rules, they can also be expressed in terms of the relationship holding between traces and their antecedents at S-structure. If a WH-
phrase moves through each CP-specifier in turn, then it will leave a trace in
each CP-specifier. The empirical differences between stating the condition as
a constraint on movement and stating it as a condition on representations are
extremely subtle, and the results are unclear. For consistency with the rest of
the theory, we will adopt a condition on representations. We can now say that
only one clause boundary (IP node) can intervene between a trace and its immediate antecedent.

Unfortunately, the matter is not quite as simple as that. Consider the contrast between (44) and (45).

(44)   Which book did Ruth report that Judith damaged?

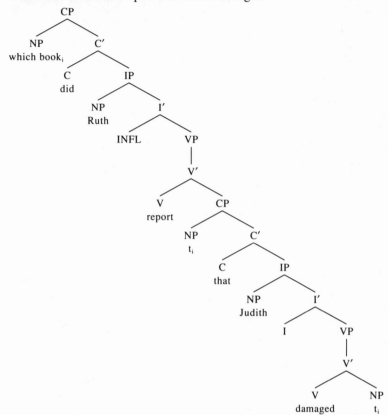

(45)   *Which book did Ruth believe the report that Judith damaged?

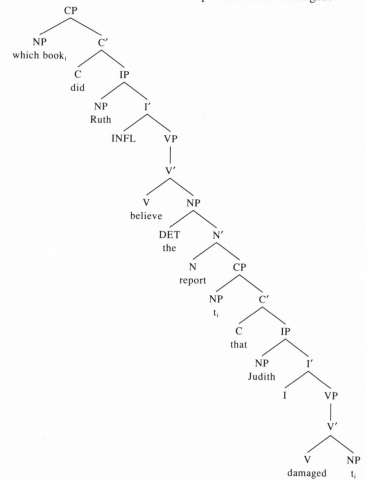

In both of these sentences, only one clause boundary intervenes between each trace and its immediate antecedent. Yet (45) is ungrammatical. The only difference between (44) and (45) is the presence of an extra NP node in (45). This NP-node intervenes between the higher of the two traces and its antecedent, the WH-phrase *which book*. It appears, then, that the locality condition on WH-movement refers not to clause boundaries, but rather to a class of nodes which we shall call *bounding nodes*. So far, it seems that the bounding nodes are NP and IP.

Let us now define *subjacency* as a measure of the structural distance between two nodes in a tree, as follows:

(46) If α c-commands β and α does not dominate β then β is n-subjacent to α iff no more than n bounding nodes dominate β which do not dominate α.

In other words, if no bounding nodes intervene between β and α, then β is 0-subjacent to α. If one or no bounding nodes intervene then β is 1-subjacent to α, and so on.

The data in (41) and (43) suggest that 1-subjacency is required of WH-movement. In other words, a trace must be 1-subjacent to its closest antecedent in a chain. This requirement is known as the *subjacency condition*.

(47) *Subjacency condition:* A trace must be 1-subjacent to its closest antedent in a chain.

The following examples show how the subjacency condition accounts for the sentences in (40) and (43). The structure in (48) corresponds to (40a), and (49) corresponds to (43a).

(48)

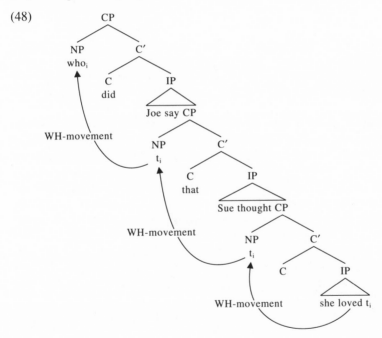

(49)

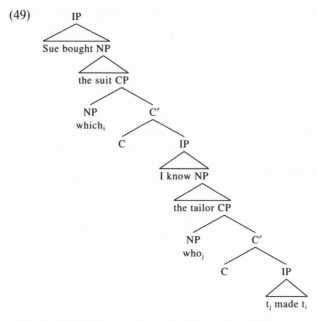

If *who_j* in (49) moves into the lowest CP-specifier first, then *which_i* must cross three bounding nodes in a single movement. This is in violation of the subjacency condition. Suppose for a moment that *which* moves first. It could move initially to the lowest CP-specifier, but it would still have to cross two bounding nodes in order to move to the higher CP-specifier. There is thus no way for *which* to move to its surface position in (49) without violating the subjacency condition. In addition, there is a problem with the second derivation just outlined. If *which* moves through the lowest CP-specifier, then it will necessarily leave a trace. This trace will then prevent *who* from undergoing WH-movement, since the lower CP-specifier is no longer empty. If *who* moves into the lower CP-specifier and obliterates the trace of *which,* we are essentially left with the first derivation, in which three bounding nodes intervene between a trace and its antecedent.

Now consider the derivation of (43b).

(50)

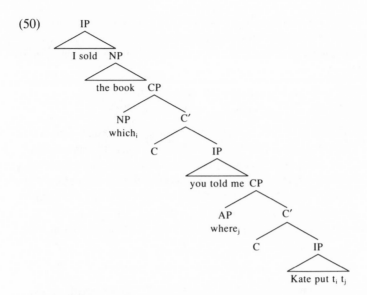

In this sentence, there are two bounding nodes between *which* and its trace. As with the previous example, *which* might have moved first, passing through the lower CP-specifier and obeying subjacency at the point of WH-movement. But at that point the trace in the lower CP-specifier would either block the movement of *where* or be obliterated by *where,* creating a subjacency violation.

The subjacency condition, together with the idea that WH-words may move from CP-specifier to CP-specifier, accounts for the sentences in (40), (42), and (43). It is easy to show that all of the instances of NP-movement discussed in chapter 5 also obey the subjacency condition. We thus conclude that the subjacency condition holds of all antecedent-trace relations.

7.7.3 Further Evidence for a Nonlexical WH-word

Recall that we proposed the null WH-word to account for sentences like (51).

(51)   a.   He found [the book [that [you wanted _____]]].
       b.   He knows [the woman [[you work for _____]]].

We said that the null WH-word moves from the position of the gap into the CP-specifier, exactly as a lexical WH-word would do. Thus, the S-structure of the sentences in (51) is as in (52).

(52)   a.   He found [the book$_i$ [e$_i$ that [you wanted t$_i$]]].
       b.   He knows [the woman$_i$ [e$_i$ [you work for t$_i$]]].

Another possibility is that in sentences like (51), no WH-movement is involved at all. The gap in the relative clause is simply coindexed with the noun that the relative clause modifies. Under this approach, the S-structure of (51) would be (53).

(53) a.   He found [the book$_i$ [that [you wanted e$_i$]]].
      b.   He knows [the woman$_i$ [[you work for e$_i$]]].

The only difference between these two approaches is that with WH-movement, as in (52), the CP-specifier is occupied, whereas without movement, as in (53), that position is vacant. However, we have discovered that even lexically empty material, such as a trace, is enough to prevent other WH-words from moving into a CP-specifier. Thus, if (52) is correct, it should be impossible to move another WH-word into such a CP-specifier. If (53) is right, such a movement should be possible. Consider the sentences in (54).

(54) a.   *I read the book (that) Sue told you who wrote.
      b.   *I read the book which Sue told you who wrote.

Under the no-movement approach, as in (53) above, (54a) is predicted to be grammatical and to have the following derivation.

(55)

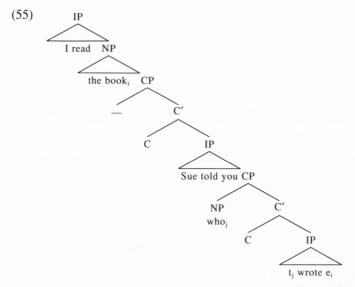

Book is simply coindexed with the empty object NP in the lowest clause. Since the CP-specifier is vacant, nothing prevents *who* from undergoing WH-movement. The no-movement analysis thus wrongly predicts that (54a) should be grammatical. In addition, it predicts that there should be a marked contrast in the grammaticality of (54a) and (54b). Since (54b) contains an overt WH-word, *which*, WH-movement must have applied. The CP-specifier in the lowest clause must therefore contain the trace of *which*, and *who* cannot undergo WH-movement. The movement analysis, on the other hand, predicts that both (54a) and (54b) are ungrammatical. The derivation of either is blocked as follows:

(56)

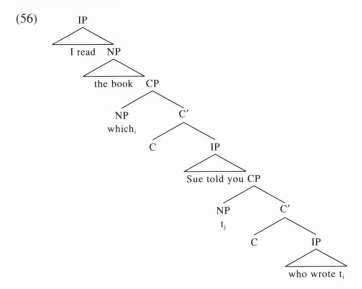

In (54a) the null WH-word has moved, leaving a coindexed trace in the lower COMP. In (54b) *which* has done the same thing. Thus, in both cases, the WH-position in the lower COMP is occupied, and *who* cannot move. From these sentences we can conclude that even if there is no lexical WH-word, WH-movement has taken place.

7.8 Summary

When WH-phrases move in questions and in relative clauses, they move to the nearest CP-specifier, and from there they may move successively to higher CP-specifiers. WH-movement, like NP-movement, obeys the subjacency condition and the θ-criterion. Unlike NP-movement, WH-movement always moves an element to a non-case position. In the next chapter, we will consider how these two movement rules can be united and treated as instances of a single process.

Readings

Chomsky, Noam. 1977. "On WH-Movement." In Culicover, Wasow, and Akmajian (1977), pp. 71–132.
———. 1981. *Lectures on Government and Binding*. Dordrecht: Foris Publications.

————. 1986b. *Barriers*. Cambridge, Mass.: MIT Press.

Culicover, Peter, Thomas Wasow, and Adrian Akmajian. 1977. *Formal Syntax*. New York: Academic Press.

Grimshaw, Jane. 1979. "Complement Selection and the Lexicon." *Linguistic Inquiry* 10:279–326.

Ross, John R. 1967. "Constraints on Variables in Syntax." Ph.D. diss., MIT, Cambridge, Mass.

8 Move α and the Theory of Movement

8.1 NP-Movement and WH-Movement: One Rule

This chapter takes another look at the two transformations developed in chapters 5 and 7. We initially treated them as separate rules in order to simplify the descriptive task facing us, but having worked out the basics of the two phenomena, we must now decide whether two rules are necessary. Considerations of simplicity suggest that if it is possible to account for both NP-movement and WH-movement by means of one rule, this should be done.

8.1.1 Why the Rules Should Be Unified

The similarities between NP-movement and WH-movement are striking. Both rules result in a structure in which the moved element c-commands its trace. Both involve the movement of a maximal projection. Both movements are structure-preserving. In both cases, the resulting chain obeys the subjacency condition. No violations of the θ-criterion or the Case Filter can be created. Thus it seems desirable to unify the two processes if possible.

8.1.2 How Move α Works

Let us now consider what would be the most general rule possible. In other words, what is the least a movement rule can say and still be a movement rule? The statement in (1) has been proposed as the minimal movement rule.

(1)   (Optional) Move α, α a category.

This rule simply states that a category may move. It says nothing about which categories actually move, which positions they move to, how far or how often a particular element may move, or whether or not traces are left behind. Initially, it seems that a rule such as this would overgenerate wildly, producing large numbers of ungrammatical sentences. However, before thinking about adding qualifications to the rule itself, let us survey the theoretical machinery already at our disposal. Perhaps the constraints and conditions already in place will suffice to limit the output of *Move α* to all and only grammatical sentences.

8.1.3 Well-formedness Conditions on S-structures

Consider some of the problems that might be created by the unconstrained application of a rule such as *Move α*. First, the rule might create structural chaos of the sort shown in (2).

(2) a.   D-structure

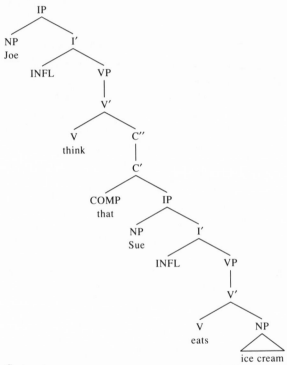

     b.   S-structure
           *Eats thinks Sue that Joe ice cream.

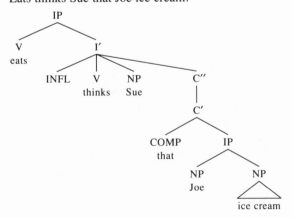

Such a derivation would be excluded by the X-bar theory, if this theory holds of S-structures as well as D-structures. Recall that X-bar theory requires that every X^n have an $X^{n/n-1}$ head and that every X^0 be the head of some X^{max}. The structure in (2b) violates this constraint in many places. The general effect of X-bar theory is to force *Move α* to be structure-preserving—in other words to produce S-structures that are essentially the same as the D-structures of the language. Thus, given this theory, the rule of *Move α* does not need to be constrained in order to prevent the generation of totally chaotic S-structures.

Another type of undesirable application of *Move α* is illustrated in (3).

(3) a. D-structure:
         Jack saw Mary.
     b. S-structure:
         Mary saw Jack.

What has happened here is that the two noun phrases, *Jack* and *Mary,* have switched places. It seems at first that this ought to have violated some principle or constraint, but in fact, the various constraints seem to be satisfied. Since the noun phrases have changed places, each occupies the position vacated by the other. There are thus no traces at S-structure. At D-structure, every noun phrase is in a θ-position. The same is true at S-structure, and since the θ-criterion does not compare the two levels, it will not "notice" that the noun phrases have been permuted. Each NP bears Case, satisfying the Case Filter. Since there are no traces, the c-command requirement and the subjacency condition have nothing to say either. What is relevant here is the principle of recoverability, mentioned in chapter 5. The principle of recoverability requires that D-structures be unambiguously recoverable from S-structures. The D-structure which would most naturally be recovered from (3b) is "Mary saw Jack," not "Jack saw Mary." Therefore the only D-structure possible for (3b) is, in fact, "Mary saw Jack." One might argue that a sentence similar to (3b) might be derived from (3a), if the two movements in question left traces giving an S-structure like (4).

(4)

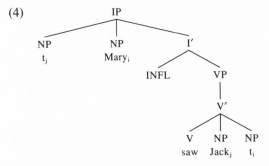

This structure may satisfy recoverability, but it violates other constraints. For example, t_j violates the c-command condition on anaphora. If t_j is removed, then *Jack* would have to be in postverbal position at D-structure. Then the sentence violates the θ-criterion, by having the NP *Mary* originate in a $\bar{\theta}$-position at D-structure and move into a θ-position at S-structure.

Another type of derivation that must be blocked is given in (5).

(5)   D-structure:
       it seems [Joe to love Sue]
       S-structure:
       *Joe$_i$ it seems [t$_i$ to love Sue]

Here, *Joe* has moved, not to subject position in the main clause, but to a position beside the subject, giving an ungrammatical sentence. Here, the Case Filter has been violated, since *Joe* cannot receive Case in either its D-structure or its S-structure position.

It is beginning to seem that the rule of *Move* α will not create as many problems as one might have thought. Let us summarize briefly the conditions and constraints currently available.

X-BAR THEORY ensures that *move* α is structure-preserving.

THE θ-CRITERION ensures that NP's originate in θ-positions and move only to $\bar{\theta}$-positions.

THE CASE FILTER ensures that lexical NP's receive Case at some point during the derivation.

RECOVERABILITY ensures that traces are left and that each unambiguous S-structure corresponds to only one possible D-structure.

SUBJACENCY guarantees that elements do not move too far—each trace must be 1-subjacent to its antecedent.

THE C-COMMAND CONDITION ON ANAPHORA ensures that movement is always structurally upwards—traces must be c-commanded by their antecedents.

Various problems remain, however. We will now discuss each of these in turn and either develop solutions or suggest where the solutions might lie.

8.2 Case Assignment and Chains

Recall that NP-movement always moves an NP from a non-Case position and that the NP must surface in a Case position. WH-movement, in contrast, moves a WH-phrase, which may be an NP, from a Case position to a CP-specifier, or from CP-specifier to CP-specifier. The WH-phrase thus surfaces in a non-Case position. The Case Filter simply states that an NP with a phonological matrix must bear Case. The question is, where does the Case Filter hold? Also, when and how is Case assigned? The Case Filter clearly cannot hold at D-structure, since sentences like (6) are grammatical.

(6) D-structure:
     e seems [Joe to love Sue] (*Joe* has no Case)
     S-structure:
     Joe$_i$ seems [t$_i$ to love Sue] (*Joe* receives Case from INFL in the main clause)

The Case Filter must therefore hold at S-structure, since many NP's originate in non-Case positions and move to Case positions. Now, where and how is Case assigned? It cannot simply be assigned to lexical NP's at S-structure, as shown by (7).

(7) D-structure:
     Sue wants what   (*what* receives objective Case from *wants*)
     S-structure:
     What$_i$ does Sue want t$_i$ (*what* is in COMP, a non-Case position)

The WH-phrase must have received Case in its pre-WH-movement position. On the face of it, it seems that Case is assigned *after* NP-movement, but *before* WH-movement. This is not a good result, since we are trying to argue that these two rules are merely instances of the same rule, *Move α*. There is no well-defined level which occurs after all applications of NP-movement and before any applications of WH-movement. We must take another look at the nature of Case assignment.

8.2.1 Chains Again

Until now, we have been tacitly assuming that Case assignment is a process, or rule, which takes place at some point in the derivation, and which marks NP's for Case. We have also assumed that once an NP has Case, it carries that Case along when it undergoes further movement. Let us now explore the idea that Case is assigned, not to NP's directly, but rather to NP **positions.** This is reminiscent of the tack we took in chapter 5, where we said that θ-roles are assigned to positions, rather than to particular noun phrases. We restated the θ-criterion in terms of chains, so that every chain required exactly one θ-role. We can now restate the Case Filter in a similar way.

(8) Every chain containing a lexically filled NP must contain a Case position.

This statement is not quite correct, as the sentences in (9) show.

(9) a.   We believe [$_{CP}$ that [$_{IP}$ Theresa$_i$ to seem [$_{IP}$ t$_i$ was arrested t$_i$]]]
     b.   I wonder [$_{CP}$ who$_i$ [$_{IP}$ t$_i$ to seem [t$_i$ was arrested t$_i$]]]

The chains in (9) contain exactly one θ-position, after *arrested,* and exactly one case position, before *was.* They therefore satisfy the θ-criterion and the case filter as given in (8). What is wrong?

The fact is that an NP undergoing only NP-movement must receive Case in the position it ends up in. An NP undergoing WH-movement, which may also have undergone NP-movement, must receive Case in the position it occupies **immediately** prior to its first move to a CP-specifier. What is needed is a way to define this position without resorting to two distinct movement rules.

8.2.2 Chains Refined

It has been proposed (Chomsky 1981) that the positions NP's may occupy can be divided into two types, *argument* positions, or A-positions, and non-argument positions, or $\bar{A}$-positions (A-bar positions). An A-position is a structural position to which a θ-role may be assigned. Object position is clearly an A-position. Subject position, in other words the IP-specifier, is also an A-position, since it is sometimes a θ-position. The CP-specifier, however, is a position to which θ-roles are never assigned and, as such, is an $\bar{A}$-position. Browning (1987) further proposes a typology of chains, as follows:

(10)   a.   A-chains—containing only A-positions.
       b. $\bar{A}$-chains—containing only $\bar{A}$-positions.
       c.   Composed chains—containing one A-position and one $\bar{A}$-position.

The chain in (11), then, is really three chains.

(11) $[_{CP}$ who$_i$ did $[_{IP}$ John say $[_{CP}$ t$_i$ $[_{IP}$ Sue thought $[_{CP}$ t$_i$ $[_{IP}$ t$_i$ had been hired t$_i]]]]]]$

The two lowest traces constitute an A-chain. *Who* and the two highest traces constitute an $\bar{A}$-chain. The lowest trace in the $\bar{A}$-chain and the highest trace in the A-chain constitute a composed chain.

Having made these distinctions, it is now possible to state the case filter as follows:

(12)   Every A-chain must contain exactly one Case position. The Case position is the head of the chain.

It has also been suggested (Chomsky 1986) that the θ-criterion and the case filter could be united as the Chain Condition, given in (13).

(13)   A maximal A-chain $(\alpha_1, \ldots, \alpha_n)$ has exactly one Case-marked position (namely, α_1) and exactly one θ-marked position (namely, α_n).

8.3 Movement of Other Categories

The two separate rules, NP-movement and WH-movement, defined fairly narrowly the class of elements that undergo movement. A rule like *Move α*, however, allows any category to move. The conditions listed above limit the possibilities somewhat, but nothing prevents, for example, a verb phrase from undergoing *Move α*. The question that arises is the following: do other categories in fact move, or is movement really limited to NP's and WH-words? Consider the following sentences.

(14) a. They said Fred would steal the car, and *steal the car* he did.
      b. *Did* Calvin like the play?

The italicized portions of these sentences have clearly been moved from their D-structure positions. The D-structures of the sentences in (14) are given in (15).

(15) a.

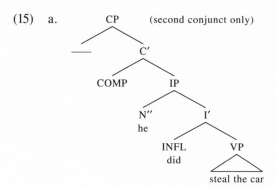

      b.

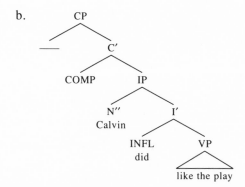

In (14a) the category undergoing movement is VP, or V^{max}. The most plausible position for VP to move to is the same place WH-phrases move to, namely the specifier of CP. The derived structure for (15a) is thus (16).

(16)

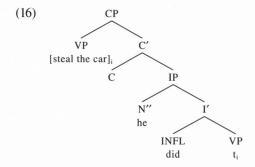

8.3.1 AUX-Inversion in English

In (14b), what is moving is INFL. This movement differs from all other instances of movement that we have seen so far in that a lexical category, rather than a maximal projection, is moving.

In the previous chapter, in the section on direct questions, the auxiliary verb *did* was placed in COMP without comment, as it was not relevant to the issue at hand. Let us now take a closer look at the structure and behavior of the English auxiliary system.

As noted earlier, person-number agreement and tense markings always appear on the first verb in the sequence. The relevant data are given in (17).

(17) a. Maureen laugh*ed*.
      b. Maureen *is* laughing.
      c. Maureen ha*s* been laughing.
      d. Maureen might have been laughing.

In early generative grammar, the English auxiliary system was accounted for by a phrase structure rule such as the one in (18).

(18) AUX → {TENSE/MODAL} (HAVE + EN) (BE + ING) (BE + EN)

The deep structure of (17d) was as shown in (19).

(19)

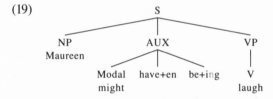

A transformation of affix-hopping, given in (20), applied to give the surface structure in (21).

(20) X aff V Y   ⇒   1 #3+2# 4
      1   2   3 4

(21)

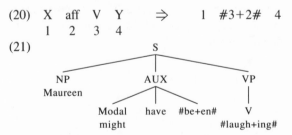

While this analysis was observationally adequate, it presupposed an unconstrained view both of phrase structure and of transformations. Neither of the structures above conforms to X-bar theory, and the rule of affix-hopping is extremely specific, in both its input and its output. No work is left for well-formedness conditions to do. Let us now figure out what our theory tells us about the English auxiliary construction.

First, consider the auxiliary verbs *have* and *be*. They are both morphologically identical to the corresponding main verbs, shown in (22).

(22)   a.   Judith *has* the measles.
       b.   Ruth *is* a student.

The simplest assumption, then, is that auxiliary *have* and *be* and main verb *have* and *be* are the same. What this means is that *have* and *be,* whether they are functioning as main verbs or as auxiliaries, belong to the category V and head a VP. This gives a structure like (23) for the sentence in (17c).

(23)

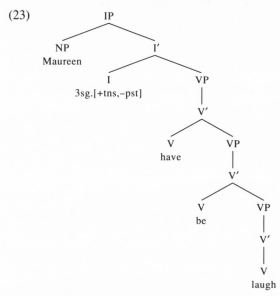

The features for person, number, finiteness ([±tense]) and tense ([±past]) originate in INFL. Modal verbs have been analyzed as lexical items of the category INFL.

The structure in (23) conforms to X-bar theory, but, at least so far, does not achieve the observational adequacy of the traditional account. There are two main problems. First, the order of elements in the auxiliary sequence is fixed, as stated explicitly in (18). There is nothing in (23) to prevent auxiliary elements from being generated in the wrong order, giving something like (24).

(24)   *Maureen was having laughed.

The second problem is that (23) says nothing about the morphology of the various verbs in the sequence, which the traditional analysis handled with the rule of affix-hopping. While these are interesting problems, the focus of this section is the phenomenon of auxiliary inversion, found primarily in direct questions. For a discussion of sentences like (24), see McCawley (1988, chapter 8).

In what follows, I shall draw fairly heavily on work by Jean-Yves Pollock (1989). Before proceeding to an analysis, we need to establish the facts of inversion. First, inversion only takes place in main clauses and a restricted set of embedded clauses, as shown in (25).

(25)   a.   Where *did* Amy live?
       b.   *Has* Amy left?
       c.   *I wonder whether *will* Amy leave.
       d.   She left because why *should* she stay? (colloquial)

Second, only a single verbal element can invert, as shown in (26).

(26)   a.   *Could* Arthur be listening?
       b.   **Could be* Arthur listening?

Third, only modals, *have,* and *be* can invert, as illustrated in (27).

(27)   a.   *Will* Tony win?
       b.   *Is* Barb washing the car?
       c.   *Has* Mary made the beds?
       d.   *Was* Murray happy?
       e.   **Likes* Katie artichokes?

Be inverts whether it is a main verb, as in (27d), or an auxiliary, as in (27b). With *have* matters are more complicated. For some speakers, *have* inverts only when it is an auxiliary, while for others, main verb *have* also undergoes inversion, giving sentences like (28).

(28)   *Has* he a new car?

If no auxiliary verb is present in the uninverted sentence, then the auxiliary *do* appears in the inverted construction.

Pollock (1989), following Koopman (1984) and others, analyzes inversion as involving movement of a verbal element from INFL to COMP. This approach is attractive for a number of reasons. First, it accounts for the impossibility of inversion in clauses containing a filled COMP. Second, it is a structure-preserving process (an X^0 moving to an X^0 position) and is thus amenable to analysis as an instance of *Move α*. Third, it accounts for the fact that person, number, and tense inflection always appear on the inverted element.

However, the structure shown in (23) cannot simply undergo INFL-to-COMP movement to produce the inverted construction. The highest auxiliary verb must first move to INFL and combine with the inflectional elements. The V+I complex then moves to COMP, giving the inverted word order.

It is possible to see direct evidence of the first stage of this two-step process. In other words, there are sentences in which one can see that an auxiliary verb has moved to INFL and remained there, rather than moving on to COMP. These involve negation and VP-initial adverbs. Examples are given in (29) and (30).

(29) a.   Daniel *was not* eating his cereal.
      b.   Meaghan *has not* finished her homework.
      c.   Michael *could not* fix the leak.
      d.   *Ruth *wrote not* the letter.
      e.   Ruth *did not* write the letter.
      f.   Judith *is not* late.
      g.   Sidonie *hasn't* enough money. (some speakers only)

(30) a.   Daniel *was quietly* eating his cereal.
      b.   Meaghan *has nearly* finished her homework.
      c.   Michael *could easily* fix the leak.
      d.   *Ruth *wrote happily* the letter.
      e.   Ruth *happily wrote* the letter.
      f.   Judith *was almost* late.
      g.   Sidonie *has seldom* enough money. (some speakers only)

If we assume that *not* and adverbs originate between INFL and V, then a process moving *have* or *be* to INFL will account for the word orders observed in (29) and (30). If anything that can move to INFL has the further possibility of moving to COMP, then the inversion facts are accounted for.

We are, however, left with the question of why only *have* and *be* can undergo verb movement. The question becomes even more intriguing when we realize that in French, for example, verb movement is not lexically restricted in this way. Any verb in French may move to INFL, as shown in (31) and (32). In French, the negative element *pas* serves as a diagnostic for verb movement, as do adverbs.

(31) a.   Pierre n'*est pas* parti.
           P. not-*be.3sg. not* left
           Pierre has not left.
      b.   Madeleine n'*a pas* fini ses devoirs.
           M. not-*have.3sg. not* finished her homework
           Madeleine has not finished her homework.
      c.   Catherine ne *mange pas* de pain ce matin.
           C. not-*eat.3sg. not* some bread this morning.
           C. isn't eating bread this morning.
           (compare: *Catherine eats not bread this morning.)

(32) a.   Pierre *est vite* parti.
           P. *be.3sg. quickly* left.
           Pierre left quickly.

b. Madeleine *a tranquillement* fini ses devoirs.
    M. *have.3sg. quietly* finished her homework.
    Madeleine quietly finished her homework.
c. Catherine *mange toujours* du pain.
    C. *eat.3sg. always* some bread
    Catherine always eats bread.
    (compare: *Catherine eats always bread)

The question of why verb movement is restricted in English, in exactly the way it is, remains to be fully answered. Pollock (1989) has one analysis, Chomsky (1989) proposes a slightly different account, and the issue is, in general, receiving a great deal of attention at the moment. We will leave this issue aside and look at the verb movement process itself.

What we have seen is that the highest verb in a clause moves to INFL and, in the inversion construction, from INFL to COMP. In each instance, the head of a projection is moving to the position of the head of the immediately dominating projection. Longer movements of heads seem to be impossible, as shown in (33).

(33)   Be$_i$ Sue might t$_i$ dancing?

In this sentence, the modal *might* originates in INFL. *Be* heads the highest VP, and has moved directly to COMP, bypassing INFL.

Notice that the subjacency condition as stated will permit the movement in (33). No bounding nodes intervene between *be* and its trace. Verb movement thus seems to be even more local than either NP-movement or WH-movement. Baker (1988), in work on noun incorporation, proposes the constraint in (34).

(34)   An X^0 may only move into the Y^0 which properly governs it.

What this constraint does is essentially to require that a moved head govern its trace. Government, which is blocked by any maximal projection, is a more restrictive relation than subjacency, which, at least so far, pays attention only to NP and IP. We will return to the matter of government in chains in chapter 9 and to locality conditions in general in chapter 12.

8.3.2 Verb-second Phenomena

It has been observed since Wackernagl (1892) that languages often accord special status to second position in a sentence. In German, the verb is found at the end of the clause, except in main clauses, where the finite verb normally appears as the second constituent in the sentence. In Warlpiri (Nash 1980), an Australian language notorious for its free word order and seeming disregard for the integrity of constituents, the auxiliary, bearing features of tense and person-number agreement, is found in second position within the clause. In Czech, which also exhibits a degree of free word order, clitics are found in second position. In Icelandic, the finite verb appears in second position in both matrix and subordinate clauses. Both Latin and Classical Greek have particles which express the relation between two constituents and which appear at the end of the first word of the second constituent—again in second position.

The second position phenomenon is interesting because it is so widespread and, at the same time, so narrow. There are no known third-position phenomena or second-from-the-last position phenomena. Grammatical processes in general do not seem to require the ability to count. Those phenomena which did seem to require counting (for example, the stressing of alternate syllables) have been found to be structurally rather than numerically based. It would thus be good to find a structural account of the second-position phenomenon.

Fortunately, the structures we have been working with provide a natural definition of the second position. Consider the structures in (35).

(35)   a.

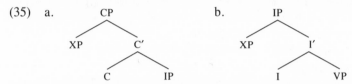

If we assume that only one constituent can be accommodated in a specifier position, then both C and I occur in second position within their respective maximal projections. The second position phenomenon can thus be accounted for by the movement of a maximal projection to the specifier position within CP or IP and the movement of a head to C or I.

What this predicts is that elements which occur in second position will be X^0's rather than maximal projections, since only X^0's can move to an X^0 position. This prediction seems to be borne out; elements which are restricted to second position are verbs, auxiliaries, clitics, and particles of various sorts.

8.4 The Theory of Movement

Let us now summarize what we know about movement.

(36)   a.   Both X^{max} and X^0 may move.
       b. X^{max} always moves to a specifier position.
       c. X^0 always moves to a head position.
       d. X^{max} movement obeys the θ-criterion, subjacency, and the Case Filter (Case Filter applies only to A-chains).
       e. X^0 movement takes place under some kind of government.

If we assume a simple rule like *Move α*, than all of the observations in (36) must follow from independent principles of the theory. Despite the progress we have made in the last few chapters, a number of questions remain.

First, if X^{max} and X^0 may move, then why not X'? It has been proposed that X' is invisible to *Move α*, but notice that this is simply a restatement of the phenomenon, not an explanation.

Second, why does X^{max} always move to a specifier position? The reason for this is that all of the other X^{max} positions are complement positions, which arise by projection from the lexicon, and are thus θ-positions. The specifier position is the only X^{max} position that is present regardless of whether it has been assigned a θ-role. Movement to anything but a specifier position would thus cause a violation of the θ-criterion.

Third, why does X^0 always move to a head position? Here again we know the answer. Since X-bar theory holds throughout the syntax, movement must be structure-preserving. The only place an X^0 can move to while preserving structure is another X^0 position—that is, a head.

Fourth, why do the θ-criterion and the Case Filter hold of X^{max} movement and not of X^0 movement? In fact, these two conditions do not fail to hold of X^0 movement in that X^0 movement does not violate them. They are simply irrelevant. The reason for this is that Case and θ-roles are assigned to arguments, and arguments are maximal projections. X^0 movement never creates an A-chain, since it never moves an argument.

Finally, why are the locality constraints on X^{max} movement apparently more lax than those holding of head movement? In order to answer this question, we must investigate the issue of locality in chains in more detail. The next chapter is the first step in this direction.

Readings

Baker, Mark. 1988. *Incorporation: A Theory of Grammatical Function Changing.* Chicago, Ill.: University of Chicago Press.

Browning, Marguerite. 1987. "Null Operator Constructions." Ph.D. diss., MIT, Cambridge, Mass.

Chomsky, Noam. 1981. *Lectures on Government and Binding.* Dordrecht: Foris Publications.

———. 1986. *Barriers.* Cambridge, Mass.: MIT Press.

———. 1989. "Some Notes on Economy of Derivation and Representation." In Laka and Mahajan (1989).

Koopman, Hilda. 1984. *The Syntax of Verbs.* Dordrecht: Foris Publications.

Laka, Itziar, and Anoop Mahajan. 1989. *Functional Heads and Clause Structure: MIT Working Papers in Linguistics, vol. 10.* Cambridge, Mass.: MIT.

McCawley, James D. 1988. *The Syntactic Phenomena of English.* Chicago, Ill.: University of Chicago Press.

Nash, David. 1980. "Topics in Warlpiri Grammar." Ph.D. diss., MIT., Cambridge, Mass.

Pollock, Jean-Yves. 1989. "Verb Movement, Universal Grammar and the Structure of IP." *Linguistic Inquiry* 20:365–424.

Wackernagl, J. 1892. "Über ein Gesetz der indogermanischen Wortstellung." *Indogermanische Forschungen* 1:333–436.

9 The Empty Category Principle

9.1 The Problem

The Subjacency Condition and its predecessors, the Island Constraints (Ross 1967), were for several years accepted as the theoretical mechanism responsible for the ungrammaticality of sentences like (1).

(1)   *Which book did you hire the woman who wrote?

However, the facts were never as clear-cut as the picture given in chapter 7. Ross first noticed the phenomenon illustrated in (2), to which he gave the rather evocative name "adverbial oil."

(2)   a.   ?This is the book which$_i$ I don't know when$_j$ I read t$_i$ t$_j$.
      b.   *This is the library where$_i$ I don't know what$_j$ I read t$_j$ t$_i$.

Ross's observation was that when a WH-island is introduced by an adverbial WH-phrase, the WH-island is easier to extract from than a WH-island introduced by a nominal WH-phrase.

As it turns out, the facts are somewhat more complicated. Consider the sentences in (3) and (4).

(3)   a.   ?This is the book which$_i$ I don't know when$_j$ I read **t$_i$** t$_j$.
      b.   ?Which book$_i$ do you wonder when$_j$ he took **t$_i$** t$_j$?
      c.   ?This is the car O$_i$ that I wonder who$_j$ t$_j$ bought **t$_i$**.
(4)   a.   *This is the place where$_i$ I don't know what$_j$ I read t$_j$ **t$_i$**.
      b.   *When$_i$ do you wonder which book$_j$ he took t$_j$ **t$_i$**?
      c.   *This is the man O$_i$ that I wonder what$_j$ **t$_i$** bought t$_j$?

The contrast between (3) and (4) is typical of the "adverbial oil" phenomenon, and in the (a) and (b) sentences, the WH-islands in (3) are indeed introduced by adverbial WH-phrases. But the (c) sentences, which exhibit the same grammaticality contrast as the (a) and (b) sentences, contain only nominal WH-phrases. In addition, consider the sentences in (5).

(5)   a.   ?Which car$_i$ did you ask when$_j$ I bought t$_i$ t$_j$?
      b.   *Which student$_i$ did you ask when$_j$ t$_i$ bought that car t$_j$?

Both sentences here contain WH-islands introduced by adverbial WH-words, yet (5b) is as bad as the sentences in (4). Something other than adverbial oil is clearly happening here.

Aoun, Hornstein, and Sportiche (1982), Huang (1981/2; 1982), and Lasnik and Saito (1984) have argued that the relevant distinction is found, not in the WH-phrase introducing the WH-island, but rather in the higher WH-phrase—the one that has moved too far, in violation of the subjacency condition.

Notice that there is a difference between the sentences in (3) and those in (4) with respect to the position of the offending, that is, nonsubjacent, trace. In (3), and in (5a), the offending trace is the direct object of the verb, while in (4) the offending trace is either the subject of a tensed clause or an adjunct to the verb phrase. By adjunct here I mean an element which is not required by the verb and to which the verb does not assign a θ-role. It seems that object traces, when nonsubjacent to their antecedents, produce a lesser degree of ungrammaticality than adjunct and subject traces do. In order to explain this, we must come up with another condition which is violated by the sentences in (4), but not by those in (3). Before making any proposal, however, we should consider another set of facts.

9.2 The That-trace Phenomenon

The sentences in (6) show that WH-movement is not normally blocked by the presence of the complementizer *that*.

(6) a. i.   What$_i$ did you claim [t_i *that* [he wanted t$_i$]]?
         ii.   What$_i$ did you claim [t_i [he wanted t$_i$]]?
     b. i.   Which book$_i$ did he say [t_i *that* [he had read t$_i$]]?
         ii.   Which book$_i$ did he say [t$_i$ [he had read t$_i$]]?

However, consider the sentences in (7).

(7) a. i.   *Who$_i$ did you claim [t_i *that* [t$_i$ won the race]]?
         ii.   Who$_i$ did you claim [t_i [t$_i$ won the race]]?
     b. i.   *Where$_i$ did you say [t_i *that* [you found the book t$_i$]]?[1]
         ii.   Where$_i$ did you say [t_i [you found the book t$_i$]]?

Here again we find a structure in which object traces are permitted, but adjunct traces and subject traces are not. Now consider the sentences in (8).

(8) a.   Which movie$_i$ did you figure out when$_j$ to go to t$_i$ t$_j$?
     b.   *[To which movie]$_i$ did you figure out when$_j$ to go t$_i$ t$_j$?

Here we see that an NP-trace which appears in a PP and which is nonsub-

---

1. For some people, the difference between these two sentences is not sufficient to warrant marking the one with *that* ungrammatical. However, even for those people, the sentence without *that* is preferable.

jacent to its antecedent is preferable to a PP-trace that is nonsubjacent to its antecedent.

9.3 An Adequate Generalization

The table in (9) sets forth what we know about traces which can be nonsubjacent to their antecedents without causing total ungrammaticality, as opposed to those which cannot.

(9)　　　?　　　　　　　　*
　　　object of V　　subject of IP
　　　object of P　　adjunct adverbial

It has been suggested that the relevant distinction is between traces which are lexically governed—governed by an X^0 head belonging to a lexical category—and those which are not.[2] The positions listed in the left-hand column in (9) are governed by V and P, both of which are lexical categories. The positions listed in the right-hand column are governed by INFL, which is not a lexical category.

Thus we can restate the generalization as (10).

(10)　　A trace that is not governed by a lexical X^0 is subject to a locality constraint which does not apply to lexically governed traces.

This additional locality constraint, which we have yet to make explicit, has been called antecedent government. The overall well-formedness condition has been called the *Empty Category Principle* (ECP) and can be formulated as in (11).

(11)　　THE EMPTY CATEGORY PRINCIPLE
　　　　A nonpronominal empty category must be properly governed. Proper government is satisfied by either lexical government or antecedent government.

9.4 Antecedent Government

Lasnik and Saito (1984) give (12) as their initial formulation of antecedent government:

(12)　　α antecedent-governs β iff:　a.　α and β are coindexed, AND
　　　　　　　　　　　　　　　　　　　　　b.　α c-commands β, AND
　　　　　　　　　　　　　　　　　　　　　c.　there is no γ, (γ an NP or S' [CP]), such that α c-commands γ and γ dominates β, unless β is the head of γ.

2. In fact, something more restrictive than government is required, as Lasnik and Saito point out. It appears that the lexical governor must also be the element θ-marking the lexically governed element.

Lasnik and Saito's paper predates the analysis of CP which places WH-words and intermediate traces in the CP specifier. As such, their account assumes that WH-words and intermediate traces are placed in COMP. In what follows, we will use Lasnik and Saito's main ideas, making adjustments where necessary to accommodate the more recent treatment of CP.

First consider the data in (3) and (4) in terms of the definition of antecedent government. In (3a) the trace of *which* is in object position and is thus lexically governed. The trace of *when* is not lexically governed and as such must be antecedent-governed. There are no NP's or CP's dominating the trace which do not also dominate *when,* so the trace is antecedent-governed. Thus (3a) contains a pure subjacency violation. Example (3b) is essentially identical to (3a). So is (3c), except that instead of an adverbial trace needing antecedent government, there is a subject trace.

The sentences in (4) contain subjacency violations equivalent to those in (3), but the situation with respect to the ECP is rather different. Consider (4b). The trace of *which book* is lexically governed by the verb and also antecedent-governed by *which book.* The trace of *when* is not lexically governed. Is it antecedent-governed? There are no intermediate traces between *when* and its original trace. The embedded clause is a CP c-commanded by *when* and dominating the trace. Thus antecedent government fails, and the sentence violates the ECP.

In (4c), the situation is the same. The trace of *what* is both lexically governed and antecedent-governed. The trace of the empty relative operator is in subject position and thus not lexically governed. It is separated from the operator by the lowest CP node and is thus not antecedent-governed. Again, the sentence violates the ECP.

Let us now turn to sentences containing that-trace phenomena. Here, a small adjustment to Lasnik and Saito's assumptions will be necessary. Lasnik and Saito assumed that all traces were in COMP, along with *that* if *that* was present. They accounted for the contrast between (7ai) and (7aii) by means of a mechanism of COMP-indexing. Essentially, they claimed that *that,* when present, is the head of COMP. COMP always takes on the index of its head. Thus any trace in a COMP containing *that* is not able to antecedent-govern a lower trace, since the trace in COMP does not itself c-command anything outside the COMP. When *that* is not present, the trace is the head of COMP and passes its index to the COMP node. It is the COMP node that c-commands the lower trace and antecedent-governs it.

Under the assumptions we are making about the derived structure of WH-movement, the that-trace phenomenon must be accounted for in a slightly different way. I will give a provisional account here and return to the question in chapter 12.

The structure of (7ai) and (7aii) is given in (13).

(13)

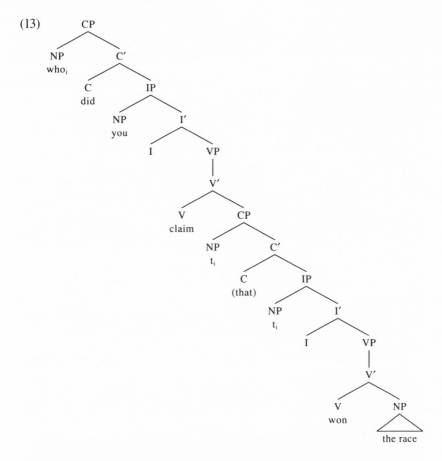

Notice that the subjacency condition has not been violated here.

There are two traces in (13) which need to be antecedent-governed. Somehow, the presence of *that* in the lower COMP must block at least one of the antecedent-government relationships. Chomsky (1986) has proposed that the complementizer *that* counts as a closer governor for the lower trace, blocking government by the intermediate trace. This is called the Minimality Condition, which will be taken up in more detail in chapter 12. Another possibility is more in line with Lasnik and Saito's approach. Suppose that the intermediate trace can only be governed from outside CP if it bears the same index as the head of CP (see clause (c) of Lasnik and Saito's definition, where an intervening CP blocks government). Suppose further that when the head of CP is empty, the element in the CP specifier assigns its index to the head of CP by a process of agreement. Then when *that* is present, the trace in the CP specifier will not be coindexed with the head of CP and as such will not be eligible for antecedent government from outside CP. Under either approach, the contrast between (7ai) and (7aii) is accounted for.

We can conclude, then, that traces are subject to two kinds of locality conditions: the subjacency condition and the empty category principle. Subjacency violations by themselves produce a mild degree of ungrammaticality while ECP violations produce a severe degree of ungrammaticality. Recall also that the relation of government, which was required for case assignment, is also a local relation. The question that remains is why there seem to be three different locality conditions in the grammar. Chapter 12 presents a recent attempt to construct a unified theory of locality.

Readings

Aoun, Joseph, Norbert Hornstein, and Dominique Sportiche. 1982. "Some Aspects of Wide Scope Quantification." *Journal of Linguistic Research* 1:69–95.

Chomsky, Noam. 1981. *Lectures on Government and Binding.* Dordrecht: Foris Publications.

———. 1986. *Barriers.* Cambridge, Mass.: MIT Press.

Huang, C-T. James. 1981/82. "Move Wh in a Language without Wh-movement." *The Linguistic Review* 1:369–416.

———. 1982. "Logical Relations in Chinese and the Theory of Grammar." Ph.D. diss., MIT, Cambridge, Mass.

Kayne, Richard. 1981. "ECP Extensions." *Linguistic Inquiry* 12:93–133.

Lasnik, Howard, and Mamoru Saito. 1984. "On the Nature of Proper Government." *Linguistic Inquiry* 15:235–89.

Pesetsky, David. 1982. "Paths and Categories." Ph.D. diss., MIT, Cambridge, Mass.

Ross, John R. 1967. "Constraints on Variables in Syntax." Ph.D. diss., MIT, Cambridge, Mass.

10 Interpretation of Nominals

In this chapter we will be concerned with rules having to do not with the position of elements within the sentence, but rather with how various elements in the sentence are to be interpreted. We will be dealing primarily with rules interpreting various types of nominals and with the general principles involved.

10.1 Lexical Anaphors

Recall from chapter 5 that the trace left by NP-movement is an anaphor. An anaphor is a nominal element which has no independent reference, but must be linked, or coindexed, with an antecedent. Now consider two types of lexical anaphors: reflexives and reciprocals.

(1)   Sue washed herself.

This sentence is grammatical only if *Sue* and *herself* are interpreted as coreferential. In other words the two NP's must be coindexed, as in (2).

(2)   Sue$_i$ washed herself$_i$.

Now consider sentence (3).

(3)   Sue$_i$ washed himself$_i$.

The coindexing tells us that *Sue* and *himself* are intended to be coreferential. However, our knowledge of English naming customs tells us that *Sue* must refer to a female, while *himself* is a masculine reflexive form. The sentence thus fails, not for any grammatical reason, but because of our knowledge of the world.

(4)   *Herself saw the movie.

This sentence is ungrammatical, because *herself,* being an anaphor, is subject to the c-command condition on anaphora (see section 5.5.3) and requires a coindexed antecedent which c-commands it. Now consider the sentences in (5).

(5)   a.   *Sue$_i$ believes that the men like herself$_i$.
      b.   *The children$_i$ want Joe to entertain themselves$_i$.

Notice that both of these sentences satisfy the c-command condition on anaphora. The subject in the higher clause c-commands the reflexive and is co-indexed with it. Nonetheless, the sentences are ungrammatical. What seems to be wrong here is that the antecedent is *too far away* from the anaphor. We must now determine exactly how close an anaphor must be to its antecedent.

10.1.1 A Structural Relation between Anaphors and Antecedents

Hypothesis 1. An anaphor must have a c-commanding antecedent in the same clause.

This statement correctly predicts that sentence (1) is grammatical and that the sentences in (5) are ungrammatical. Consider, however, the sentences in (6).

(6)   a.   Charles$_i$ believes [himself$_i$ to be a genius].
      b.   *Charles$_i$ believes [himself$_i$ is a genius].

In neither (6a) nor (6b) does the reflexive have an antecedent in the same clause. By hypothesis 1, both sentences should be ungrammatical. Yet (6a) is fine while (6b) is ungrammatical. There are two related differences between these two sentences. The S-structures are shown in (7).

(7)   a.   Charles$_i$ believes [himself$_i$ INFL[−tense] be a genius].
      b.   Charles$_i$ believes [himself$_i$ INFL[+tense] be a genius].

In (7a), the lower clause has a [−tense] INFL. Since *believe* can exceptionally govern, and thus assign Case, into a lower clause, *himself* receives objective Case from *believe* (see section 6.6). In (7b), there is a [+tense] INFL in the lower clause which assigns nominative case to *himself*. Thus the **governor** of *himself* in (7a) is in the higher clause, while the governor of *himself* in (7b) is in the lower clause.

Hypothesis 2. An anaphor must have an antecedent in the same clause as its governor.

This statement accounts for sentences like (1) and (5) and, in addition, predicts the difference between (6a) and (6b). However, consider the sentences in (8).

(8)   a.   Mary$_i$ saw [$_{NP}$ a picture of herself$_i$].
      b.   *Mary$_i$ saw [$_{NP}$ Ted's picture of herself$_i$].

Hypothesis 2 wrongly predicts that both (8a) and (8b) should be grammatical. *Herself* is governed by the preposition *of* in both sentences, and in both cases the antecedent, *Mary,* is in the same clause as the governor. The difference between (8a) and (8b) is that in (8a), the bracketed NP has no subject, while in (8b), the bracketed NP has a subject. (Review section 4.4.2 for subjects of NP's). Consider also sentence (9).

(9)   Mary saw [$_{NP}$ Ted's$_i$ picture of himself$_i$].

It seems that not only IP, but also NP, serves as a limit to the distance between an anaphor and its antecedent. In addition, the presence or absence of a subject seems to make a difference.

Hypothesis 3. The antecedent of an anaphor must be within the smallest NP or IP which contains the governor of the anaphor and which also contains a subject that could potentially serve as antecedent for the anaphor.

10.1.2 Governing Category and Accessible Subject

The statement of this hypothesis can be tidied up by defining a few terms.

GOVERNING CATEGORY FOR X: any NP or IP dominating the governor of X.

MINIMAL GOVERNING CATEGORY FOR X: the lowest governing category for X.

BINDING: An element is bound if it is coindexed with another element which c-commands it.

ACCESSIBLE SUBJECT FOR X: a subject which may be coindexed with X.

Hypothesis 3 restated. An anaphor must be bound within its minimal governing category containing an accessible subject.

Let us test this hypothesis on a variety of sentences.

(10)   Ted saw [Mary's$_i$ picture of herself$_i$].

Herself is governed by *of*. The bracketed NP is thus a governing category for *herself*. Since the NP contains an accessible subject, *Mary, herself* must be bound within the NP. It is, so the sentence is good.

(11)   *Ted$_i$ saw [Mary's picture of himself$_i$].

By exactly the same reasoning as with (10), *himself* must be bound within the bracketed NP. It is not, so the sentence is bad.

(12)   Louis$_i$ knows that [[a picture of himself$_i$] is hanging in the post office].

In this case, *himself* is governed by *of*. The bracketed NP is thus a governing category for *himself*. However, it contains no accessible subject, so the anaphor need not be bound within it. The embedded IP is also a governing category for *himself*. However, since *himself* is contained within the subject, the subject is not accessible to *himself*. If *himself* and the subject were coindexed, we would have a structure in which an element is coindexed with another element properly containing it. May (1977) has proposed that such structures are universally to be excluded. He proposes a filter, known as the

i-within-i filter, to block such structures. The i-within-i filter excludes not only the situation described above, but also sentences like (13) below.

(13)   *This is [a picture of [itself]$_i$]$_i$

The lower clause in (12) above thus contains no accessible subject for *himself*, and *himself* therefore need not be bound within it. The minimal governing category containing an accessible subject for *himself* is thus the main clause. Since *himself* is coindexed with *Louis*, it is bound within the main clause, and the sentence is good.

(14)   *Sue$_i$ wants [Ron to hire herself$_i$]

Here, *herself* is governed by *hire*. The lower clause contains an accessible subject, *Ron*. Thus *herself* must be bound within the lower clause. It is not, so the sentence is bad.

10.1.3 Nominative Anaphors

(15)   a.   Glenn$_i$ believes himself$_i$ to be a genius.
        b.   *Glenn$_i$ believes that himself$_i$ is a genius.

Sentence (15a) is correctly predicted to be grammatical by hypothesis 3, as follows. The governor of *himself* is the main verb *believes*. The minimal governing category for *himself* is thus the main clause. The main clause contains an accessible subject, *Glenn*, and *himself* is bound within the main clause. Sentence (15b), on the other hand, poses a problem. *Himself* is governed by INFL in the lower clause. However, since *himself* is the subject of that clause, there is no subject which could be coindexed with *himself*. Thus, hypothesis 3 predicts that the relevant governing category for *himself* is the main clause. Since *himself* is bound in the main clause, the sentence should be grammatical, according to hypothesis 3. Unfortunately, the sentence is ungrammatical.

It turns out that hypothesis 3 makes correct predictions, except for a very well defined class of cases. These cases, like sentence (15b), all contain anaphors governed by a [+ finite] INFL in subordinate clauses. In other words, counterexamples to hypothesis 3 all involve *nominative* anaphors. There have been various proposals attempting to modify hypothesis 3 to account for nominative anaphors. The first one we shall look at was proposed in Chomsky (1980). In that work, he suggested that anaphors simply cannot be nominative. This was called the "Nominative Island Condition" and is repeated here as the second clause of hypothesis 4.

Hypothesis 4: An anaphor must be:
   a. bound within its minimal governing category containing an accessible subject
   AND
   b. non-nominative.

The problem with the Nominative Island Condition is that it offers no explanation for the ill-formedness of nominative anaphors.

A second proposal, put forth in Chomsky (1981), attempts to derive the Nominative Island Condition from the first clause of hypothesis 4. What is involved here is an abstract morpheme in INFL, called AGR. According to Chomsky, AGR is a nominal element bearing features for person and number. It must agree with, and be coindexed with, the NP in subject position, and it is also involved in transmitting person and number features to the finite verb. Nonfinite clauses, it has been suggested, lack the AGR morpheme.

Assuming the existence of the AGR morpheme, Chomsky then extends the definition of subject so that it includes this morpheme. In a finite clause, then, AGR counts as an accessible subject for the NP in subject position. It follows from clause (a) of hypothesis 4 above that nominative anaphors must be bound in the clause of which they are the subject. AGR cannot count as an antecedent, for reasons which will be explored later. Thus nominative anaphors will always be ill-formed.

Hypothesis 5: (The Binding Condition for Anaphors)
An anaphor must be bound within its minimal governing category containing an accessible subject.

A quick glance at the following sentences will show that the reciprocal *each other* is subject to exactly the same conditions as the reflexives. The only difference is that *each other*, by virtue of its meaning, must be coindexed with an NP referring to more than one individual, as shown by (16).

(16) a. *The boy$_i$ saw each other$_i$.
      b. The boys$_i$ saw each other$_i$.
(17) a. *Each other were leaving. (no antecedent)
      b. *The men$_i$ believe that each other$_i$ are leaving. (nominative anaphor)
      c. The men$_i$ believe each other$_i$ to be geniuses.
      d. *The women$_i$ bought [Sue's pictures of each other$_i$].
      e. The women$_i$ bought [pictures of each other$_i$].
      f. The newlyweds$_i$ expected that [[pictures of each other$_i$] would be sent to their parents].
      g. *The children$_i$ believe that the teacher hates each other$_i$.

10.2 Lexical Pronouns

We have established that anaphors (reflexives and reciprocals) must be bound in their minimal governing category containing an accessible subject. Let us now turn to the binding conditions on another set of elements, which we will call *pronouns*.

10.2.1 Binding Conditions

Included in the set of pronouns are the personal pronouns *she/her, he/him, they/them,* the possessive pronouns *his, her, their,* and the referential pronoun *it.* Consider the sentences in (18) below.

(18)   a.   *Mary$_i$ saw her$_i$.
       b.   *Sue$_i$ believes her$_i$ to be beautiful.
       c.   *I heard [Joe's$_i$ story about him$_i$].
       d.   ?Fred$_i$ saw [a picture of him$_i$] in the post office.

In sentences (18a)–(18c), the pronoun is bound in its minimal governing category. The sentences are ungrammatical with the intended reading. Notice that in these three sentences, the minimal governing category contains an accessible subject. Now consider (18d). The pronoun in (18d) is free in its minimal governing category, the bracketed NP. However, this governing category contains no accessible subject. The lowest governing category containing an accessible subject is the entire sentence. The pronoun is, in fact, bound in this governing category. Notice also that the sentence is not entirely ungrammatical. Nor is it perfect; a reflexive would be preferable to a pronoun in this context. Now consider the sentences in (19).

(19)   a.   Sue$_i$ thinks that she$_i$ is winning.
       b.   She$_i$ likes apples.
       c.   Joe$_i$ thinks that she$_j$ is happy.

These sentences illustrate two points. First, it is clear that pronouns, unlike anaphors, can be nominative. In all of the sentences in (19) the pronoun receives nominative Case from INFL. Second, it is apparent that although a pronoun may have an antecedent within the sentence as in (19a), it may also be completely free within the sentence, as in (19b) and (19c). Thus, any statement in the form of (20) will undoubtedly be wrong.

(20)   A pronoun must be bound in . . .

Let us define the notion **free,** meaning 'not bound'; that is, not coindexed with a c-commanding antecedent. The binding condition for pronouns could then be something like (21).

(21)   A pronoun must be free in its minimal governing category.

This statement correctly predicts that (18a)–(18c) are ungrammatical, since in these cases, the pronoun is bound in its minimal governing category. It also makes the right predictions for the sentences in (19). Since the pronouns in (19) are governed by INFL, the minimal governing category for the pronouns in (19a) and (19c) is the subordinate clause. Since *she* is free in the subordinate clause in (19a), condition (21) is satisfied. In (19b) and (19c) the condition is also satisfied, since the pronoun is entirely free.

The one case so far that (21) does not seem to handle is (18d). The pronoun in (18d) is free in its minimal governing category; thus (21) predicts that it should be grammatical. We will return to this problem shortly.

10.2.2 Pronoun-anaphor Overlap

Consider the sentences in (22).

(22)   a.   [John$_i$ found [his$_i$ book]].
       b.   John$_i$ thinks that [Sue$_j$ has [his$_i$ book]].

The minimal governing category for the pronoun in both of these sentences is the bracketed NP. The minimal governing category containing an accessible subject is the bracketed IP. In both cases the pronoun is free in the bracketed NP. In (22a) the pronoun is bound in the bracketed IP.

These sentences provide evidence that accessible subjects are not relevant to the binding condition on pronouns. If we assume that condition (21) is basically correct, we are left with the task of explaining the difference between sentence (18d) on the one hand and sentences like (22a) on the other. The relevant difference seems to be that in (18d) an anaphor is also possible, as shown in (23).

(23)   Cary$_i$ saw a picture of herself$_i$ in the office.

This is in contrast with (22), where no anaphors are possible. No anaphors are possible in this case because English has no possessive reflexives, so no reflexive could occur in place of the pronouns in (22). The principle in (24) thus seems to describe what is going on.

(24)   If a pronoun and an anaphor are both possible in a given context, the anaphor is preferable.

Principles similar to this have been proposed by Bouchard (1983) and Burzio (1986). Other approaches have been proposed by Huang (1983) and Chomsky (1986).

To sum up, then, we have one statement governing the distribution of anaphors and one statement governing the distribution of pronouns. These are called the binding conditions. The principle in (24) applies to both anaphors and pronouns.

10.3 Binding Conditions for Pronouns and Anaphors

A. An anaphor must be bound in its minimal governing category containing an accessible subject.

B. A pronoun must be free in its minimal governing category.

In a position where a pronoun and an anaphor are both possible, the anaphor is preferable.

10.4 Lexical Names, or R-expressions

We have looked at elements that must be bound (anaphors) and at elements that may be bound (pronouns). We now turn to elements that must not be bound. These are called names, or more properly, referring expressions (R-expressions). Consider the sentences in (25).

(25) a.   *Carla$_i$ thinks that *Carla*$_i$ will win.
      b.   *John$_i$ thinks that the *boy*$_i$ will win.
      c.   *Sue$_i$ believes that Mary wants *Sue*$_i$ to win.

The italicized noun phrases in (25) cannot be coreferential with the subjects of the main clauses. Thus if they are coindexed, the sentences are ungrammatical.

Hypothesis 1. A referring expression cannot be coindexed with any other NP in the sentence.

This statement accounts correctly for the data in (25), but consider the sentences in (26).

(26) a.   John said that Mary$_i$ would lose, but Mary$_i$ won.
      b.   Sue$_i$ saw me and I saw Sue$_i$.

In these sentences, an R-expression is coindexed with another NP, and the sentences are grammatical. The crucial diference between the sentences in (25) and (26) has to do with c-command. The structures in (27) illustrate this difference.

(27) a.

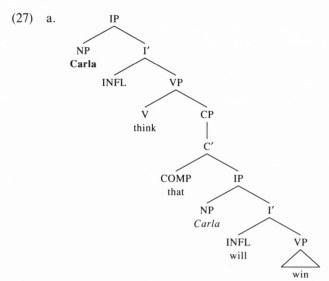

b.

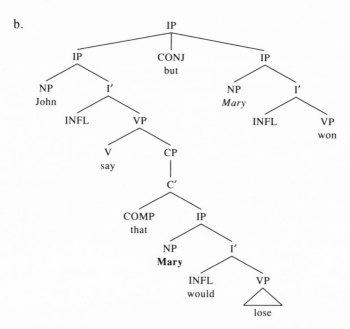

In (27a), which corresponds to (25a), the boldface NP **Carla** c-commands the italicized *Carla*. In (27b), which corresponds to (26a), the boldface NP **Mary** does not c-command, nor is it c-commanded by, the italicized NP *Mary*. This shows that what is relevant here is not simply coindexing, but *binding*. Recall that an NP is bound if it is coindexed with an NP that c-commands it. Thus the binding condition for R-expressions can be stated as follows.

(28) *Binding Condition for R-expressions:* An R-expression must be free.

We can now state the binding conditions for all three types of NP's, as follows.

10.5 The Binding Theory

A. An anaphor must be bound in its minimal governing category containing an accessible subject.

B. A pronoun must be free in its minimal governing category.
In a position where a pronoun and an anaphor are both possible, the anaphor is preferable.

C. An R-expression must be free.

10.6 Empty Anaphors

We have seen that there are three types of lexical noun phrases: anaphors, pronouns, and R-expressions. We will now investigate various types of "gaps," or empty noun phrases, and see whether they can be classified in the same way.

10.6.1 NP-trace

In the section on NP-movement, we made use of the idea that the coindexed trace left behind by NP-movement was an anaphor. We noted that an NP-trace must be c-commanded by its antecedent. If NP-trace is truly an anaphor, then it should be subject to the binding theory developed in the previous section. The sentences in (29) illustrate that NP-trace cannot be nominative.

(29) a. *Michael$_i$ seems that t$_i$ is tired
      b. *The book$_i$ is believed that t$_i$ was stolen

The sentences in (30) illustrate that NP-trace must be bound in its minimal governing category containing an accessible subject. The relevant governing category in each case is bracketed, and the accessible subject is italicized.

(30) a. [*Trish$_i$* seems t$_i$ to have left]
      b. *Sue$_i$ seems that [*Joe* loves t$_i$]
      c. *Eleanor$_i$ was believed that [*George* saw t$_i$]

The sentences in (31) illustrate some differences between the surface distribution of lexical anaphors and that of NP-trace. These differences are due to three things. First, lexical anaphors *must* receive Case (the Case Filter, section 6.7), while NP-trace must lack Case. Second, since NP-trace arises through movement, the trace must always be subjacent to its antecedent. Lexical anaphors, in contrast, are not constrained by subjacency. Third, since traces arise through movement, a trace and its antecedent share a θ-role. A lexical anaphor has a θ-role independent of that of its antecedent.

(31) a. *John$_i$ seems [himself$_i$ to be tired]
          himself has no Case
          John has no θ-role
          (compare: John$_i$ seems [t$_i$ to be tired].)
      b. *Alison$_i$ seems that [$_{IP}$ [$_{NP}$ pictures of t$_i$] were sold]
          violates subjacency
          (compare: Alison$_i$ believes that [[pictures of herself$_i$] were sold].)

We see, then, that various general principles (the θ-Criterion, the Case Filter, the Subjacency Condition, the Binding Conditions) can interact in interesting ways. The properties shared by lexical anaphors and NP-trace are accounted for by the fact that they are both anaphors and subject to the binding conditions. The differences between them can be shown to follow from the fact that one is lexical and the other not, and from the fact that one arises by movement while the other is present at D-structure. We thus conclude that NP-trace is an anaphor.

10.7 Missing NP's—PRO

Consider the following sentences:

(32)   a.   Judith tried to swim.
     b.   Sue wants to eat dinner.

In both of these sentences, the subject of the embedded verb is missing. Yet speakers of English have no trouble understanding that the subject of *swim* in (32a) is intended to be *Judith* and that the subject of *eat* in (32b) is *Sue*. One possible way to account for this might be to use NP-movement, as it was used earlier to account for sentences like (33).

(33)   John$_i$ seems t$_i$ to have won the race.

However, there are two serious problems with this approach. First, the θ-criterion permits movement only to a $\bar{\theta}$-position. If the sentences in (32) were derived as in (34), we would have an instance of movement to a θ-position.

(34)   a.   e tried [Judith to swim]
        Judith$_i$ tried t$_i$ to swim
     b.   e wants [Sue to eat dinner]
        Sue$_i$ wants t$_i$ to eat dinner

Try assigns the role of agent to its subject, while *swim* assigns the role of theme/agent to its subject. If *Judith* moves as in (34a), it is moving to a θ-position, violating the θ-criterion. The same problem arises with (34b).

The second serious problem with the movement approach has to do with the subjacency condition. The movements shown in (34) do not violate the subjacency condition, but consider the sentences in (35).

(35)   a.   *Sue* thinks that [it would be fun [*e* to paint herself green]].
     b.   *Mary* knows that [[*e* to confess] would be a mistake].

In both of these sentences, the empty NP in the lowest clause is interpreted as coreferential with the subject in the highest clause. However, if the sentences were derived as in (36), the subjacency condition would be violated. Notice also that the θ-criterion would be violated, just as in (34).

(36) a.

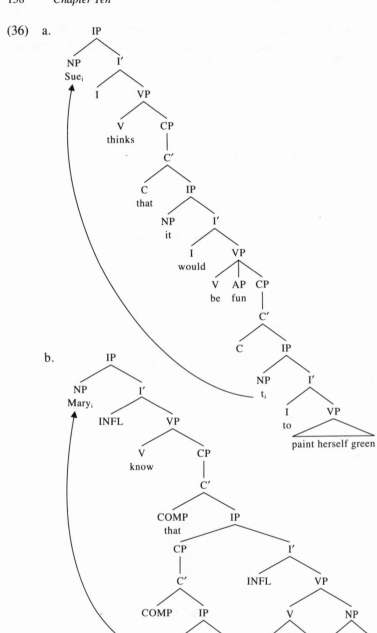

b.

We must therefore conclude that if the θ-criterion and the subjacency condition are to be preserved, the empty NP's in (32) and (35) cannot be the traces of NP-movement. The other alternative is that these NP-e pairs are simply present, both at D-structure and at S-structure. They are interpreted as coreferential by means of a simple coindexing operation. Since these empty noun phrases can be coindexed with other noun phrases, it is necessary to determine which, if any, of the binding conditions are involved. In other words, are empty NP's anaphors, pronouns, R-expressions, or something else entirely? We shall henceforth call these underlying empty NP's **PRO,** to distinguish them from traces. Traces will continue to be represented as t.

Possibility A: PRO is an anaphor.

If PRO is an anaphor, then it will satisfy condition A of the binding theory. It will be bound in its minimal governing category containing an accessible subject and, as such, will never be nominative.

(37)   *Suzannah believes that PRO is a genius.

This sentence illustrates that PRO cannot be nominative. So far, PRO seems to be behaving like an anaphor.

(38)   a.   George$_i$ wants [PRO$_i$ to leave]
         b.   *George$_i$ wants [PRO$_j$ to leave]

Here, PRO is again behaving like an anaphor, in that it *must* take *George* as its antecedent. If *George* and PRO are not coindexed as in (38b), the sentence is ungrammatical. If PRO were simply a pronoun, it ought to be able to be free, as represented in (38b). Now consider the sentences in (39).

(39)   a.   *Madelyn$_i$ admires PRO$_i$.
         b.   *Madelyn$_i$ sold a picture of PRO$_i$.

In both of these sentences, PRO is bound in its minimal governing category containing an accessible subject. It therefore satisfies condition A of the binding theory. Nonetheless, the sentences are ungrammatical.

We must therefore conclude that, although PRO shares some characteristics of anaphors—it cannot be nominative, and there are some structures in which it must be bound—it is nonetheless not a true anaphor.

Possibility B: PRO is a pronoun.

Consider the sentences in (39) and (40).

(40)   a.   It is unclear what PRO to do.
         b.   The police stopped PRO drinking on campus.
(41)   a.   It is unclear what he did.
         b.   The police stopped their drinking on campus.

Like the pronoun *he* in (41a), PRO in (40a) is entirely free. Examples (40b) and (41b) are both ambiguous. Under one reading, the police used to drink on campus, but have stopped doing so. In the other reading, the police stopped other people's drinking. In these sentences, PRO may be either completely free or bound. In this respect, it is behaving like a pronoun.

However, consider the following sentences.

(42) a.   Ruth$_i$ expects PRO$_i$ to leave.
      b.   The children$_i$ expect each other$_i$ to do the dishes.
      c.   *Dan$_i$ expects him$_i$ to leave.

It is not clear what governs PRO in (42a). If anything, the governor is *expects*. Thus the minimal governing category is the entire sentence. If PRO is a pronoun, it should have to be free in its minimal governing category (condition B of the binding theory). In (42c) we see that a real pronoun, such as *him*, cannot be bound in this sentence. However, PRO must be interpreted as coreferential with *Ruth* in (42a) and, thus, is bound, as an anaphor would be. Example (42b) shows that anaphors can occur in this position. Thus, it seems that PRO behaves in some respects like a pronoun and in other respects like an anaphor.

A number of proposals have been put forward in recent years to account for this seemingly inconsistent behavior of PRO. We will consider a few of these so as to gain some appreciation of the issues involved.

10.7.1 The PRO Theorem

Chomsky (1981), in a logical *tour de force*, excludes PRO from the binding theory altogether. First, it should be noted that the binding theory developed in that work is slightly different from the one given here. In Chomsky (1981), both conditions A and B of the binding theory make reference to accessible subjects, so that the theory allows for no pronoun-anaphor overlap whatsoever. The binding conditions from Chomsky (1981) are given in (43).

(43) *Governing Category:*
      β is a governing category for α if and only if β is the minimal category containing α, a governor of α, and a SUBJECT accessible to α.
      Binding Theory:
      A.   An anaphor is bound in its governing category.
      B.   An pronominal is free in its governing category.

Assuming such a theory, Chomsky claims that PRO is both an anaphor and a pronoun. PRO is thus subject to both condition A and condition B of the binding theory, which means that it must be both free and bound in its minimal governing category containing an accessible subject. As Chomsky points out, this contradiction disappears in exactly one situation: when PRO has no governor. If PRO lacks a governor, then it has no governing category. The domain in which it must be both free and bound is thus undefined. The prediction is, then, that PRO will only be possible in ungoverned positions. Let us investigate the correctness of this prediction.

Recall that Case is assigned to an NP under government by V, P, or INFL. It therefore follows that if an element is always ungoverned, it will never receive Case. We therefore predict that PRO will never occur in a Case-marked position.

Nominative Case: We have already seen that PRO cannot be nominative. This is illustrated again in (44).

(44)   a.   *PRO took the notebook.
       b.   *It is unclear what PRO did.
            (Compare: It is unclear what PRO to do.)
       c.   *Ruth expects that PRO will win.
            (Compare: Ruth expects PRO to win.)

Objective Case:

(45)   a.   *Jennifer saw PRO
       b.   *Jennifer believes PRO to be a genius. (exceptional case marking)
       c.   *She put the book beside PRO

In fact, the only position in which PRO can occur is subject position in a nonfinite clause where exceptional case marking does not apply. This is the only position which is ungoverned. If PRO is both a pronoun and an anaphor, this distribution follows automatically from the binding theory in Chomsky (1981).

The foregoing conclusions about PRO have come to be known as the PRO theorem. The theorem is stated informally as follows:

1. PRO is both an anaphor and a pronoun.

2. In order for PRO to occur in sentences without causing a contradiction in the binding theory, PRO must always lack a governing category.

3. In order for PRO to lack a governing category, PRO must not be governed.

4. Therefore, PRO will only occur in ungoverned positions.

The PRO theorem accounts for the restricted distribution of PRO, but is silent on the matter of when PRO must be coindexed with an antecedent and when it may be free. Since PRO, lacking a governing category, falls outside the domain of the binding theory, the term **control** has come to be used to refer to the relationship between PRO and its antecedent. Chomsky (1981) treats control as a separate subtheory. He does not formulate a comprehensive theory of control, but points out that more than just structural considerations must play a role. The sentences in (46) show that PRO is sometimes controlled by a higher subject and sometimes by a higher object.

(46)   a.   John$_j$ persuaded Sue$_i$ [PRO$_{i/*j}$ to feed herself$_i$/*himself$_j$]
       b.   Sue$_i$ promised John$_j$ [PRO$_{i/*j}$ to feed herself$_i$/*himself$_j$]

The examples in (47) illustrate that when the lower verb is passive, and especially when the lower verb is "be allowed," PRO is controlled by a different NP from the one that it is controlled by when the lower verb is active.

(47)   a.   George$_j$ begged Judith$_i$ [PRO$_i$ to feed the baby]
       b.   Peter$_j$ begged Trish$_i$ [PRO$_j$ to be released from prison]
       c.   Emily$_j$ begged Michael$_i$ [PRO$_j$ to be allowed [t$_j$ to go home]]

While the specific choice of controller seems to depend on nonstructural factors, the question of when PRO must be controlled and when it can be free does seem to have a structural answer. The data in (48) show that when PRO occurs in an embedded question, it may be free, even if there is a possible controller in the immediately dominating clause. When PRO is entirely free, it receives an arbitrary interpretation, indicated by the subscript index *arb*.

(48)   a.   Joanne asked Katherine [how [PRO$_{arb}$ to best prepare oneself for a sea voyage]
       b.   Joseph wondered [where [PRO$_{arb}$ to place oneself for the best view]

When PRO occurs in an embedded declarative, as in (49), with a potential controller in the immediately dominating clause, then PRO must be controlled.

(49)   a.   Joanne told Katherine$_i$ [PRO$_{i/*arb}$ to prepare herself/*oneself for a long trip]
       b.   Joseph$_i$ wanted [PRO$_{i/*arb}$ to place himself/*oneself in the front row]

If there is no potential controller in the immediately dominating clause, as in (50), PRO can be free.

(50)   a.   Joanne told Katherine [that it would be a good idea [PRO$_{arb}$ to prepare oneself for a long trip]]
       b.   Joseph said [that it would be rude [PRO$_{arb}$ to place oneself in the front row]]

While Chomsky (1981) assumes that control is a subtheory separate from the binding theory, other authors have attempted to eliminate it and derive its effects from other components. We will briefly look at two such attempts, to give some notion of the range of possibilities. Note, however, that we will not adopt either of them, nor will we attempt to investigate how the theory as a whole would have to change if we were to adopt one or the other of them. The reader is referred to the primary literature for more details.

10.7.2 PRO as Pure Anaphor

Manzini (1983) claims that PRO is an anaphor, subject to the binding theory. However, she adopts Chomsky's claim that PRO is an ungoverned element. In order to bring PRO into the binding theory, she proposes the definitions in (51).

(51) a. *c-domain*
          γ is the c-domain of α iff
          γ is the minimal maximal category [i.e., lowest XP] dominating α
      b. *domain-governing category*
          γ is a domain-governing category for α iff
          i. γ is a governing category for the c-domain of α, AND
          ii. γ contains a subject accessible to α.

She then extends condition A of the binding theory to include (52).

(52) An anaphor without a governing category is bound in its domain-governing category.

Manzini's paper predates the reanalysis of S and S' as IP and CP. As such, since she assumes that S' is a higher projection of S, she does not regard S as a maximal category. This must be kept in mind as we look at some examples to see how Manzini's theory works.

(53) Tina wants [$_{S'}$ [$_S$ PRO to shampoo the carpet]]

In this example, S' is the c-domain of PRO, since it is the lowest maximal category dominating PRO. The main verb *want* is the governor of the S'. By Manzini's definition, then, the matrix clause, which contains an accessible subject, *Tina*, is the domain-governing category for PRO. The theory correctly predicts that PRO must be coindexed with *Tina*.

(54) Tina thinks [$_{S'}$ that [$_S$ it would be stupid [$_{S'}$ [$_S$ PRO to shampoo the carpet]]]].

Here, the lowest S' in the c-domain of PRO. This clause is governed by INFL in the middle clause and is coindexed with the expletive subject pronoun *it*. The domain-governing category for PRO would thus have to be the middle clause. However, this clause does not contain a subject accessible to PRO. Since *it* is coindexed with the clause containing PRO, the coindexing of *it* and PRO would violate the i-within-i constraint (see pages 149–50 for this constraint). PRO in (54) thus lacks a domain-governing category and, as such, may be free.

It is easy to see that this analysis will distinguish between cases where there is a potential controller in the immediately dominating clause and cases where there is no potential controller. Now consider the other structure in which PRO may be free, namely, sentences containing an embedded question.

(55)   Sue asked Mary [$_{S'}$ how [$_S$ PRO to prepare oneself for a flood]]

By the definitions given, the c-domain of PRO is the embedded S'. Since the S' is governed by the verb *asked,* and since the matrix clause contains a subject (*Sue*) accessible to PRO, it seems that the domain-governing category for PRO in (55) ought to be the matrix clause. The prediction is, then, that PRO must be bound in the matrix clause. This is clearly a wrong prediction, since PRO in (55) is free, and the sentence is perfectly grammatical. Manzini proposes that in cases where COMP is non-null, in other words when COMP contains a question word, S behaves as a maximal projection. Under the CP/IP analysis, we have a different problem. The problem in that case is that the theory predicts that IP should always behave like a maximal projection. This means that the c-domain of PRO will always be IP. Since IP is governed by COMP in CP, the domain-governing category for PRO would be the immediately dominating CP. Under the CP/IP analysis, then, some stipulation that IP is nonmaximal, or defective in some way, would be required in order for a theory such as Manzini's to distinguish between (53) and (54).

While there are some problems remaining to be worked out in the details of Manzini's theory, the general approach is interesting. Overall, her goal was to define the domain in which PRO must be controlled and to incorporate this domain into the binding theory. The exceptional behavior of PRO follows from its being an ungoverned element, as it did in Chomsky (1981).

10.7.3 PRO as Either Anaphor or Pronoun

Bouchard (1983) attributes the restricted distribution of PRO not to government per se, but rather to Case theory.

He quite rightly points out that it is desirable to have the behavior of PRO follow from independent principles of the theory, rather than to have a separate subtheory whose sole purpose is to account for the relationship between PRO and its antecedent. He proposes a principle of lexicalization, stated in (56), which holds at the level of PF (phonetic form).

(56)   Principle of Lexicalization (Bouchard 1983:41):
        A noun N will be lexicalized if and only if Ψ-features are present in the entry of N at PF, where Ψ = person, number, gender, Case.

The effect of this principle is to require that lexical noun phrases have all Ψ-features and that empty noun phrases have no Ψ-features, at PF.

It follows from the principle of lexicalization that PRO, an empty NP, will occur only in positions to which no Case is assigned. Bouchard claims that there is nothing wrong with PRO being governed, provided that it is not Case-marked.

There are many other differences between Bouchard's theory and that of Chomsky (1981). For example, the principle of lexicalization would not allow there to be *any* case-marked empty NP's. As we shall see shortly, the theory we are using requires two types of case-marked empty NP's. Since these differences have far-reaching consequences for the theory as a whole, and since we will not be adopting the principle of lexicalization in any case, we will not explore them here. We will, however, consider the main points of Bouchard's treatment of the control phenomenon.

According to Bouchard, PRO can be either an anaphor or a pronoun. In his theory, there is in fact only one empty category, and its properties follow from the environment in which it appears. If PRO is locally bound, then it is an anaphor, whereas if it is locally free, then it is a pronominal.

Bouchard's version of condition A, the binding condition for anaphors, is more restrictive than the one proposed by Chomsky. Bouchard argues that an anaphor must be governed by its antecedent in order to be well-formed. He assumes that S′ is the maximal projection of V. Thus when PRO is behaving like an anaphor, it must be because it is governed by an antecedent. This means that in sentences like (57), there cannot be an S′ between *Mary* and PRO.

(57)   Mary$_i$ tried [PRO$_i$ to feed the baby]

If no S′ intervenes between *Mary* and PRO, note that PRO is governed, not only by *Mary*, but also by the verb *tried*. What then prevents *tried* from assigning the Ψ-feature of Case to PRO, forcing it to be lexicalized? Bouchard's answer to this is to claim that Case-assignment and θ-role assignment normally go together, and since *tried* does not assign a θ-role to PRO, it cannot assign Case either. Exceptional Case marking, such as is found in (58), arises when a verb exceptionally permits its θ-marking and Case-marking properties to be separated.

(58)   Mary$_i$ believes [herself$_i$ to have fed the baby]

When PRO is not governed by a possible antecedent, then it is a pronoun and may corefer freely. If it is not coindexed with any other NP, then it receives the index *arb*.

For the purposes of the rest of the chapter, we will assume that PRO must be ungoverned and that it is interpreted by a theory of Control, essentially along the lines of Chomsky (1981).

10.8 Distinctive Features for Nominals

How can we account for the fact that there is an element which is both a pronoun and an anaphor, while there do not seem to be any which are both

R-expressions and anaphors, or both R-expressions and pronouns? Suppose that there are two distinctive features involved, [±pronominal] and [±anaphor]. These will be abbreviated as [±p] and [±a]. If these features are correct, then there would be four types of nominals, with the following specifications:

		Lexical	Nonlexical
[+a, −p] true anaphors		reflexives reciprocals	NP-trace
[−a, +p] true pronouns		he, she, etc.	??
[+a, +p] pronominal anaphors		??	PRO
[−a, −p] R-expressions		John, etc.	??

10.9 Gaps in the Nominal Inventory

There are three gaps in the inventory. If the theory is to hold, these gaps must be accounted for. It must be shown either that there are, in fact, nominal elements bearing these features, thus filling the gap, or that the gap must exist for independent reasons.

10.9.1 Lexical [+a, +p]

Let us first deal with the gap in the first column. Are there any lexical elements with the features [+a, +p], and if not, why not? Recall that elements which bear these two features must always be ungoverned. Since Case is always assigned under government, an ungoverned element will never receive Case. But the Case Filter states that a lexical NP must always have case. Lexical NP's will thus always occur in governed positions. It therefore follows that no lexical element can have the features [+a, +p], since such an element would always either violate the Case Filter or cause a contradiction in the Binding Theory. This gap is thus explained.

10.9.2 Nonlexical [−a, +p]

A nonlexical element bearing the features [−a, +p] would be a true null pronoun. It could occur in governed positions, since its status with respect to the binding theory is well defined. Lacking a phonological matrix, however, the question arises as to how its features of person and number might be identified. Before trying to answer this question, however, let us try to find an example of a null pronoun, similar to PRO, but which can occur in governed positions. It is not obvious that this element occurs in English, but fairly clear examples can be found in other languages. Recall that in some languages, the place-holder pronoun, like *it* in (59), does not occur.

(59)   *It* seems that Mary is tired.
(60)   _____ parece que María está cansada   (Spanish)
            seems that   is   tired

In these languages, personal pronouns in subject position often do not occur either, as illustrated in (60).

(61)   dice   que está   cansada
        says(3sg.) that is(3sg.) tired(f.sg.)   'S/he says that she is tired'

The missing subject pronouns cannot be PRO, since they are apparently governed and Case-marked by a [+tense] INFL. Lexical NP's can occur in this position, as can personal pronouns, which are used for emphasis.

(62)   a.   María dice que Juan está cansado.
        b.   El dice que *e* está cansado.
             he

We saw earlier that PRO never occurs in a Case-marked position, so the empty NP's in (60) and (61) cannot be PRO. Since the empty categories in (60) and (61) are governed, they have a minimal governing category. It thus makes sense to ask whether they are free or bound in their minimal governing category. In (61), each empty category is governed by INFL[+tense]. The minimal governing category is therefore the clause of which the empty category is the subject. The empty category is, in each case, free in its minimal governing category and therefore satisfies condition B of the binding theory. It would seem, therefore, that the empty categories in (61) are true pronouns. Additional evidence that they are not anaphors is provided by the fact that they are in a nominative Case-marked position. Anaphors, as we have seen, cannot be nominative. Also, they can be entirely free, as shown in the main clause of (61). The empty NP in these Spanish sentences seems to fit the description of a nonlexical element bearing the features $[-a, +p]$. We will call it pro, or "little pro," to distinguish it from PRO, or "big PRO," which bears the features $[+a, +p]$.

Now consider the question of what governs the distribution of pro. Why can we not say 'Want to leave' meaning 'They want to leave'? Intuitively, one answer can be found in a consideration of what information pronouns contain and how this information might be transmitted if the pronoun is phonologically null. First, what information can a pronoun carry? It is in general marked for person (*I* vs. *you* vs. *she*), often for number (*she* vs. *they* but *you*(sg.) vs. *you*(pl.)) and sometimes for gender (*he* vs. *she*). That is in general all the information that a pronoun contains. Now, in many languages, finite verbs are marked (i.e., agree) for the person, number, and sometimes for the gender of their subjects. So, in Spanish, we have *quiero/quieres/quiere* (I/you/(s)he wants) and *quiero/queremos* (I/we want). Verbs are marked for person and number. In Russian, also a language which has pro, some verbs, in addition to being marked for person and number, are also marked for gender, as in *byl/byla/bylo* (he/she/it was).

In these languages, the information which would be carried by the subject pronoun is also present on the verb. Thus the subject pronoun is, in some sense, redundant. Not surprisingly, it turns out that pro normally can occur in subject position in those languages where the finite verb is inflected to show person and number. In languages like English, where the inflectional system is not rich enough to carry this information, pro cannot occur, and a lexical subject must be present. This difference between English and Spanish has been attributed to the nature of the agreement (AGR) morpheme in INFL.

It has also been argued (Rizzi 1986, Roberge 1990, and others), that pro occurs in French in sentences like (63).

(63)   Louise le   prend
        Louise it(masc.sg.) takes
        'Louise takes it'

In French, direct object NP's normally occur after the verb, as shown in (64).

(64)   Louise prend le   crayon.
        Louise takes the pencil.

However, pronominal direct objects appear as preverbal clitics, as in (63). Roberge (1990) argues that these clitics are base-generated attached to V and coindexed with pro in postverbal object position. In a sentence like (63), the clitic provides the person and number features necessary for pro to be identified.

Subject pronouns in French can be treated in essentially the same way. The pronoun is a clitic, base-generated in INFL and coindexed with pro in subject position. The clitic serves to identify the person and number features of pro.

Under this view, the fact that clitic pronouns and so-called "rich" AGR serve essentially the same purpose is nicely accounted for, since subject clitics and AGR both originate in INFL. The relation between pro and a clitic on the one hand, and between pro and AGR on the other hand, is exactly the same.

Languages with clitic pronouns also provide interesting evidence bearing on the question of whether pro has Case. Some languages with clitic pronouns exhibit a phenomenon known as **clitic doubling,** in which both a clitic and a full NP appear. The following data from Pied Noir French are taken from Roberge (1990).

(65)   a.   Marie l'aime   à Jean
              Marie him(3.sg)-likes to Jean
              'Marie likes Jean.'

   b.   *Marie l'aime   Jean
        Marie him(3.sg)-likes Jean
        'Marie likes Jean.'
   c.   Marie l'aime   pro
        Marie him(3.sg)-likes pro
        'Marie likes him.'

What is interesting about these sentences is that when a full NP object appears with a clitic pronoun, the object NP must be marked with a preposition. The most obvious reason for the presence of this preposition, which doesn't seem to contribute anything to the meaning of the sentence, is to provide the object NP with Case. If the object NP in (65a) cannot receive Case from the verb, then something else must have received, or absorbed, the verb's Case feature. It is commonly believed that the clitic pronoun absorbs the case feature from the verb. Assuming this, then pro in (65c) cannot be receiving Case from the verb. Notice that this result is consistent with Bouchard's Principle of Lexicalization: if pro were Case-marked, then it would have a Ψ-feature and would have to be phonologically realized.

While the data from object doubling strongly suggest that clitics absorb Case and that pro is therefore not Case-marked, data from doubling of subject clitics suggest the opposite. With subject doubling, the NP does not require a preposition, as shown in (66).

(66)   a.   Un homme il vient
          a man (he) comes
     b.   Le soleil il brille pour tout le monde
          the sun (it) shines for everyone

Roberge considers this apparent contradiction in some detail and proposes two possible solutions, neither of which is without problems. The reader is referred to Roberge (1990: 113–16) for details.

Unfortunately, the picture is even more complicated. While pro occurs in languages with rich agreement, such as Spanish, and seems not to occur in languages with weak agreement, such as English, it appears to occur in languages such as Mandarin and Japanese, which have no agreement whatsoever. Huang (1982, 1984) discusses this phenomenon with respect to Mandarin and analyzes it as involving an abstract discourse topic (an operator that appears in an $\bar{\text{A}}$ position c-commanding the sentence), which is coindexed with the empty category. The empty category is thus similar to a WH-trace in being bound by an operator. Again, the reader is referred to Huang's work for details.

We can conclude from the foregoing that there is a phonologically null pronoun, bearing the features [−a, +p], which occurs in governed positions. It may or may not be Case-marked, and its features of person and number must be identified, either by rich inflection (AGR in INFL) or by a clitic.

10.9.3 Nonlexical [−a, −p]

The only remaining gap in the nominal system is that corresponding to non-lexical R-expressions. In the next section, we will see that the trace of WH-movement bears the features [−a, −p].

10.10 Two Kinds of Binding

10.10.1 The Problem of WH-trace

Until now, I have used the notion "bound" to mean simply coindexed with a c-commanding element. This section shows that, in fact, there are two kinds of binding, distinguished by the type of position in which the c-commanding element occurs. Consider the sentences in (67).

(67) a.   *Which girl$_i$ [did she$_i$ think [t$_i$ would win the race]]?
      b.   Which girl$_i$ [t$_i$ thought [she$_i$ would win the race]]?

The question we are considering here is why (67a) is ungrammatical. Notice that in both (67a) and (67b), the pronoun *she* satisfies condition B of the binding theory. Its minimal governing category is the IP of which it is the subject, and in both cases, it is free in that IP. The problem must therefore have to do with the trace in (67a). Notice that, like the pronoun *she*, the trace is in nominative subject position and is therefore free in its minimal governing category containing an accessible subject. If WH-trace were an anaphor, then (67a) would violate condition A of the binding theory. However, the trace in (67b) is in exactly the same situation, and the sentence is grammatical. Thus WH-trace cannot be an anaphor. It cannot be a pronoun either. Since it satisfies condition B in both (67a) and (67b), if it were a pronoun, both sentences ought to be grammatical. It cannot be a pronominal anaphor, since it is in a governed position. The only category of nominals remaining is the category of R-expressions. However, condition C of the binding theory states that R-expressions must be entirely free. The trace in the grammatical (67b) is bound by the c-commanding WH-phrase *which girl*.

The difference between (67a) and (67b) is that in (67a), the WH-trace is bound by a pronoun in subject position, while in (67b), the closest binder of the WH-trace is the moved WH-phrase, which is in the CP-specifier. This difference has been exploited to restrict the domain of the binding theory, as follows.

Assume that the binding theory refers only to binding by elements in argument positions. Recall that an argument position is a structural position in a clause to which a θ-role may be assigned. The specifier position in CP is a non-argument position. Since the WH-phrase *which girl* is in the CP specifier, it does not count as an antecedent for the purposes of the binding theory. The WH-trace in (67b), since it is bound only by the WH-phrase, is free for the purposes of the binding theory. The WH-trace in (67a), however, is also bound by the pronoun *she*, which is in an argument position. The trace is therefore bound in the sense relevant to the binding theory.

10.10.2 A Revised Binding Theory

We can now reformulate the binding theory, as follows.

(68)   Definitions:
    a.   A-BOUND: An element is A-bound if it is coindexed with a c-commanding element in an A-position.
    b. $\bar{\text{A}}$-BOUND: An element is $\bar{\text{A}}$-bound if it is coindexed with a c-commanding element in an $\bar{\text{A}}$-position.
    c.   A-FREE: An element is A-free if it is not coindexed with a c-commanding element in an A-position. (NOTE: an element may be A-free and $\bar{\text{A}}$-bound at the same time.)

THE BINDING THEORY

A. An anaphor must be A-bound within its minimal governing category containing an accessible subject.

B. A pronoun must be A-free within its minimal governing category.
In structures where both a pronoun and an anaphor are possible, the anaphor is preferable.

C. An R-expression must be A-free.

Given this revision of the binding theory, WH-traces can be treated as R-expressions, and the sentences in (67) are accounted for. Sentence (67a) is ungrammatical because the WH-trace is A-bound by *she;* (67b) is grammatical because the WH-trace, though $\bar{\text{A}}$-bound, is A-free.

Readings

Bouchard, Denis. 1983. *On the Content of Empty Categories*. Dordrecht: Foris Publications.

Burzio, Luigi. 1986. *Italian Syntax*. Dordrecht: Reidel.

Chomsky, Noam. 1980. "On Binding." *Linguistic Inquiry* 11:1–46.

———. 1981. *Lectures on Government and Binding*. Dordrecht: Foris Publications.

———. 1986. *Knowledge of Language: Its Nature, Origin and Use*. New York: Praeger.

Huang, C-T. James. 1982. "Logical Relations in Chinese and the Theory of Grammar." Ph.D. diss., MIT, Cambridge, Mass.

———. 1983. "A Note on the Binding Theory." *Linguistic Inquiry* 14:554–61.

———. 1984. "On the Distribution and Reference of Empty Pronouns." *Linguistic Inquiry* 15:531–74.

Manzini, Maria Rita. 1983. "Control and Control Theory." *Linguistic Inquiry* 14:421–46.

May, Robert. 1977. "The Grammar of Quantification." Ph.D. diss., MIT, Cambridge, Mass.

Rizzi, Luigi. 1986. "Null Objects in Italian and the Theory of pro." *Linguistic Inquiry* 17:501–57.

Roberge, Yves. 1990. *The Syntactic Recoverability of Null Arguments*. Montreal: McGill-Queen's University Press.

11 Clauses and Categories

The discovery that S and S' are best treated as normal X-bar projections of INFL and COMP (IP and CP) was merely the beginning of an entire area of investigation that has come to be known as the theory of functional categories. The term functional category is opposed to the term lexical category because functional and lexical categories exhibit different clusters of properties, as listed in (1).

(1)   a.   LEXICAL CATEGORIES (N, V, A)
           —have substantive meaning
           —assign θ-roles to their arguments
           —are open classes (new words can be created)
           —permit indefinite recursion on X' (see chapter 2)
      b.   FUNCTIONAL CATEGORIES (COMP, INFL, DET)
           —lack substantive meaning
           —do not assign θ-roles
           —are closed classes (no new words can be created)
           —do not permit recursion on X'

Several dissertations have been written which attempt to develop a theory of lexical and functional categories. Abney (1987) argues in some detail that what we have always called a noun phrase is really a projection of the determiner. Fukui (1986) proposes that many of the differences between Japanese and English can be accounted for if Japanese lacks functional categories entirely. More recently, Pollock (1989) and Chomsky (1989) argue that INFL is not a single functional category, but rather a complex of distinct functional categories, each of which heads its own XP projection.

The theory of functional categories is in its infancy, and it is impossible to give a complete, coherent, widely accepted picture of the entire theory for the simple reason that many fundamental issues are still being debated. This chapter aims to present as clearly as possible some of the more important proposals made by Pollock and by Chomsky concerning the functional categories involved in clause structure. We will steer clear of many of the technical details of these analyses, aiming instead for a basic understanding of the general approach and of the kinds of data that are brought to bear. For more than this, the reader is referred to the (rapidly growing) primary literature.

We now turn to the structure of INFL.

11.1 The Articulation of INFL

Pollock (1989), cited earlier with respect to verb movement, presents an analysis of English and French clause structure which involves splitting INFL into two separate categories, tense (T) and agreement (AGR). An embedded finite clause in English thus has the D-structure shown in (2).

(2)   . . . that Mary eats the cake

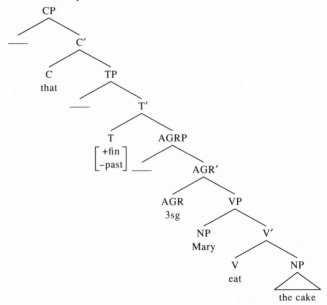

Pollock argues that in French, V normally moves to AGR, and then to T. The subject NP moves from the VP-specifier through the AGRP-specifier to the TP-specifier, to receive nominative Case. In English, only the auxiliary verbs *have* and *be,* main verb *be,* and for some speakers main verb *have,* can undergo movement from V to AGR. Thus, in English, when there is no auxiliary verb, affix movement takes place to lower the tense morpheme and the agreement morpheme to attach to V. The S-structures of the English and French versions of (2) are given in (3).

(3)   a.

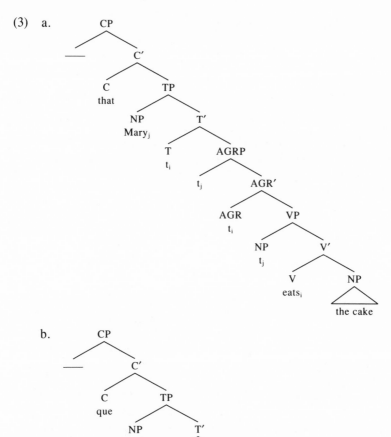

b.

Notice that in English, the verb remains within VP at S-structure, while in French, the verb moves up to occupy the head of TP. Pollock argues that certain adverbs occur at the left edge of the VP and shows that, as predicted by this analysis, these adverbs precede the main verb in English and follow it in French. An example is given in (4).

(4)   Marie mange souvent du gâteau
      Marie eats often (of) cake
      'Marie often eats cake' (compare *Marie eats often cake)

Since English auxiliary verbs do move from V to AGR and to T, adverbs such as *often* appear after the auxiliary verb, as shown in (5).

(5)   Marie has often eaten cake.

All of the foregoing can be accounted for with the IP structure we have been working with. In fact, as Pollock points out, these data were analyzed by Emonds (1976) and Jackendoff (1972) in terms of movement from V to AUX in the structure shown in (6).

(6)

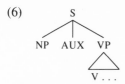

Pollock shows, however, that the verb movement in (4) must be treated as taking place in two steps. He shows that there is a position between V and INFL, in which the verb sometimes surfaces. The theory of movement dictates that this intermediate position must also be an X^0 heading its own projection. Thus Pollock proposes that INFL be split into T and AGR, giving the structures shown in (2) and (3).

Let us briefly review the evidence Pollock presents for two-step verb movement. First, he assumes that the negative element *pas* does not undergo movement. It can therefore be used as a diagnostic for the movement of other elements in the sentences. Second, he shows that while all finite verbs in French must surface to the left of *pas,* infinitival verbs behave differently. The relevant data are given in (7) and (8).

(7)   a.   Marie ne *regarde pas/*pas regarde* la télévision.
           Marie does not watch television.
      b.   Marie *n'est pas/*ne pas est* heureuse.
           Marie is not happy.
      c.   Marie *n'a pas/*ne pas a* de voiture.
           Marie does not have a car.

(8)   a.   Ne *pas regarder/*regarder pas* la télévision consolide l'esprit critique.
           Not to watch television strengthens one's independence.
      b.   *Ne pas être/n'être pas* heureux est une condition pour écrire des romans.
           Not to be happy is a prerequisite for writing novels.
      c.   *Ne pas avoir/n'avoir pas* de voiture rend la vie difficile.
           Not to have a car makes life difficult.

What we see in these sentences is that in infinitives, only the verbs *être* (be) and *avoir* (have) can move to the left of *pas*. Main verbs such as *regarder* must surface to the right of *pas*. Pollock shows that in infinitives in French, verb movement is restricted in much the same way as it is in all sentences in English.

We have still not seen any evidence for two-step verb movement. In order to show this, Pollock compares the behavior of *pas* in infinitives with that of adverbs. Consider the sentences in (9) and (10).

(9) Pierre *parle à peine/*à peine parle* l'italien.
     Pierre hardly speaks Italian.
(10) *A peine parler/parler à peine* l'italien après cinq ans d'étude dénote un
     manque de don pour les langues.
     To hardly speak Italian after five years of study means you lack a gift
     for languages.

These sentences show that in finite clauses, the verb must move to the left of the adverb. In infinitives, the verb may or may not move to the left of the adverb. What is important is the contrast between (10) and (8a). We know from (8) that infinitival verbs other than *avoir* and *être* cannot move to the left of *pas*. On the other hand, (10) shows that infinitival verbs can move leftward. Pollock calls the leftward movement shown in (10) "short V movement" and proposes that this involves movement to AGR. In order to account for the facts, he claims that adverbs originate at the left edge of the verb phrase, while *pas,* and indeed sentential negation in general, originates between T and AGR, as shown in (11).

(11)

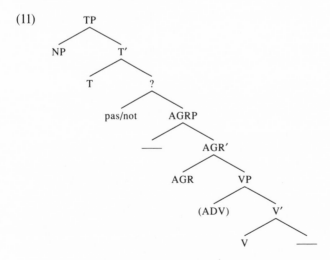

The table in (12) sets forth the permissible movements of verbs in English and French finite and infinitival clauses.

(12)

		V-AGR	AGR-T
English	finite	only have/be	any V in AGR
	infinitival	only have/be	??(depends on analysis of *to*)
French	finite	all verbs	all verbs
	infinitival	all verbs	only have/be

The rest of Pollock's paper is devoted to explaining why verb movement is always lexically restricted in English and only sometimes in French. In addition, he argues that negation, like T and AGR, heads its own projection. The point to be made here, however, is that unless INFL is split into at least two separate projections, the facts of English and French verb movement cannot even be described, much less explained.

Other functional categories have been proposed as part of the clausal superstructure in various languages. Tenny (1987) claims that Aspect is one of these. Rivero (1988) proposes that the Balkan languages (Albanian, Bulgarian, Modern Greek, and Romanian) have Modal and Tense as two separate projections, whereas it is normally assumed that in English, modals belong to the category Tense. Chomsky (1989) argues for two separate AGR projections, one for subject agreement and one for object agreement. Lefebvre, Massam, and others have argued that clauses in Haitian are headed by determiners. It is fair to say that there is no coherent overall cross-linguistic picture of the number and nature of the functional categories in the clausal superstructure. However, a number of questions can be posed at this point.

(13)   a.   What constitutes evidence for a new functional projection?
       b.   What are the distinctive features, or other defining criteria, determining the set of possible functional projections?
       c.   What are the possible structural relationships between the various functional projections?
       d.   Which category, if any, defines the clause?
       e.   How much can clausal superstructure differ from language to language and from clause-type to clause-type within a language?

Since we assume that phrase structure is projected from the lexicon, we could say that for every functional category F, there must be at least one lexical item of category F in a language in order for F and its maximal projection FP to appear in phrase structures of that language. This answer is not sufficiently well defined, however. For example, does an affix count as a lexical item, or must there be an independent word of that category? Also, perhaps the set of functional categories is universally available, and no language-particular evidence is required for a specific category. If this is the case, then one would expect a fair degree of cross-linguistic uniformity, both with respect to which functional categories appear and also with respect to their hierarchical arrangement within the clause.

None of the questions listed in (13) have been answered in a way that is widely accepted. The reader is referred to the authors mentioned above for various attempts to answer some or all of them.

Readings

Abney, Steven. 1987. "The English Noun Phrase in its Sentential Aspect." Ph.D. diss., MIT, Cambridge, Mass.

Chomsky, Noam. 1989. "Some Notes on Economy of Derivation and Representation." In Laka and Mahajan (1989).

Emonds, Joseph. 1976. *A Transformational Approach to English Syntax*. New York: Academic Press.

Fukui, Naoki. 1986. "A Theory of Category Projection and Its Applications." Ph.D. diss., MIT, Cambridge, Mass.

Jackendoff, Ray. 1972. *Semantic Interpretation in Generative Grammar*. Cambridge, Mass.: MIT Press.

Laka, Itziar, and Anoop Mahajan. 1989. *Functional Heads and Clause Structure: MIT Working Papers in Linguistics, vol 10*. Cambridge, Mass.

Lefebvre, Claire. 1982. "L'expansion d'une Catégorie Grammaticale: Le Déterminant LA." In C. Lefebvre, H. Magloire-Holly, and N. Piou, *Syntaxe de l'Haïtien*. Ann Arbor, Michigan: Karoma Publishers.

————, and Diane Massam. 1988. "Haitian Creole Syntax: A Case for DET as Head." *Journal of Pidgin and Creole Languages* 3:213–43.

Pollock, Jean-Yves. 1989. "Verb Movement, Universal Grammar and the Structure of IP." *Linguistic Inquiry* 20:365–424.

Rivero, Maria-Luisa. 1988. "The Structure of IP and V-movement in the Languages of the Balkans." Unpublished ms., University of Ottawa.

Tenny, Carol. 1987. "Grammaticalizing Aspect and Affectedness." Ph.D. diss., MIT, Cambridge, Mass.

12 A Unified Approach to Locality Constraints

Throughout this text, and in fact throughout the history of generative grammar, much effort has been devoted to determining the nature of locality constraints. A locality constraint is any theoretical device whose effect is to limit the structural distance that can be covered by any other theoretical device. The subjacency condition is an obvious example of a locality constraint.

In this chapter we will review the various locality constraints in the theory presented so far and, in some cases, look at their historical antecedents. We will then turn to a recent attempt (Chomsky 1986b) to provide a unified, principled theory of locality.

12.1 An Inventory of Locality Constraints and What they Constrain

12.1.1 The Subjacency Condition

The subjacency condition is a locality constraint on movement. It limits the number of NP or IP nodes that can intervene between adjacent traces in a chain. If more than one NP or IP intervenes between two adjacent traces in a chain, then the sentence is ungrammatical. As we saw in chapter 9, violations of the subjacency condition produce a mild degree of ungrammaticality.

The subjacency condition was itself a unification of a number of other constraints proposed by Ross (1967). The Ross constraints were essentially a listing of the types of structures out of which elements could not move. Some of these are given, very schematically, in (1).

(1) a. THE COMPLEX NP CONSTRAINT
No element may be moved out of a sentence dominated by an NP with a lexical head.

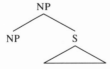

e.g., *Which car did you kiss the man who was driving?

b. THE SENTENTIAL SUBJECT CONSTRAINT
No element may be moved out of a sentence dominated by an NP which is itself immediately dominated by S.

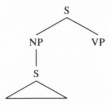

e.g., *Which house did that she bought surprise you?

c. THE LEFT BRANCH CONDITION
No element which is the leftmost constituent of another constituent may be moved out of that constituent.

e.g., *Whose did you sell book?

The subjacency condition is a clear improvement over the Ross constraints in that it extracts what they all have in common and expresses it as a single locality constraint on movement. Questions remain, however. First, why does the subjacency condition refer only to NP and IP? In fact, it has been proposed (Rizzi 1982) that, in Italian, the subjacency condition is sensitive to NP and CP and not to IP. We clearly require a theory that delimits what cross-linguistic variation is possible and gives a principled account of why certain nodes are relevant and others not. Second, why does the subjacency condition hold only of adjacent elements in a chain and not of other relations, such as that between PRO and its antecedent? What makes traces different from other empty categories in this respect?

12.1.2 Government

The relation of government is relevant in many areas of the grammar. It must hold between any two elements which exhibit selectional restrictions (see chapter 4). It is required for Case assignment and for most instances of θ-role assignment. Government, unlike subjacency, pays attention to all maximal projections.

There are also questions that remain to be answered about government. Recall the phenomenon of exceptional case marking, discussed in chapter 6. This phenomenon has been analyzed in a number of ways over the years. One way involves attributing to certain verbs the ability to govern in a special way. Whereas government is normally blocked by a maximal projection, these verbs can govern the subject of their complement. Another treatment depended on the assumption that S' (CP) is a maximal projection while S (IP) is not. In this analysis, verbs exhibiting exceptional case marking either undergo a lexically governed rule of S'-deletion or are marked to take an S rather than an S' complement at D-structure. In either case, the result is that no maximal projection intervenes between the verb and the subject of its complement.

Such treatments are not available under the CP/IP analysis, since both CP and IP are maximal projections under X-bar theory.

Other types of exceptional case marking have been discussed by Massam (1985). She claims that in some languages (Fijian, for example), noun phrases move from the embedded clause into the CP-specifier so as to receive Case from the higher verb. Massam concludes that government generally holds between α and β in structures such as (2).

(2)

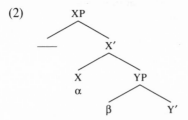

In other words, a maximal projection does not generally block government of its own specifier position.

12.1.3 Proper Government

As outlined in chapter 9, proper government, according to Lasnik and Saito (1984), is really two rather different notions. Lexical government is a subset of what has been called government, in that any category may govern, but only a lexical, as opposed to a functional, category may lexically govern. Antecedent government is something else entirely. First, it is a relationship between coindexed elements in a chain, rather than between a head and its complement. Second, it seems not to be blocked by all maximal projections, since an element in a CP-specifier can directly antecedent-govern an element in a lower CP-specifier, as shown in (3).

(3) $[_{CP}$ when$_i$ did $[_{IP}$ he $[_{VP}$ say $[_{CP}$ t$_i$ $[_{IP}$ he would $[_{VP}$ arrive] t$_i$]]]]]

If we grant Massam's claim that XP does not block government of its own specifier, then the lower CP should not block government of the intermediate trace. Lasnik and Saito argue in some detail that a trace in COMP cannot be lexically governed by the immediately c-commanding verb. We will therefore assume that *say* cannot govern the intermediate trace in (3). However, VP and IP still intervene between *when* and the intermediate trace and might be expected to block government. Lasnik and Saito eventually conclude that only NP and S' (CP) block antecedent government. They note that this makes antecedent government look very similar to subjacency, but show that the two relations are nonetheless independent.

12.1.4 Binding of Anaphors

Another relationship that must be local is that between an anaphor and its antecedent. Government is relevant to this relation only in that it is the governor of the anaphor, rather than the anaphor itself, which determines the domain within which the antecedent must be found. Again, NP and IP are listed in the definition, since the governing category is always NP or IP and never, for example, VP.

12.1.5 Summary

The chart in (4) sets forth the various theoretical devices which ensure that syntactic relations are local and highlights both the categories relevant to each device and the operations and relations each device constrains.

(4) CONSTRAINT	HOLDS OF:	PAYS ATTENTION TO:
Subjacency	move α	NP and IP (English) NP and CP (Italian)
Government	Case assignment θ-role assignment selection	all XP's (government OK into specifiers)
Lexical government (ECP)	traces	all XP's only lexical X^0's govern
Antecedent government	traces if not lexically governed	NP and CP
Binding condition A	anaphors	NP and IP (in definition of governing category)
Binding condition B	pronominals	NP and IP (in definition of governing category)

12.2 The *Barriers* Approach

Chomsky (1986b) is a monograph devoted to exploring the possibility of a unified theory of locality constraints. It deals primarily with various types of government and with bounding (subjacency). The central goal is to develop a theory of barriers. A barrier is a node that blocks some relation, such as government or movement, from holding between two positions in a structure. Ideally, anything that is a barrier for one relation should be a barrier for all other relations. Chomsky notes at the outset that the subjacency condition seems to be looser than the locality conditions on government. This was noticed in chapter 9, where we saw that pure subjacency violations were mildly ungrammatical, while ECP violations were severely ungrammatical. Chomsky proposes, as an initial hypothesis, that "one barrier suffices to block government, whereas more than one barrier inhibits movement, perhaps in a graded manner" (Chomsky 1986b:1).

12.2.1 Outline

The purpose of this chapter is not to provide a detailed commentary on the theory of barriers, or even an exposition of all its details. For that, the reader is referred to the primary literature. What I will do here is give a fairly brief and, I hope, clear outline of the main points of the theory and illustrate how the theory works with a few carefully chosen examples. The final section will raise some questions that the theory still must answer.

It has long been known that complement clauses are more amenable to extraction than adjunct clauses, as illustrated in (5).

(5)   a.   Which car do you believe [that he stole t]?
       b.   *Which car did you cry [when he sold t]?

The difference between (5a) and (5b) is that in (5a), the embedded sentence is assigned a θ-role by the verb *believe*, while in (5b), the embedded sentence is an adverbial adjunct not assigned a θ-role by the verb.

Huang (1982) proposes to account for this with the condition stated in (6).

(6)   CONDITION ON EXTRACTION DOMAIN: A phrase A may be extracted out of a domain B only if B is properly governed.

This insight survives in the theory of barriers as the notion of L-marking, defined in (7). The embedded CP in (5a) is L-marked, while the one in (5b) is not.

(7)   a.   DIRECT θ-MARKING: α directly θ-marks β if and only if β is the complement of α in the sense of X-bar theory.
       b.   L-MARKING: α L-marks β if and only if α is a lexical category, and α directly θ-marks β.

The definition of barrier will have to refer to L-marking in order to distinguish between pairs of sentences like (5a) and (5b).

The next thing to notice is that often two categories seem to block government when it is clear that neither category on its own will do so. Consider the sentences in (8) (taken from Chomsky 1986b:11).

(8)   a.   Terry decided [$_{CP}$ e [$_{IP}$ PRO to [$_{VP}$ see the movie]]]
       b.   How did Terry want [$_{CP}$ t [$_{IP}$ PRO to fix the car t]]

Assuming the PRO theorem, PRO in both of these sentences must be un-governed. Therefore, government cannot extend from the main verb through CP and IP to PRO. We also know from exceptional case marking that IP is not a barrier to government of its own subject position. It thus appears that CP is the barrier blocking government of PRO by the higher verb. However, let us take a closer look at (8b). Here, we have an adjunct adverbial that has under-gone WH-movement from the lower IP, through the lower CP-specifier, to the higher CP-specifier. The lowest trace, being an adjunct trace, is not lexically governed. Since the sentence is grammatical, we know that it must satisfy the ECP. Antecedent government must therefore hold between *how* and the inter-mediate trace and between the intermediate trace and the lower trace. Since the embedded CP intervenes between *how* and the intermediate trace, it can-not possibly be a barrier to government all by itself. There is something about the interaction of CP and IP which creates a barrier between the higher verb and PRO, but which does not create a barrier between *how* and the interme-diate trace.

It is important to notice that we are now talking about barriers relative to a particular element. A node may be a barrier for PRO in (8) without being a barrier for something else. Thus the definition of a barrier will have to incor-porate reference to the element with respect to which the barrier holds. In (8) it appears that CP is a barrier for elements within IP but not for elements within CP but outside IP. This behavior is accounted for by defining another notion, that of **blocking category** (BC).

(9)   BLOCKING CATEGORY: γ is a blocking category for β if and only if:
       γ is a maximal projection, AND
       γ is not L-marked, AND
       γ dominates β.

There are two ways in which a node can be a barrier. First, a node can be a barrier by inheritance, and, second, it can be an inherent barrier (a barrier all on its own). The definition of barrier is given by Chomsky as (10).

(10)   BARRIER: a maximal projection γ is a barrier for β if and only if:
       (a) γ immediately dominates[1] δ, δ a blocking category for β,
       OR
       (b) γ is a blocking category for β and $\gamma \neq$ IP.

Let us test this definition against (8b), bearing in mind that PRO must not be governed by *want*, while the intermediate trace must be governed by *how*. The structure of (8b) is given in (11).

---

1. The phrase **γ immediately dominates δ** in this context means that γ is the lowest maximal projection dominating δ, not that γ is the lowest node dominating δ.

(11)

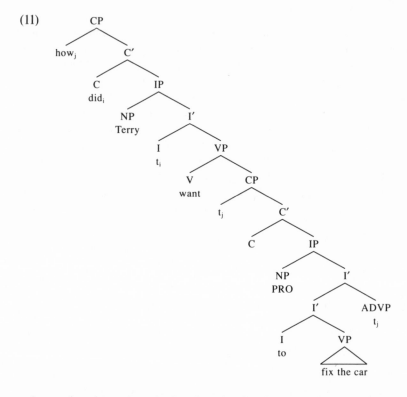

Let us first determine whether there is a barrier protecting PRO from government by *want*. There are two maximal projections, CP and IP, between *want* and PRO. CP is L-marked by *want* and, as such, cannot be a blocking category. It thus cannot be an inherent barrier for PRO. The possibility still exists that CP might inherit barrierhood from a lower blocking category. IP is not L-marked and, as such, is a blocking category for PRO. Is it a barrier? No, because clause (b) of (10) stipulates that IP can never be a barrier inherently.

Thus we see that neither CP nor IP is an inherent barrier for PRO. IP is a blocking category for PRO, since it is not L-marked. Let us now consider clause (a) of (10). CP is a maximal projection immediately dominating IP, which is a blocking category for PRO. CP is therefore a barrier for PRO, not inherently, but by inheritance from IP. PRO is thus not governed by *want*.

Having established that CP is a barrier for PRO, we now turn to the intermediate trace. There are three maximal projections between the trace and *how:* the lower CP and the VP and IP of the higher clause. The lower CP is L-marked and thus not a blocking category for the trace. It does not dominate another blocking category for the trace, since the trace is in the CP specifier. There is thus no way the lower CP can be a barrier for the trace in its own specifier. The higher IP node is not L-marked and is thus a blocking category. It cannot be an inherent barrier because of the stipulation that IP is never an inherent barrier. It could, however, inherit barrierhood from a lower blocking category. The question of whether *how* governs its trace thus reduces to whether VP is a blocking category for the trace. If it is, then it is itself an inherent barrier, and, in addition, it transmits barrierhood to IP. If it is not a blocking category, then it is not a barrier and also does not transmit barrierhood to IP.

Clearly, since the sentence is grammatical, and since we want to maintain the ECP, we want *how* to govern its trace. We must therefore figure out why VP is not itself a barrier, and why it fails to transmit barrierhood to IP. Chomsky (1986b) chooses to account for the non-barrierhood of VP by appealing to the theory of adjunction. Adjunction falls under the theory of movement and involves a process not yet discussed in this text. All the movements we have looked at were substitutions. In substitution, an element moves to fill a slot provided by X-bar theory. In adjunction, a new position is created, as shown in (12).

(12)

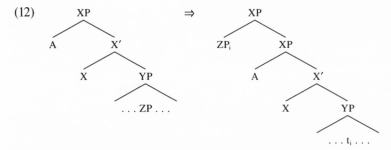

Chomsky assumes that adjunction is possible only to a maximal projection which is a non-argument. This means that it is never possible to adjoin something to an NP or to a complement CP, but that it is generally possible to adjoin an element to VP.

The question of how to interpret adjunction structures with respect to barrierhood is an interesting one. Do the two XP's in (12) count as separate maximal projections or do they count as a single projection? If they count as a single projection, then what is the status of the adjoined material? Is it inside the complex projection, or is it outside? Drawing on work by May (1985), Chomsky makes the following assumptions concerning adjunction structures:

(13) a. Adjunction structures constitute a single maximal projection consisting of two **segments.**

  b. α is **dominated** by β only if it is dominated by every segment of β.

  c. α **excludes** β if no segment of α dominates β.

He then redefines government in terms of the notion of exclusion, as in (14).

(14)   α governs β iff α c-commands β and there is no γ, γ a barrier for β, such that γ excludes α.

These assumptions make it possible to analyze sentence (8b) in such a way that VP does not constitute a blocking category or a barrier. What is required is the assumption that when *how* moves from the lower CP-specifier, it adjoins to VP and then moves from there to the higher CP-specifier, leaving a trace in the adjoined position. Let us examine this structure in terms of the definitions we have so far. The revised structure is given in (15).

(15)

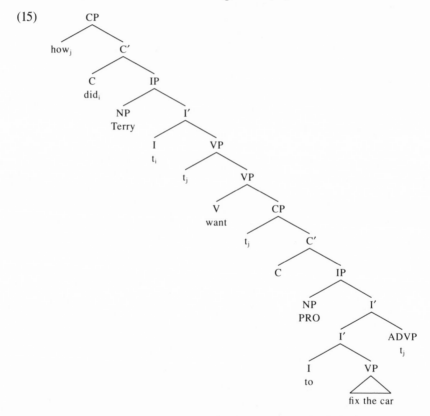

We now have two antecedent-government relations where before we only had one. Look first at the relation between *how* and the VP-adjoined trace. We saw earlier that IP is a blocking category for the trace, but cannot be an inherent barrier. In this new structure, VP cannot be a blocking category or a barrier for the adjoined trace. Since only one segment of VP dominates the trace, the VP as a whole does not dominate the trace. Only dominating elements can be blocking categories or barriers. There are therefore no barriers between *how* and the adjoined trace.

Now consider the relation between the adjoined trace and the trace in the lower CP-specifier. The lower CP, being L-marked, is neither a blocking category nor a barrier. VP cannot be a blocking category or a barrier intervening between the two traces since VP does not exclude the adjoined trace. There are, therefore, no barriers between the two traces. Antecedent government holds, and the sentence is well-formed.

Adjunction is also crucially involved in the derivation of (16).

(16)   Who did [$_{IP}$ Jane [$_{VP}$ see t]]

If *who* moves directly from object position to the CP-specifier, then two barriers intervene between the moved *who* and its trace. VP is a blocking category and a barrier, and IP is a barrier by inheritance from VP. This wrongly predicts that (16) should contain a fairly severe subjacency violation.

If *who* adjoins to VP before moving to the CP-specifier, then the situation is rather different. Consider the structure in (17).

(17)   Who did [$_{IP}$ Jane [$_{VP}$ t^1 [$_{VP}$ see t^2]]]

Since VP does not exclude t^1, VP does not constitute a blocking category or a barrier between t^1 and t^2. Since only one segment of VP dominates t^1, the VP as a whole does not dominate t^1, and VP therefore is neither a blocking category nor a barrier for t^1. IP is a blocking category, but, as we have seen, IP can only be a barrier by inheritance. Since VP is not a blocking category, IP is not a barrier. There are therefore no barriers crossed in the derivation of (16).

Since subjacency violations are weaker than ECP violations, and since subjacency violations are more ungrammatical as they involve more bounding nodes, or barriers, Chomsky proposes (Chomsky 1986b:30) that subjacency be defined in a gradient manner, as in (18).

(18) β is n-subjacent to α iff there are fewer than n+1 barriers for β that exclude α.

What is required for a chain to be acceptable is 1-subjacency between adjacent elements in the chain. If 0-subjacency holds, then the sentence is even more acceptable, but if only 2-subjacency holds, the sentence is ungrammatical.

Let us now look at how the *Barriers* account handles the data which motivated the Ross constraints. In (19) we have an example of a violation of the Complex NP Constraint.

(19)   *Which car did you see the man who was driving?

The structure of (19) is given in (20), assuming that adjunction takes place wherever possible.

(20)

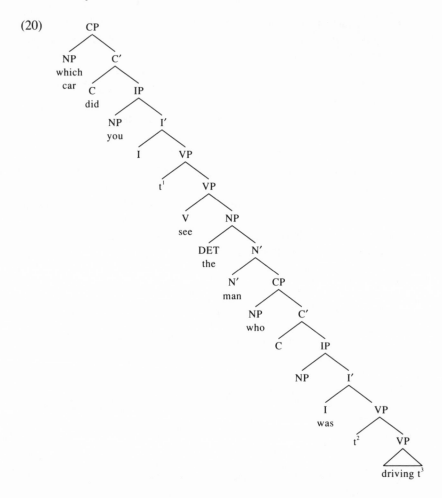

There are no barriers between t^2 and t^3, since VP does not exclude t^2. There are also no barriers between *which car* and t^1, since VP does not dominate t^1 and IP can only be a barrier by inheritance. The problem must therefore be between t^1 and t^2. The lower IP is a blocking category for t^2, but not a barrier. The lower CP is not L-marked and, as such, is both a blocking category and a barrier. The NP dominating the relative clause is L-marked by *see* and is thus not a blocking category, but it dominates the blocking category CP and is therefore a barrier by inheritance. We see that there are two barriers, NP and CP, between t^1 and t^2, and the ungrammaticality of (19) is accounted for.

Now consider (21), a violation of the sentential subject constraint.

(21)   *Who did [that Sue married t] surprise you?

Analyses of sentences like (21) differ as to whether the sentential subject is dominated by NP. Let us assume that it is not, since an extra NP node would only increase the number of barriers. The structure of (21) is given in (22).

(22)

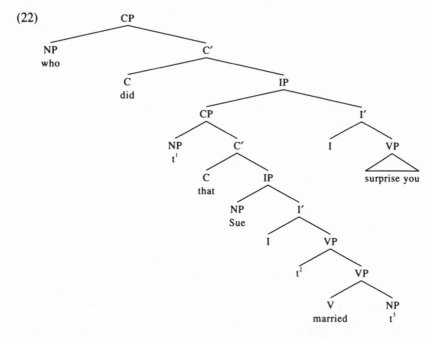

There are no barriers between t^2 and t^3. The only maximal projection that dominates t^2 and excludes t^1 is IP, which can never be a barrier except by inheritance. The subjacency violation must therefore be between *who* and t^1. The CP immediately dominating t^1 is not L-marked and is therefore a blocking category and a barrier. The IP dominating the CP is a barrier by inheritance from CP. There are thus two barriers between *who* and t^1, and the ungrammaticality of (21) is accounted for.

An advantage of the *Barriers* approach over the specific bounding nodes approach to subjacency has to do with WH-movement in sentences involving exceptional case marking. Consider (23).

(23)   Which car do [$_{IP}$ you [$_{VP}$ t [$_{VP}$ expect [$_{IP}$ Sue to [$_{VP}$ t [$_{VP}$ buy t]]]]]]]

Under the original formulation of subjacency, two bounding nodes intervened between *which car* and its trace in object position. This predicts that (23) ought to be at least mildly ungrammatical, on a par with WH-island violations such as (24).

(24)   Which car$_i$ did [$_{IP}$ you wonder [$_{CP}$ when$_j$ [$_{IP}$ they bought t$_i$ t$_j$]]]

Here, two bounding nodes intervene between *which car* and its trace.

Chomsky (1981) suggests that (23) might be accounted for as follows. First, he assumes a rule of S'-deletion to account for exceptional case marking. Second, he assumes that subjacency is actually a constraint on movement rules, rather than on the structures the rules create. This gives (23) the derivation in (25).

(25)   D-structure:
   $[_S$ you (do) expect $[_{S'}$ $[_S$ Sue to buy which car]]]
   Wh-movement, inversion:
   $[_{S'}$ which car$_i$ do $[_S$ you expect $[_{S'}$ t$_i$ $[_S$ Sue to buy t$_i$]]]]]
   S'-deletion, exceptional case marking:
   $[_{S'}$ which car$_i$ do $[_S$ you expect $[_S$ Sue to buy t$_i$]]]

The subjacency condition is satisfied, since the WH-phrase crossed only one bounding node at a time.

Under the *Barriers* approach, the analysis is significantly more straightforward. Subjacency can be stated as a condition on chains, and no deletions are required. Consider (23) again. Assuming adjunction to VP, neither VP will be a blocking category or a barrier. The lower IP is L-marked and thus not a blocking category. In any case, IP can only be a barrier by inheritance from a lower blocking category, and here there is no blocking category for IP to inherit barrierhood from. The higher IP, though not L-marked and therefore a blocking category, again has nothing to inherit barrierhood from. There are therefore no barriers between *which car* and its trace.

Returning to the ECP, let us consider the contrast between (26) and (27).

(26)   Which student did you claim $[_{CP}$ t $\varnothing$ $[_{IP}$ t had failed]]
(27)   *Which student did you claim $[_{CP}$ t that $[_{IP}$ t had failed]]

Lasnik and Saito (1984) proposed to account for these facts by the mechanism of COMP-indexing. Recall that they assumed that WH-phrases moved into COMP in the traditional S' structure. We suggested that essentially the same account might hold in a CP structure, if the specifier and head of CP had to share an index. Leaving indexing aside, let us see what the *Barriers* approach has to say about these sentences, the structure of which is given in (28).

(28)   Which student did $[_{IP}$ you $[_{VP}$ t^1 $[_{VP}$ claim $[_{CP}$ t^2 (that) $[_{IP}$ t^3 had failed]]]]]]

The only difference between (26) and (27) is the presence of the lexical complementizer *that* in (27). In neither sentence is there a barrier between t^2 and t^3, since the only maximal projection intervening is IP, which can never be an inherent barrier. Equally, no barriers intervene between t^1 and t^2 because CP is L-marked and VP does not exclude t^1. Between *which student* and t^1 there are again no barriers, since VP does not dominate t^1 and IP cannot be an inherent barrier. By the current definitions, both sentences are predicted to be grammatical.

To account for this, as well as for some other facts, Chomsky proposes the minimality condition, which is given in (29).

(29) In the structure . . . α . . . [γ . . . δ . . . β . . .],
      α does not govern β if γ is a projection of δ excluding α.

Incorporating this into the definition of barrier gives (30).

(30) γ is a barrier for β if and only if:
      I   (holds for both government and movement)
           γ is a maximal projection, AND
           a. γ immediately dominates δ, δ a blocking category for β
           OR
           b. γ is a blocking category for β and $\gamma \neq$ IP
               OR
      II   (holds only for government)
           γ is the immediate projection of δ, a zero-level category distinct from β

The effect of this modification is to prevent the complements of a head from being governed by anything but that head. This makes intuitive sense with respect to Case marking and has the desired effect for the that-trace phenomenon illustrated in (26) and (27). Assuming that the lexical complementizer *that* is visible to the minimality condition, and that the null complementizer, lacking any features, is not visible, then C' will count as a barrier for the trace in subject position in (27). This barrier prevents the trace from being antecedent-governed by the trace in the CP-specifier, producing an ECP violation.

12.2.2 Remaining Problems

So far, the *Barriers* approach seems to be a very promising attempt to provide a unified treatment of locality constraints. Some problems remain to be solved, however. First and foremost is the stipulation that IP, alone among all maximal projections, can only be a barrier by inheritance. The general idea behind the *Barriers* approach was to avoid such category-specific stipulations. In fact, the situation with IP is even more murky, since Chomsky stipulates that I' can never be a barrier by virtue of the minimality condition. Clearly, more work is needed in order to understand what makes IP different from the other categories. A promising avenue to pursue here is the idea that IP is not actually IP, but rather a constellation of different functional projections along the lines discussed in the previous chapter. It has been proposed that head movement from, for example, AGR to T voids the barrierhood of AGRP by allowing it to be L-marked by the moved item. See Rivero (1988) for work along these lines.

Another question has to do with VP. Since it is always possible to adjoin to VP, VP is *never* a blocking category or a barrier for either subjacency or antecedent government (note that V' can be a barrier by minimality). Given the number of new assumptions that were required once crucial use was made of adjunction to VP, it would be desirable to find some independent evidence for the VP-adjoined trace. If none can be found, then another explanation might be sought for the non-barrierhood of VP. Again, it might be productive to investigate the relationship between the verb and the inflectional category heading the immediately dominating projection. If head movement voids barrierhood, then it is entirely possible that the barrierhood of VP might be eliminated without recourse to adjunction.

Finally, the question remains of why minimality is relevant only for government. The conditions on the two parts of the definition of barrier given in (30) begin to chip away at the unified nature of the theory of barriers.

All of these questions, while serious, do not detract from the general thrust of the *Barriers* approach; namely that the phenomenon of locality should receive as unified a treatment as possible in the theory of grammar. It appears at the moment that the emerging theory of functional categories may provide interesting solutions to some of the more obvious problems in the theory of barriers, and that the theory of barriers may raise some interesting problems for the theory of functional categories.

Readings

Chomsky, Noam. 1981. *Lectures on Government and Binding*. Dordrecht: Foris Publications.

————. 1986b. *Barriers*. Cambridge, Mass.: MIT Press.

Huang, C-T. James. 1982. "Logical Relations in Chinese and the Theory of Grammar." Ph.D. diss., MIT, Cambridge, Mass.

Lasnik, Howard, and Mamoru Saito. 1984. "On the Nature of Proper Government." *Linguistic Inquiry* 15:235–89.

Massam, Diane. 1985. "Case Theory and the Projection Principle." Ph.D. diss., MIT, Cambridge, Mass.

May, Robert. 1985. *Logical Form*. Cambridge, Mass.: MIT Press.

Rivero, Maria-Luisa. 1988. "The Structure of IP and V-movement in the Languages of the Balkans." Unpublished ms., University of Ottawa.

Rizzi, Luigi. 1982. *Issues in Italian Syntax*. Dordrecht: Foris Publications.

Ross, John R. 1967. "Constraints on Variables in Syntax." Ph.D. diss., MIT, Cambridge, Mass.

References

Abney, Steven. 1987. "The English Noun Phrase in Its Sentential Aspect." Ph.D. diss., MIT, Cambridge, Mass.

Aoun, Joseph, Norbert Hornstein, and Dominique Sportiche. 1982. "Some Aspects of Wide Scope Quantification." *Journal of Linguistic Research* 1:69–95.

Baker, Mark. 1988. *Incorporation: A Theory of Grammatical Function Changing.* Chicago, Ill.: University of Chicago Press.

———, Kyle Johnson, and Ian Roberts. 1989. "Passive Arguments Raised." *Linguistic Inquiry* 20:219–52.

Bouchard, Denis. 1983. *On the Content of Empty Categories.* Dordrecht: Foris Publications.

Browning, Marguerite. 1987. "Null Operator Constructions." Ph.D. diss., MIT, Cambridge, Mass.

Burzio, Luigi. 1986. *Italian Syntax.* Dordrecht: Reidel.

Chomsky, Noam. 1965. *Aspects of the Theory of Syntax.* Cambridge, Mass.: MIT Press.

———. 1970. "Remarks on Nominalization." In Jacobs and Rosenbaum (1970).

———. 1973. *The Logical Structure of Linguistic Theory.* New York: Plenum.

———. 1977. "On WH-Movement." In Culicover, Wasow, and Akmajian (1977).

———. 1980. "On Binding." *Linguistic Inquiry* 11:1–46.

———. 1981. *Lectures on Government and Binding.* Dordrecht: Foris Publications.

———. 1986a. *Knowledge of Language: Its Nature, Origin and Use.* New York: Praeger.

———. 1986b. *Barriers.* Cambridge, Mass.: MIT Press.

———. 1989. "Some Notes on Economy of Derivation and Representation." In Laka and Mahajan (1989).

Culicover, Peter, Thomas Wasow, and Adrian Akmajian. 1977. *Formal Syntax.* New York: Academic Press

Dresher, B. Elan, and Jonathan D. Kaye. 1990. "A Computational Learning Model for Metrical Phonology." *Cognition* 34:137–95.

Emonds, Joseph. 1976. *A Transformational Approach to English Syntax.* New York: Academic Press.

Fiengo, Robert. 1977. "On Trace Theory." *Linguistic Inquiry* 8:35–62.

Fillmore, Charles J., and D. Terence Langendoen. 1971. *Studies in Linguistic Semantics.* New York: Holt, Rinehart and Winston.

Fukui, Naoki. 1986. "A Theory of Category Projection and Its Applications." Ph.D. diss., MIT, Cambridge, Mass.

Grimshaw, Jane. 1979. "Complement Selection and the Lexicon." *Linguistic Inquiry* 10:279–326.

———. 1990. *Argument Structure.* Cambridge, Mass.: MIT Press.

Gruber, Jeffrey. 1965. "Studies in Lexical Relations." Ph.D. diss., MIT, Cambridge; Indiana University Linguistics Club, Bloomington, Ind. Reprinted as part of Gruber (1976).

———. 1976. *Lexical Structures in Syntax and Semantics.* Amsterdam: North-Holland.

Hale, Kenneth, and Samuel Jay Keyser. 1987. "A View from the Middle." *Lexicon Project Working Papers 10.* Cambridge, Mass.: MIT.

Huang, C-T. James. 1981/82. "Move Wh in a Language without Wh-movement." *The Linguistic Review* 1:369–416.

———. 1982. "Logical Relations in Chinese and the Theory of Grammar. Ph.D. diss., MIT, Cambridge, Mass.

———. 1983. "A Note on the Binding Theory." *Linguistic Inquiry* 14:554–61.

———. 1984. "On the Distribution and Reference of Empty Pronouns." *Linguistic Inquiry* 15:531–74.

Hyams, Nina M. 1986. *Language Acquisition and the Theory of Parameters.* Dordrecht: Reidel.

Jackendoff, Ray. 1972. *Semantic Interpretation in Generative Grammar.* Cambridge, Mass.: MIT Press.

———. 1977. *X-bar Syntax: A Study of Phrase Structure.* Cambridge, Mass.: MIT Press.

———. 1983. *Semantics and Cognition.* Cambridge, Mass.: MIT Press

———. 1987. "The Status of Thematic Relations in Linguistic Theory." *Linguistic Inquiry* 18:369–412.

Jacobs, Roderick, and Peter Rosenbaum. 1970. *Readings in English Transformational Grammar.* Waltham, Mass.: Ginn & Company.

Jaeggli, Osvaldo. 1986. "Passive." *Linguistic Inquiry* 17:587–622.

Katz, Jerrold J., and Paul M. Postal. 1964. *An Integrated Theory of Linguistic Descriptions.* Cambridge, Mass.: MIT Press.

Kayne, Richard. 1981. "ECP Extensions." *Linguistic Inquiry* 12:93–133.

Koopman, Hilda. 1984. *The Syntax of Verbs.* Dordrecht: Foris Publications.

Laka, Itziar, and Anoop Mahajan. 1989. *Functional Heads and Clause Structure: MIT Working Papers in Linguistics, vol 10.* Cambridge, Mass.

Lakoff, George. 1971. "On Generative Semantics." In Danny D. Steinberg and Leon A. Jakobovits, *Semantics,* pp. 232–96. London: Cambridge University Press.

Lasnik, Howard, and Mamoru Saito. 1984. "On the Nature of Proper Government." *Linguistic Inquiry* 15:235–89.

Lefebvre, Claire. 1982. "L'expansion d'une Catégorie Grammaticale: Le Déterminant LA." In C. Lefebvre, H. Magloire-Holly, and N. Piou, *Syntaxe de l'Haïtien.* Ann Arbor, Michigan: Karoma Publishers.

———, and Diane Massam. 1988. "Haitian Creole Syntax: A Case for DET as Head." *Journal of Pidgin and Creole Languages* 3:213–43.

Lightfoot, David. 1982. *The Language Lottery.* Cambridge, Mass.: MIT Press.

McCawley, James D. 1968. "The Role of Semantics in Grammar." In Emmon Bach and Robert T. Harms, *Universals in Linguistic Theory*, pp. 125–69. New York: Holt, Rinehart and Winston.

———. 1988. *The Syntactic Phenomena of English*. Chicago, Ill.: University of Chicago Press.

Manzini, Maria Rita. 1983. "Control and Control Theory." *Linguistic Inquiry* 14: 421–46.

Marantz, Alec. 1984. *On the Nature of Grammatical Relations*. Cambridge, Mass.: MIT Press.

Massam, Diane. 1985. "Case Theory and the Projection Principle." Ph.D. diss., MIT, Cambridge, Mass.

May, Robert. 1977. "The Grammar of Quantification." Ph.D. diss., MIT, Cambridge, Mass.

———. 1985. *Logical Form*. Cambridge, Mass.: MIT Press.

Muysken, Pieter, and Henk van Riemsdijk. 1985. *Features and Projections*. Dordrecht: Foris Publications.

Nash, David. 1980. "Topics in Warlpiri Grammar." Ph.D. diss., MIT, Cambridge, Mass.

Newmeyer, Frederick J. 1980. *Linguistic Theory in America*. New York: Academic Press.

———. 1983. *Grammatical Theory: Its Limits and Its Possibilities*. Chicago, Ill.: University of Chicago Press.

Partee, Barbara H. 1971. "On the Requirement that Transformations Preserve Meaning." In Fillmore and Langendoen (1971).

Pesetsky, David. 1982. "Paths and Categories." Ph.D. diss., MIT, Cambridge, Mass.

Pollock, Jean-Yves. 1989. "Verb Movement, Universal Grammar and the Structure of IP." *Linguistic Inquiry* 20:365–424.

Reuland, Eric. 1985. "A Feature System for the Set of Categorial Heads." In Muysken and van Riemsdijk (1985).

Rivero, Maria-Luisa. 1988. "The Structure of IP and V-movement in the Languages of the Balkans." Unpublished ms., University of Ottawa.

Rizzi, Luigi. 1982. *Issues in Italian Syntax*. Dordrecht: Foris Publications.

———. 1986. "Null Objects in Italian and the Theory of pro." *Linguistic Inquiry* 17:501–57.

Roberge, Yves. 1990. *The Syntactic Recoverability of Null Arguments*. Montreal: McGill-Queen's University Press.

Ross, John R. 1967. "Constraints on Variables in Syntax." Ph.D. diss., MIT, Cambridge, Mass.

———. 1970. "On Declarative Sentences." In Roderick A. Jacobs and Peter S. Rosenbaum, *Readings in English Transformational Grammar*, pp. 222–72. Waltham, Mass.: Ginn and Company.

———. 1972. "Auxiliare als Hauptverben." In Werner Abraham and Robert Binnick, *Generative Semantik*, pp. 95–115. Frankfurt am Main: Athenäum Verlag.

Selkirk, Elisabeth. 1984. *Phonology and Syntax: The Relation Between Sound and Structure*. Cambridge, Mass.: MIT Press.

Stowell, Timothy A. 1981. "Origins of Phrase Structure." Ph.D. diss., MIT, Cambridge, Mass.

Tenny, Carol. 1987. "Grammaticalizing Aspect and Affectedness." Ph.D. diss., MIT, Cambridge, Mass.

Travis, Lisa. 1984. "Parameters and Effects of Word Order Variation." Ph.D. diss., MIT, Cambridge, Mass.

Wackernagl, J. 1892. "Über ein Gesetz der indogermanischen Wortstellung." *Indogermanische Forschungen* 1:333–436.

Wasow, Thomas. 1977. "Transformations and the Lexicon." In Culicover, Wasow, and Akmajian (1977).

Index

Page references in boldface indicate where definitions can be found.